Tic Tac Toe

Making the Move Toward Effective Classroom Management

S. Michael Putman

Amy J. Good

University of North Carolina Charlotte

Kendall Hunt
publishing company

www.kendallhunt.com
Send all inquiries to:
4050 Westmark Drive
Dubuque, IA 52004-1840

Printed in the United States of America
10 9 8 7 6 5 4 3 2 1

Table of Contents

Appendix B – Constructing the Management Intervention Study

CHAPTER I

Introduction to Classroom Management

No other topic in education receives greater attention or causes more concerns for teachers and parents

and students than classroom discipline. . . . The lack of effective classroom discipline or behavior

management skills is the major stumbling block to a successful career in teaching.

Nicholas Long and William Morse (1996) *Conflict in the Classroom*

This chapter will serve as a foundation and guide you as you read the rest of this book. In it, we will provide an introduction to the idea that classroom management represents more than the traditional notion of discipline – it now encompasses multiple facets within the classroom. We will also describe how classroom management models and philosophies can be represented on a continuum of philosophical views. As you read this chapter, you will be introduced to relevant vocabulary, presented with philosophical underpinnings for classroom management, and introduced to pertinent concepts. In sum, the information will help you consider the answer to the question "How will I manage my classroom?" This question represents an important consideration as you create, reconsider, and potentially implement a plan that is successful with all children.

Guiding Questions
As you read and explore the concepts introduced within this chapter, use the following questions to guide your thinking:
- What is meant by the term "classroom management"?
- How do philosophies of classroom management differ?
- How do differing degrees of control impact classroom management and philosophy?
- What style of classroom management best matches what I envision for my classroom?

Reflect and Act:
Think about what you already know about classroom management. Using p. 155, write a definition for classroom management, then develop a short list of 5-10 items that describes your knowledge of and perceptions about classroom management, including why it may be difficult or challenging for teachers.

BACKGROUND

21st Century classrooms present multiple challenges for today's teachers. Like no other time in history, teachers are under pressure to increase student achievement while simultaneously balancing the multiple complexities presented by the changing composition of the students in their classrooms. In a context that is increasingly filled with children from diverse backgrounds, the teaching profession has remained primarily female, Caucasian, and middle class (National Education Association, 2010). As a result, it is not surprising that teachers cite classroom management and diversity as being aspects of teaching that cause apprehension (Chambers, 2003; Evertson & Weinstein, 2006; Melnick & Meister, 2008). These concerns appear regardless of age or experience; yet teachers in the earliest phases of their career appear to experience the most significant concerns regarding overall classroom management and student behavior (Moore, 2003; Veenman, 1984). In fact, teachers unsuccessful in establishing themselves in the area of classroom management are more likely to leave the field within the first 5 years of their teaching career (Rinke, 2007).

Explanations of what constitutes classroom management are ever-evolving. Traditionally, classroom management was primarily associated with the organization of the classroom, the creation of rules, routines, and procedures, the engagement of students during instruction, and interventions for displays of improper behavior (Doyle, 2006; Evertson & Weinstein, 2006). In 1988, Brophy generalized classroom management as "the actions taken to create and maintain a learning environment conducive to attainment of the goals of instruction" (p. 2). Kellough and Roberts (2002) focus on classroom management as a process that includes organizational as well as instructional components to ensure student learning. Recent literature has begun to recognize the multiple facets that encompass what has been referred to as comprehensive classroom management (see Jones & Jones, 2012). Within this view, classroom management encompasses "commitment to and skills in working collaboratively with all adults in the building as well as parents/guardians to implement the most effective methods for assisting students in developing age-appropriate academic and behavior skills" (Jones & Jones, 2012, p. 6). It also involves factors associated with teaching students skills to successfully interact and connect with other students. Teachers must be able to communicate, model, and effectively reinforce attitudes and behaviors that facilitate classroom interactions (Brophy, 2006). According to several experts, these actions improve both teacher-student and student-student interactions and relationships and, subsequently, the overall climate of a classroom (see Pianta, 2006; Wentzel, 2006).

Understanding this information is critical as teachers must possess pedagogical knowledge in addition to the ability to successfully maintain an environment conducive to teaching and learning to meet the multiple behavioral and instructional needs within today's classrooms. In my classes, I (Mike) often refer to the "big three" of teaching: curricular design, instructional strategies, and classroom management (Larrivee, 2005). Others (see Jones & Jones, 2012) refer to classroom management as an element within a system that includes the classroom environment, instructional methods, and individual student's needs, including external conditions that may impact behavior. Regardless of your chosen definition, there is little doubt skills related to planning, instruction, and management are important for both new and experienced teachers and ones that all teachers must constantly work on to improve.

This information is also important in helping you realize that classroom management is NOT solely focused on discipline. It is much more. For example, when some think of classroom management, they immediately associate it with the administration of consequences for unacceptable behavior. While consequences may be an important piece of an individual management plan, they represent only a piece of the puzzle and may be dependent upon your philosophical orientation towards successful management.

Recognizing this, what characterizes effective classroom managers? Experts on classroom management (see Bloom, 2009; Jones & Jones, 2012) have proposed that effective managers:

1. Demonstrate caring
2. Communicate regularly and clearly with students
3. Have established rules or behavioral guidelines
4. Hold high expectations
5. Model positive behavior
6. Are proactive, rather than reactive
7. Utilize procedures and routines that provide structure to activities
8. Teach students methods to develop self-control and responsibility
9. Create an engaging curriculum

Teachers who are successful in this area also understand students' needs and react accordingly, treating each as individuals (Jones & Jones, 2012). We will continue to explore these characteristics and how they are manifest in teaching behaviors as we examine the multiple considerations that go into building a classroom management plan that is effective with all learners.

THEORY TO PRACTICE

> **Reflect and Act:**
> What constitutes misbehavior? Create a list of the behaviors that will be strictly forbidden in your classroom. Discuss the list with a colleague. How do the two lists differ? Together, form a list to represent the most common forms of misbehavior that you think you will see in the classroom.

What's My Philosophy of Classroom Management?

Before any teacher can implement a system of classroom management, questions regarding her views of the role of the teacher, the child, and the interaction between the two need to be examined. The old saying *"different strokes for different folks"* applies to the area of classroom management. If I am a teacher who likes to have control of a classroom and wants to develop strict guidelines and procedures regarding management of the classroom, management theories which advocate approaches that allow students ownership and empowerment will not resonate with me. On the other hand, if I believe children should take an active role in the construction of an overall system, but attempt to implement a theory where the teacher is the ultimate authority, there's a significant chance that it will not be successful. To some degree classroom management styles are reflective of an individual's personality. Incongruence between personality and theory may cause a teacher to be inconsistent which, in turn, may limit classroom success of both the students and teacher.

It's important for teachers to consider what they believe represents acceptable behavior as well as the actions that will construe misbehavior in their classroom. For example, some teachers may view it as acceptable for a student to get out of his seat to sharpen his pencil while they are teaching. You, on the other hand, may view this as unacceptable and may administer a verbal warning or consequence. The key idea is that all of us have views of behavior that will shape and influence how children act in our classroom. Taking this a step further, behavior can be defined as any action that can be taken, while misbehavior represents any given behavior that is not acceptable or appropriate within the context it is demonstrated. For example, if I am attending a birthday party, it is acceptable to talk very loud to peers as well as sing. However, if I am in a crowded movie theater, generally, both of these actions would be unacceptable. For that reason, before examining your philosophy and creating your management plan, you must direct particular attention to what behaviors are acceptable or unacceptable within your classroom.

Defining the Continuum

Teachers typically exhibit beliefs relating to classroom management (and children's behaviors) that fall into a consistent pattern. This general pattern is easily shown in a continuum that reflects varying levels of power in the teacher/student relationship. Figure 1 provides a visual reference to the management continuum. In general, teacher-in-charge (TIC) would be described as teacher behaviors that utilize assertive or controlling techniques to cause students to change their behavior to better match what is desired by the educator or educational setting. In the center of the continuum is the Teacher-and-Child (TAC) philosophy. Here the relationship could be described as mutually inclusive as the teacher and students communicate to develop and agree upon behaviors and interventions. The final portion of the continuum is Toward Empowerment/Ownership (TOE). Teachers who exhibit this orientation ultimately cede the majority of control of power to the students in the classroom, providing them an authentic environment to experience problem-solving and relationship-building.

Figure 1. Continuum of Classroom Management Philosophy

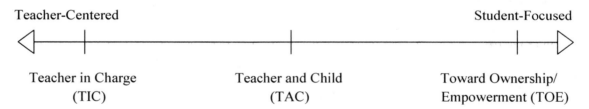

Teacher-Centered   Student-Focused

| Teacher in Charge | Teacher and Child | Toward Ownership/ |
| (TIC) | (TAC) | Empowerment (TOE) |

Teacher in Charge (TIC)

The Teacher in Charge would be most aligned with a behavioristic orientation towards effective classroom management. Teachers with this philosophy envision the classroom as an orderly, structured environment and are likely to emphasize a system of reinforcement or consequences to increase the likelihood that children demonstrate acceptable behavior. There is a focus on rules and procedures that ensure children "know" how to act properly. In short, students who demonstrate appropriate behavior are reinforced, either tangibly or verbally, while inappropriate behavior is extinguished or diminished with the use of punishments that increase in the level of severity as the magnitude or significance of misbehavior rises.

Teacher and Child (TAC)

Teacher and Child is exemplified by a partnership between the teacher and students. Behavioral expectations are established jointly as the teacher and children discuss elements of the classroom that

4

allow the teacher to teach and the students to learn. The role of consequences is diminished and when they are used, they are likely to be logical consequences, meaning they are directly related to the inappropriate conduct. For example, if a student writes on a desk, he may have to clean the desk as well as others in the classroom. The ultimate goal of the teacher in such a system is to help children take responsibility for their own behavior while simultaneously altering behavior that results from children's lack of understanding of methods to fulfill their own needs.

Toward Ownership/Empowerment (TOE)

Towards Ownership/Empowerment is characterized by students having an active part in determining the overall classroom climate with respect to management. The teacher is likely to acknowledge student views and work with students to determine methods that will empower the student to make her own choices within the classroom climate. For example, teachers who subscribe to this philosophy may utilize classroom meetings where students in the classroom collaboratively develop rules or discuss a solution to a classroom situation. In short, the teacher listens and offers suggestions for the child to consider as opposed to overpowering the student's view in an effort to exert control.

> **Reflect and Act:**
> **Re-examine your definition of classroom management. Has it changed? Where do you fall on the continuum? With this in mind, on p. 156, write three statements that will form a foundation for your classroom management plan, e.g. Students in my classroom will take an active part in establishing the behavioral standards that will be enforced in my classroom.**

Previous research has established other names for the continuum of classroom management and linked the various theories to the levels of control. For example, Glickman and Tamashiro (1980) described the levels as Interventionist (TIC), Interactionalist (TAC), and Non-Interventionists (TOE). Table 1 lists several theorists which could be associated with each category of the continuum. It is important to note that the various theorists may espouse actions/strategies that may align at various points along the continuum. The location in the table is meant to illustrate the level of the continuum that we feel the theory is most aligned with.

APPLICATION WITH DIVERSE LEARNERS

As previously mentioned, teachers experience a certain amount of trepidation related to working with students who come from linguistically or culturally diverse backgrounds. While this chapter serves to introduce general concepts associated with developing an understanding of what constitutes classroom management, later chapters will incorporate specific principles for working with diverse learners, including culturally responsive classroom management. The latter "requires that teachers set high expectations for students, ensure that students meet their expectations, and maintain a caring, structured, cooperative classroom environment that addresses students' lived experiences and cultural backgrounds" (Adkins-Coleman, 2010, p. 41). Culturally responsive management frameworks also "incorporate elements of students' home, personal, and community lives into the classroom" (Monroe & Obidah, 2004, p. 259). When the teachers possess (or have the skills and opportunities to acquire) the knowledge, skills, dispositions, and beliefs that are necessary to meet the needs of and be responsive to their students, equitable classroom management and learning opportunities for all students are possible.

Table 1. Theories and Theorists Aligned with TAC-TAC-TOE Continuum

Teacher in Charge (TIC)	Teacher and Child (TAC)	Toward Ownership/Empowerment (TOE)
Assertive Discipline Lee and Marlene Canter **Positive Discipline** Fredric Jones **Behavior Modification** B.F. Skinner	**Positive Discipline in the Classroom** Jane Nelsen, Lynn Lott, and H. Stephen Glenn **Cooperative Discipline** Linda Albert **Discipline with Dignity** Richard Curwin and Allen Mendler **Noncoercive Discipline** William Glasser **Win-Win Discipline** Spencer Kagan, Patricia Kyle, and Sally Scott	**Beyond Discipline** Alfie Kohn **Teaching with Love and Logic** Jim Fay and David Funk **Discipline as Self-Control** Thomas Gordon **Inner Discipline** Barbara Coloroso

CASE STUDY – Developing Your Philosophy

As the bell rang, Mr. Johnson's fifth grade math class began according to what had been rehearsed over the preceding four weeks. Mr. Johnson asked the students to begin thinking about the "Problem of the Day" and to attempt to come up with a correct solution. This was the opening procedure that Mr. Johnson had implemented to get his students working the moment class started, as advocated by Fred Jones (Jones, 1987), whom he had studied as an undergraduate education major. As had also been typical over the four week period, Daniel was the last person to get started on the problem. First, he had to locate his pencil, then he had to sharpen it before he could start writing. When he finally got his pencil ready and came back to his desk, there was the matter of finding a piece of paper. This process took three to four minutes, and, even though he tried to be patient, Mr. Johnson was beginning to get frustrated.

"Daniel, please get working on the problem because time is almost up," said Mr. Johnson. Daniel looked at the problem for a moment, wrote a few numbers, and then stopped working.

"What's the matter, Daniel?" Mr. Johnson asked.

"I don't know how to do this problem," Daniel replied.

"You haven't tried it yet," Mr. Johnson said.

At this point other students were beginning to talk around the classroom as they had already solved the problem. Mr. Johnson glanced around the room, used his best "teacher look" to get the students who were beginning to get off-task back to work, and proceeded to try and help Daniel.

"You have the numbers you need to solve the problem written down correctly," said Mr. Johnson trying to use Jones' idea of "be positive, be brief, and be gone" (Jones, 1987).

"But I don't know what to do now," whined Daniel.

"We covered a very similar problem to this on Monday… if you pull out your notes, you should be able to use what we did to help you with this problem," countered Mr. Johnson.

Mr. Johnson then spent another minute trying to get Daniel to find his notebook and to begin working on the problem, but with no success. Daniel refused to work any further and kept saying he couldn't do the work and didn't want to try. As the majority of the class was finished at this point, Mr. Johnson was forced to abandon his attempts to get Daniel working and attend to the rest of the students.

As Mr. Johnson and the rest of the class discussed possible solutions for the "Problem of the Day," Daniel tapped the desk with his pencil or looked out the window. He did not engage in the conversation, nor did he note how he could have solved the problem. Mr. Johnson ignored these behaviors and continued with class.

This was not unusual behavior from Daniel. In truth, it always seemed Daniel was doing something he shouldn't be. When Mr. Johnson was giving instructions regarding how to complete the steps necessary to solve the math problems he was doing in class, Daniel would often draw on his notebook paper, instead of taking notes. As students worked out problems on their own, Daniel liked to turn and look at the paper of the girl who sat behind him or complain that he couldn't do the problem. Sometimes he would stare blankly into space and refuse to work, even when Mr. Johnson threatened consequences. Mr. Johnson was now at the point where he was not sure how to be successful with Daniel.

Reflect on the following questions before moving on to the descriptions:

1. What are some of the behaviors being exhibited by Daniel?
2. Are any of these behaviors disrupting other students?
3. What actions has Mr. Johnson taken to help Daniel get to work? Were any successful?
4. What are some potential reasons Daniel may be exhibiting the behaviors he is?
5. How would you handle this situation?

After you have answered the discussion questions and decided how you would handle the situation, read all three of the choices that follow. Select one that most closely matches your ideas. Or if you read one that you like better than your own ideas, choose it as your own. Then follow the directions for the activities that follow the explanations of the options.

Case Study: Response Choices
Choice A

If I were Mr. Johnson, at the first sign of misbehavior, I would have asked Daniel to pull a card or sign the discipline book as a warning for his lack of following the classroom routine and getting right to work. He is clearly disobeying authority and does not show respect for the teacher or other students as evidenced by his off-task behavior. Continued misbehavior by Daniel beyond the warning card or signature would result in some consequence such as the loss of a privilege or, eventually, a note sent home to his parents. As this behavior has been happening for four weeks, I would also consider creating a positive behavior system that would focus on giving Daniel some type of mark for when he displayed positive behavior. If he accumulated enough positive behavior marks, he would be given some type of reward.

If you chose this option, then examine the information under the Choice A section that follows on this page and read the underlying ideas of this response from recognized classroom management theorists.

Choice B

If I were this teacher, I would examine Daniel's behavior to note potential reasons for the misbehavior. Was he acting out to get attention or to avoid failure as he felt he did not understand what was being taught? If the reason behind the behavior appeared to be attention related, I would look for opportunities to provide positive attention to Daniel when he behaved acceptably. On the other hand, if I thought Daniel exhibited his misbehaviors because he didn't want to appear to not understand the content in front of his classmates, I would hold a private talk with Daniel acknowledging the situation. We would then begin to examine potential solutions for helping Daniel – peer tutoring, hand signals by Daniel to indicate that he needs help, or other methods that would allow Daniel to learn the material being taught.

If you chose this option, then turn to page 9 and read Choice B to learn about the underlying ideas of this response from recognized classroom management theorists.

Choice C

If I were this teacher, I would ask Daniel why he thinks he is not able to complete the problem of the day or focus on instruction. As we talked, I would be sure to allow him to express feelings about the situation. I would acknowledge these opinions and ask him what could be done to help him. I would listen to Daniel's response and consider giving Daniel opportunities to work with peers on the "Problem of the Day" or during instruction if he indicated these options would help him. Alternatively, if Daniel expressed disinterest in the topic, I would look for opportunities to allow Daniel to choose his own topic or course of study that utilized similar concepts. Since this appears to be a recurring problem, I would also examine the method I was using to teach the content to determine how well it matched Daniel's preferred learning style.

If you chose this option, then turn to page 10 and read Choice C to learn about the underlying ideas of this response from recognized classroom management theorists.

Case Study: Using TIC-TAC-TOE
Choice A

If your response was aligned with the teacher behaviors in Choice A, you may find elements of Lee and Marlene Canter's *Assertive Discipline* (see Canter & Canter, 2002) and Fred Jones' *Positive Discipline* (see Jones, 1987) appealing. These theories fall into the TIC category.

In this scenario, Mr. Johnson already exhibits several strategies recommended in *Positive Discipline* including bell work and the idea of "be positive, be brief, and be gone." Jones advocates the use of "bell work" to get students started on a task as soon as they enter the classroom. This is effective as it limits opportunities for misbehavior as students start doing something academic immediately. His idea of "be positive…" comes from his research that showed teachers spending too long helping individual students, resulting in increased misbehaviors by students who were waiting for help. Using this theory allows the teacher to maximize the amount of students that can be given assistance in a minimal amount of time and helps the teacher to maintain an active presence around the room.

In handling misbehaviors, Jones and the Canters stress the use of consequences that become progressively more severe as misbehaviors repeatedly occur. Jones refers to this as backup systems, while the Canters call it the discipline hierarchy. In choice A, the warning and eventual loss of a privilege for Daniel would be representative of these aspects of the respective theories. To help students learn proper behavior, Jones cites the use of a positive incentive system as beneficial. He refers to students earning what he calls preferred activity time (PAT) whereby students earn time to engage in academically-based, free choice activities. The Canters advocate a system of positive recognition for compliance with behavioral expectations in the form of praise, positive notes, or by giving special activities or privileges. Finally, Choice A also mentions the idea of respect – *Assertive Discipline* maintains that all students must respect the teacher's right to teach and students' right to learn. Any behavior that inhibits either of these rights is met with a swift and consistent administration of some consequence.

Choice B

The response emulated by Choice B would fall into the category of the teacher and child (TAC) working together to formulate a solution. Elements included in the response are drawn from Linda Albert's *Cooperative Discipline* (see Albert, 2003) and Richard Curwin and Allen Mendler's *Discipline with Dignity* (see Curwin & Mendler, 1999).

Linda Albert maintains that teachers need to help students feel connected, capable, and that they can contribute to the classroom. She refers to these as the 3 C's in her theory of *Cooperative Discipline*. Two of these traits are exhibited in choice B as the solution allows the teacher to help Daniel by listening and acknowledging his feelings (connected), and helping him succeed (capable). Albert also states that students typically misbehave to satisfy one of four basic goals: attention, power, revenge, and avoidance of failure. To determine which of these goals the student was trying to meet, choice B outlines the examination of Daniel's behavior to note potential reasons for the misbehavior. Using this technique, choice B narrows down the reasons for misbehavior as fulfilling the need for attention or avoiding of failure.

Allowing Daniel to maintain his dignity through the use of signals would be consistent with the ideas of Curwin and Mendler. By giving the student an opportunity to control his/her learning environment, problems associated with powerlessness are alleviated and the teacher is demonstrating the knowledge of the preventive dimension of *Discipline with Dignity*. Here the teacher focuses on what can be done to prevent discipline problems before they happen – a critical ingredient in any successful classroom management plan.

The key notion behind the TAC behaviors seen in choice B is the teacher and child working together to help the student behave responsibly. Developing a plan of action that is mutually acceptable to both the teacher and student will not only help when problems occur, but it may also limit misbehavior due to the student's feeling of ownership in the plan. In regards to consequences, the TAC teacher would enforce them, but they are often developed in conjunction with the students and applied in a manner that allows students to make connections between the misbehavior and consequence. For example, failure to turn in an assignment results in the loss of points – there is a logical relationship that exists between grades and work completion.

Choice C

As the goal of the TOE teacher is to look for ways for students to empower themselves, the teacher in choice C chose to engage the student in conversation regarding what was causing his misbehaviors. Ginott refers to this as inviting cooperation through congruent communication (Ginott, 1972). Doing this allows the student to express him or herself and makes them active participants in the potential solutions. Ginott stresses the importance of the teacher acknowledging and accepting these student feelings as justifiable. Overpowering student feelings, in this case, will continue to make Daniel reluctant to start work without teacher direction. The focus here is on the child becoming more self-reliant and making decisions that help him control his own behavior.

Since this appears to be a recurring problem, another area of focus for the teacher would be the instruction that's taking place. Does the student understand what content is being taught? Is content being taught in such a way as to promote understanding? Kohn (1996) states the importance of not focusing on making the students adapt to the needs of the adult, but for the teacher to ask herself, "What do students require in order to flourish and how can I provide those things?" This information would come from listening to the student and observing antecedents to the problem. Is the problem occurring only when the student is forced to complete individual work? In choice C, the question of learning style is mentioned. It may become necessary for the teacher to consider adapting instruction or instructional settings to provide the greatest opportunities for all students. Alternatively, if a student expresses disinterest in the topic, the teacher may consider looking for opportunities to allow the student to choose his own topic or course of study that utilizes similar concepts.

SUMMARY

In this chapter you have defined classroom management, been introduced to the TIC-TAC-TOE continuum of classroom management, and have begun to reflect on your own management style with theories in mind. The continuum and connection to other theories of managing the learning environment will provide a context as you develop and design your own management plan. The facets of management have been introduced allowing for you to see that discipline is only one aspect of overall management. Please continue to reflect on your own answer to the question, "How will I manage my classroom?" you are now closer to creating and implementing a plan that is successful with all children in your classroom.

MOVING ON: Reflection Assignments
1. Form a discussion group whose members represent all three options. Discuss together everyone's answers to the 5 questions on p.7 you answered before selecting an option.
2. Create a Venn Diagram with a circle representing each of the three management perspectives. Fill in the diagram noting similarities and differences between the potential and actual responses by a teacher representing each of the perspectives.
3. Individually, describe in writing how you could use observation as an important component within classroom management to help limit misbehaviors.

REFERENCES

Adkins-Coleman, T. (2010). "I'm not afraid to come into your world": Case studies of facilitating engagement in urban high school English classrooms. *The Journal of Negro Education, 79*(1), 41-53.

Albert, L. (2003). *A teacher's guide to cooperative discipline: How to manage your classroom and promote self-esteem.* Circle Pines, MN: American Guidance Service Publishing.

Bloom, L. (2009). *Classroom management: Creating positive outcomes for all students.* Upper Saddle River, NJ: Merrill/Pearson.

Brophy, J. (1988). Educating teachers about managing classrooms and students. *Teaching and Teacher Education, 4*, 1-18. doi:10.1016/0742-051X(88)90020-0

Brophy, J. (2006). History of research on classroom management. In C. M. Evertson and C. S. Weinstein (Eds.), *Handbook of Classroom Management: Research, Practice, and Contemporary Issues* (pp. 17-43). Mahwah, NJ: Lawrence Erlbaum Associates.

Canter, L., & Canter, M. (2002). *Assertive discipline: Positive behavior management for today's schools* (3rd ed.). Bloomington, IN: Solution Tree.

Chambers, S. M. (2003, February). *The impact of length of student teaching on the self-efficacy and classroom orientation of preservice teachers.* Paper presented at the Annual Meeting of the Southwest Educational Research Association, San Antonio, TX. Retrieved from http://www.eric.ed.gov/PDFS/ED477509.pdf

Curwin, R. L., & Mendler, A. N. (1999). *Discipline with dignity.* Alexandria, VA: Association for Supervision and Curriculum Development.

Doyle, W. (2006). Ecological approaches to classroom management. In C. M. Evertson and C. S. Weinstein (Eds.), *Handbook of Classroom Management: Research, Practice, and Contemporary Issues* (pp. 97-126). Mahwah, NJ: Lawrence Erlbaum Associates.

Evertson, C. M., & Weinstein, C. S. (2006). Classroom management as a field of inquiry. In C. M. Evertson and C. S. Weinstein (Eds.), *Handbook of Classroom Management: Research, Practice, and Contemporary Issues* (pp. 1-16). Mahwah, NJ: Lawrence Erlbaum Associates.

Ginott, H. (1972). *Teacher and child.* New York: Macmillan.

Glickman, C. D., & Tamashiro, R. T. (1980). Clarifying teachers' beliefs about discipline. *Educational Leadership, 37*, 459-464.

Jones, F. H. (1987). *Positive classroom discipline.* New York: McGraw-Hill.

Jones, V., & Jones, L. (2012). *Comprehensive classroom management: Creating communities of support and solving problems* (10th ed.). Upper Saddle River, NJ: Pearson.

Kellough, R. & Roberts, P. (2002). *A resource guide for elementary school teaching: Planning for competence* (5th ed.). Columbus, OH: Merrill Prentice Hall.

Kohn, A. (1996). *Beyond discipline: From compliance to community.* Alexandria, VA: Association for Supervision and Curriculum Development.

Larrivee, B. (2005). *Authentic classroom management: Creating a learning community and building reflective practice.* Boston, MA: Allyn & Bacon.

Melnick, S. A., & Meister, D. G. (2008). A comparison of beginning and experienced teachers' concerns. *Educational Research Quarterly, 31*(3), 39-56.

Monroe, C. R., & Obidah, J. E. (2004). The influence of cultural synchronization on a teacher's perceptions of disruption: A case study of an African-American middle school classroom. *Journal of Teacher Education, 55*, 256-268.

Moore, R. (2003). Reexamining the field experiences of preservice teachers. *Journal of*

11

Teacher Education, 54, 31-42.

National Education Association. (2010). *Status of the American public school teacher 2005-2006.* Washington, D.C.: National Education Association.

Pianta, R. C. (2006). Classroom management and relationships between children and teachers: Implications for research and practice. In C. M. Evertson and C. S. Weinstein (Eds.), *Handbook of Classroom Management: Research, Practice, and Contemporary Issues* (pp. 685-710). Mahwah, NJ: Lawrence Erlbaum Associates.

Rinke, C. (2007). Understanding teachers' careers: Linking professional life to professional path. *Educational Research Review, 3,* 1–13. doi:10.1016/j.edurev.2007.10.001

Veenman, S. (1984). Perceived problems of beginning teachers. *Review of Educational Research, 54*(2), 143-178.

Wentzel, K. R. (2006). A social motivation perspective for classroom management. In C. M. Evertson and C. S. Weinstein (Eds.), *Handbook of Classroom Management: Research, Practice, and Contemporary Issues* (pp. 619-643). Mahwah, NJ: Lawrence Erlbaum Associates.

CHAPTER II

Creating Positive Relationships

"Nobody cares how much you know, until they know how much you care"-
Theodore Roosevelt

This chapter will introduce the importance and rationale for creating and maintaining positive relationships between teachers and students in the classroom. You will read about setting up a classroom community and getting to know your students. The process of creating positive relationships starts before you even meet the children. It starts with reflecting on your own behavior as a person and a teacher. The previous chapter introduces the development of your own philosophy. At the center of your philosophy is your ability for creating relationships. How do you think people should be treated? Do you believe in treating others the way you would want to be treated? Are you assertive? Do you have a controlling personality? Do you delegate or share the work load? Are you inviting of others? Are you complimentary? Cooperative? A good listener? You will be introduced to teacher behaviors that influence student behavior in a positive manner as well as a negative manner. You will learn ways to get to know your students and how to appreciate individual differences. The steps and procedures for setting up a classroom community will be discussed and you will be asked to stop and reflect on this process. You will read about the importance of communicating you care and support your students, including a closer look at dialog and non-verbal communication in the classroom. Finally, you will analyze some practical ways to build positive relationships with students every day.

Guiding Questions
As you read and explore the concepts introduced within this chapter, use the following questions to guide your thinking:
- What are your own teacher behaviors that can impact both positive and negative relationships with your students?
- What are some ways to get to know your students and appreciate individual differences?
- How will you set up a classroom community?
- In what ways will you communicate you care and support your students? Why is your dialogue and non-verbal communication important?
- What are some practical ways to build positive relationships with students in the classroom every day?

BACKGROUND

Chapter 1 introduces the importance of developing a philosophy of management and the remaining chapters will help guide you to develop a style of managing the learning environment. A guiding question of this chapter asks that you examine your own teacher behaviors. First, we must provide some background and descriptions of teacher behaviors, so that you may examine your own. According to Barbara Coloroso (2010) there are three types of teachers, 1) Brick wall teachers have a strict and rigid style, 2) Jellyfish teachers are wishy-washy, with no guidelines, and 3) Backbone teachers provide support and structure necessary for students to be successful. A teacher who uses punishments, humiliation, threats, and bribes is considered to be a brick wall teacher. This type of teacher behavior should be avoided and will not lead to positive relationships with students. A teacher who is lax in discipline, has little recognizable structure or consistency can allow students to do whatever they want, until provoked and then they resort to irrational behaviors. When a teacher provides opportunities for students to make decisions and correct their own mistakes, they develop independence and feel valued. The Backbone teacher neither tells them what to do, nor does the work for them, he trusts in the students and provides support to get the work done. Which of these three types do you identify with today?

There are many philosophies on how to create positive relationships with students. At the center of most positive discipline plans is the theme of developing and earning mutual respect. Involving students with the responsibilities of the classroom is essential, including sharing the role of managing the classroom and active involvement of all students. Democratic teaching involves the teachers and students designing class rules and regulations together. The students have a voice in the classroom, choose their behavior, are invited to participate, and feel as though they matter in a democratic classroom. Dreikers and Stoltz (1964) teach the premise that good discipline occurs best in a classroom led by a democratic teacher who shares responsibilities for managing the learning environment. In contrast, an autocratic teacher makes all of the decisions and imposes them on students. The permissive teacher is one who does not have rules, regulations, and the students have no consequences for their behavior. Which type of teacher would have the best opportunities for creating positive relationships? So it seems a jellyfish teacher may work well in a permissive classroom and a brickwall teacher would fit in an autocratic classroom. Do you see yourself as a backbone teacher in a democratic classroom? Which style do you most identify?

Cooperative discipline theory (Albert, 2003) is based on involving students and families in the creation of rules and consequences. This shared responsibility encourages students to feel a sense of belonging in the classroom, they feel they are a capable member, and they can contribute every day. Gordon (2008) also promotes participative classroom management, where students and teachers share in the planning and management of a classroom. Albert (2003) shares the Three C's of Cooperative Discipline, where the teacher helps the students to feel capable, connected with others, and provides opportunities for the students to feel as though they are contributing members of the class. In order to make a child feel capable, connected, and contributing, teachers should provide many opportunities for students to participate in teams and other cooperative scenarios. Cooperative learning theory (Johnson & Johnson, 1990) suggests that students participate in shared problem solving, shared learning experiences, and team building with their peers. There should be plenty of time with positive face to face peer interaction, positive interdependence, and individual accountability for group work. Often, teachers shy away from cooperative learning because of classroom noise, management, assessment, and inexperience. Teachers who plan for cooperative learning experiences can set the tone for a more positive relationship with their students because it shows the students they trust them and can share the responsibility of teaching and learning.

Nelsen, Lott, and Glenn (2000) contribute there are certain teacher behaviors that act as barriers to developing caring relationships with students, while other behaviors help to build. They identify five pairs of contrasting behaviors: 1) assuming versus checking, 2) rescuing versus exploring, 3) directing versus inviting, 4) expecting versus celebrating, and 5) "adult-isms" versus respecting. When considering your own teacher behaviors, think of these relationship builders and barriers. The following questions will help guide you as you create your own philosophy of educating children: Do you often make assumptions about others' feelings and abilities or do you seek the truth? Do you feel you need to do it yourself, because that is the only way to be sure it is done correctly? Do you enjoy engaging students and discovering with your students? Are you more comfortable lecturing and being the "keeper of the information" or do you feel comfortable welcoming the students into a less structured cooperative teaming experience. Do you find yourself saying things like, "…because I said so" and "How come you never?" "Why don't you *ever* do it right?" Teachers who are interested in creating positive relationships do not say these "adultisms", they get energy from encouraging and respecting others because they know if respect is given, it will be received, in return.

Creating positive relationships starts with developing mutual respect. All people need to feel a sense of dignity. It would be impossible to create a positive relationship with students when the students do not feel a sense of dignity. Richard Curwin and Allen Mendler (1992) outline principles relating to disciplining with dignity and always treating students in a dignified manner. They advise teachers to reflect on allowing the students to regain and maintain a sense of hope that things will improve and they will learn how to behave and overcome barriers. They suggest teachers should not attack a student's dignity but instead offer hope. Curwin and Mendler would like for teachers to reflect on the following: How would you feel if you were the student? What am I doing to my student's dignity? Am I motivating? Am I helping the student to become responsible or just obedient? How am I being encouraging?

15

When considering establishing positive relationships, the manner of which a teacher talks to students is important to examine. Thomas Gordon (2008) teaches about "I- messages" and "you-messages" and how they can be used to influence behaviors. He contends that I messages can be used in a positive way to help students to cease unacceptable behavior. For example, an I-message is a statement in which people tell how they feel, such as, "I am having difficulty reading because there is so much noise in the room." You-messages are statements that are not as productive, where blame is assigned to a person or people, for example, "You boys are causing us to not get work done!" More examples include, "I am so glad to hear about your exciting weekends, but I can't hear when everyone talks at once." There are also negative you-messages that should be avoided if possible, "You were the worst class at the assembly, you embarrassed me in front of the school." Instead, the teacher could have given a preventative I-message before the assembly, "I hope you remember to be quiet during the assembly today, I want us to remind each other with our class quiet sign". Gordon (2008) also further examines how teachers speak to students. He has identified "door openers" words and actions that encourage others to share what is on their mind and "communication roadblocks" which are comments that shut down a student's willingness to communicate. An example of a "door opener" is asking a child who is non-compliant, "Do you feel like talking to me later at lunch about anything?" On the contrast, the teacher could put up a communication "roadblock" and tell the non-compliant student what he ought to be doing and how his behavior is wrong.

authoritarian

As you reflect on your own style of teaching and your positive relationship builders, are you a teacher who dictates procedures and berates students? Or are you a teacher who inspires learning and provides an encouraging environment? William Glasser (2011) distinguishes these two types of teachers as "lead" teachers or "boss" teachers. He promotes that "lead" teachers are most effective in the classroom and they have what he refers to as "7 Connecting Habits", including caring, listening, supporting, contributing, encouraging, trusting, and befriending. Boss teachers are thought to limit productivity and just encourage students to complete the task. He shares the "7 Deadly Habits" of boss teachers include, criticizing, blaming, nagging, complaining, threatening, punishing, and rewarding students. On the contrary, a lead teacher will inspire, motivate, and plan powerful experiences for the students. Think of the terms "leader" and "bossy", what is the difference between these two terms? What does it mean to be bossy? Is it effective for a positive relationship in the classroom? What does it mean to be a leader? Which type of teacher do you identify?

THEORY TO PRACTICE

> **Reflect and Act:**
>
> **Creating positive relationships with your students can start with an examination of your own personality and your own behaviors. What are your pet peeves? What type of environment do you work best? Are you a leader or a boss? List how others would describe you. Create a graphic where you brainstorm your attributes.**

Rationale: Why should you want to create positive relationships in the classroom?

Once the school year begins, greeting your students at the door can set the tone for the day. A "Hello", high-five, hug, or a handshake can really make children feel welcomed and a sense of belonging in your classroom community is more likely to start, with this simple gesture. As members of the classroom community, students will have rights and responsibilities, where they can contribute, allowing the students to share the responsibility for the discipline in the class- in other words, students need jobs and responsibilities in the classroom, even young children can share the load. If the students learn anything they will learn you. If you present yourself in a hostile manner or have a need to control every aspect of the classroom, the students will learn their place and unfortunately, they may not be inspired to learn anything else, except the knowledge they do not get along with their teacher. It is possible the child will disengage and there will not be an opportunity to teach the child, which is your job. Do you respond well to someone who berates you or are you motivated by someone who inspires? Children need to be inspired to learn, berating helps no one. If you take the time to build a positive classroom atmosphere, you will be perceived as a successful teacher and the positive energy is contagious. Your students have a better chance of learning in a positive atmosphere.

Teacher behaviors impact both positive and negative student relationships

Teachers, who want to create positive relationships with their students, should not only think about "getting along" with their students but they should think about planning powerful instruction that will inspire and motivate learning. Creating positive relationships with students is not about becoming friends. Teachers need to think about being friendly, not becoming the students' friends. There should be a balance of time spent on designing your management plan and planning lessons and units of study. Instruction and management are linked and when teachers plan for active, relevant integrative, challenging, and value-based (NCSS) lessons, there is little "down time". Down time, is when misbehavior can occur (Snyder, Cramer, Afrank, & Patterson, 2005). When you have taken time to plan active, integrative, relevant, and challenging units of study, the students will be so focused on the powerful learning, they will behave, naturally. They will be so busy; there is no time for misbehavior. This does not mean you need to have the students physically active, they can be mentally active. The integrative aspect of their learning can be instruction integrated with a value, such as respect, responsibility, or other character traits. When the students see relevance in what they are learning, they are more likely to maintain interest, and may not choose distracting misbehaviors. Similarly, when students are challenged, they may try to achieve success, finish tasks, and not want to be involved in misbehavior.

Earlier, "backbone" teachers were introduced. They focus management on respect, responsibility, caring, and success. Backbone teachers are able to give respect and they expect to get respect in return from the students. They model respectful behaviors every day and establish and practice routines with smooth transitions. They do not just go text to text, lecturing all day. If you want to be an effective manager, practice powerful teaching, while exhibiting the skills of a backbone teacher. The lead teachers, who were introduced earlier, use positive words and praise often. When they do, they make it genuine and empower individual students to resolve conflicts. It is possible to train students in conflict resolution and peer mediation. Conflict resolution programs allow students to share responsibility for discipline and hopefully learn from their mistakes. Having set times for class meetings each week is a way to allow students to express their voice and concerns. These meetings can be productive if simple rules relating to mutual respect are followed by all participants.

Teachers who care set up individual conferences with students. When there are concerns, the students can record them in a notebook to be discussed at a classroom meeting. Teachers who care express interest in students clubs, sports, and extracurricular activities. They may have lunch with their students and often send positive notes home. A suggestion box can be utilized to let the students know you value their opinion and suggestions for improving their learning experiences. The caring teacher will participate on the playground, participate in art, physical education, and music performances. The caring teacher is involved in the school events and the community. Finally, the caring teacher will collaborate with other elementary teachers or pair up with lower elementary teachers for reading buddies, pen pals, and correspondence journals.

involved outward acts

Classroom community
Brophy and Alleman (2007) suggest four steps for setting up a classroom community: 1) Formulate overall classroom goals specific to a social education learning community, 2) Focus on the physical environment, 3)Establishment of rules, norms, roles, and procedures, and 4) Create a vision for how all of this will function-"What should our classroom look like to us?". When setting up a classroom community, student interest is at the center. Give the students an interest inventory where they can share their personal interests with you. The students should feel safe, secure, respected, valued, and have positive contact with their peers. According to Sapon-Shevin (2010) the five characteristics of a learning community are: security, open communication, mutual liking, shared goals, and connectedness. Students need to feel as an important part of the whole group.

Arrange your classroom so that it encourages collaboration, structure, and order. Be ready to change the seating arrangement often. The physical classroom needs to be set up conducive to a community. There are several ways to allow students to feel as though they are contributing members of the class. Set up your classroom like a society and call them citizens. Use the Constitution as a guide. Develop your rules and procedures together. All age groups respond well to a democratic classroom style because they are going to be citizens soon, so give them time to practice. Make sure you share responsibility for tasks and jobs in the classroom. The students can assume roles in the classroom and contribute to things such as leading class meetings, refilling supplies, collecting papers, etc.

share responsib.

Talking to your students: Communicating care and support
There are many ways to communicate that you care, including "get to know you" experiences. In the beginning of the year, the students can complete interest inventories. The inventory asks the children to report their personal favorites (foods, movies, music, tv shows,

actors, books, colors, etc). This information can be used to design incentive plans and contract incentives. As a teacher, you can communicate you care by interacting with the students regarding their life outside of school, expressing interest in their hobbies, sports teams, and families. The students know you care when you provide feedback immediately regarding their work. Practicing active listening is another way to show you care. The students will also appreciate and respond to any attempts to prevent misbehavior through planning powerful teaching experiences.

Be sure to build a support system with family involvement. You can start by setting up a class web page, involve the students in newsletters, involve parents in creative ways, such as a class showcase. Be sure to document and celebrate the learning going on in your elementary classrooms. This topic will be discussed more in depth in chapter 9. When you must respond to negative behavior, allow students to "save face" and maintain hope they will be successful in the class. Whenever you respond, no matter the behavior, try to keep it positive, in that you are not going to disrespect the child. You can share you are disappointed with the behavior, not with the child.

Practical ways to build positive relationships with students in the classroom

Positive behavior is contagious. *Be the person you want your students to be.* Think about theater and drama, use your voice, body language, and non-verbals, they are more powerful than you think. Smile and be energetic. Be firm, but friendly. Use volume, inflection, and energy, these are powerful tools.

- Be sure to check-in with your students, show them you care by working the room and checking for understanding, "Show me that you understand and I will be around to check"
- The way you speak to your students helps to create positive relationships. Use your clear voice and an affirmative tone. For example, "Raise your hand. Wait for me to call on you. Tell me your idea..." Give clear instructions and make sure they know them and always allow time for compliance.
- Non-verbals are amazing- tell the class, "Class we are going to choose a SECRET class sign, no other class will know about it. The sign will be what we use to get each other's attention. Give the students some examples, and state, "Let's vote on our secret sign, you choose".
- Try motivating incentives, such as a lottery.
- Communicate in a clear, upbeat tone. Think of how powerful your voice can be.
- Follow-through on your promises or requests. Think about the importance of follow through with sports. Would you have a good golf swing, batting swing, serve, free throw if you did not follow through? If you notice that you only threaten to take away or move clips and tickets, then you have no follow- through. Do not be afraid to act on your management plan and communicate though non-verbals where students lose a privilege. Follow through fairly, quietly, and always allow the child to maintain hope he will be able to come back to the activity and if he behaves for the next 5 minutes.

- When communicating with children, it is important to be on their eye level. Do not hover above them. They need to know you are talking to them.
- Model the behavior you want to see in your students.
- Students appreciate individual conferences on books they are reading, they like to have lunch with you 1 on 1 or in small groups. These conferences are opportunities to set goals and create contracts. It is a good idea to implement class meetings. Have a classroom economy where everything costs and it is similar to the game of "life" where you can assign jobs, give paychecks, and have them work for what they do. The students can maintain a checkbook, accounts. A classroom economy integrates well with management.

Student behavior and academic performance can be associated with a positive teacher and student relationship (Albert, 2003). Imagine a child excitedly walking into class with news to share, when he begins to share the news, his teacher tells him, now is not the time, and that he needs to get out his homework instead. What message does this send to the child? Perhaps the child will give the same behavior back to the teacher when asked to get out his math book, by ignoring the teacher's request and misbehaving. If children are given a routine and a process for sharing- and know when they can share important news- perhaps the students will feel welcome- and more likely, will be compliant.

Reflect and Act:

How do you plan to avoid favoritism? How will you be fair? How will you motivate students to learn? Why do you think some teachers treat children differently? Is it possible to treat a child differently because of dress, hygiene, skin color, parents, neighborhood, or any other reason? Why? How? How will you avoid this?

APPLICATION WITH DIVERSE LEARNERS

Students are worth all the effort teachers can expend on them. They are worth it not just when they are bright, good looking, or well-behaved, but always (Colorosso, 2010). Diversity in classrooms requires the creation of a safe, secure, supportive learning community with many opportunities to say nice things to one another, complete tasks together, and to learn from one another. What are your own biases when it comes to starting relationships with people- including your students? Students perform well for teachers who do not make an issue of race- but instead celebrate the differences.

Talking with students about their behavior is one of the most complex aspects of teaching. How does classroom talk differ from talking other places? There are cultural definitions of "foul" language, use of slang, sarcasm, jokes, etc. Take cautions here. Loudness and repetition does not necessarily improve the relationships with all of your students. Avoid ambiguity, be polite and clear when giving instructions, use visuals, and find cues that will work for certain requests and reminders. Nagging has negative effect on students. You will be tuned out eventually. Always

no power struggle

allow the student to "save face" when communicating with the child regarding negative behaviors. Remain calm and speak in a non-aggressive tone. When helping a child with emotional issues to change a behavior, do not take any interaction personally, do not allow the other students to treat the child any differently, suggest a "change of scenery" or change the subject. Do not respond to a student who may state, "I hate you!" Do not become an angry teacher, it is your job to help discipline, an opportunity to teach acceptable behavior. It is not productive to take this personally.

"Tough" students benefit from several one-on-one meetings. Give them respect and allow them time to process what they have done. Remember, the purpose of discipline is self-discipline. With individuals, it is best to first, find out what motivates the child, through an interest inventory, set up a contract, where target behaviors are identified and when they are reduced, the student can fulfill the contract (earn a privilege or other motivator). The target behaviors must be observable and measurable (Rhode, Jenson & Reavis, 1992).

It may be helpful to go through the following checklist, regarding your own teacher behaviors. A checklist for negative teacher behaviors- DO I:
1. Seat low expectation students far away? Do you exclude them from the group, never to let them have hope in returning?
2. Pay less attention to certain students?
3. Call on the same students? Do you show favoritism?
4. Give less time to certain students to reply?
5. Only criticize certain students? Praise some and criticize others?
6. Interrupt student? Demand less of certain students?
7. Use negative tones with certain students? Spend more or less time working with and helping certain students?
8. Treat a child differently because of parents, former student sibling, origin, race?
9. Treat a child differently because of dress, hygiene, etc?
10. Treat a child differently because of a former teacher sharing information?

A checklist for positive teacher behaviors. Do I:
1. Use test data to inform my teaching?
2. Use flexible grouping where it is not always the same groups of students (always the high flyers together)
3. Challenge all students?
4. Use ethnically diverse materials for all students?
5. Use fair discipline for all students?
6. Communicate higher expectations for all?
7. Monitor my own verbal and non-verbal communication?
8. Involve all students in their learning process?
9. Change seating arrangement often?
10. Provide opportunities to include all students, often?

CASE STUDY – Building Positive Relationships with Students

The hallways were bustling with children as the buses were leaving the parking lot, another Monday has begun at David Parks Elementary. The children happily chatter about family events from the weekend- and catch up with their peers...as they enter their third grade classroom, they are greeted with Mrs. Pratt firmly stating, "Hurry up, get in here and be quiet!"... there are no formal greetings and Mrs. Pratt is busying herself with some posters and a bulletin board-multi-tasking, because she is going to be observed today and wants her classroom to look 'just right'. She announces (while not looking at the children) to "quickly put away your things, and open up your math book to page 67"....the children have questions for her and want to tell her about their weekends- but she needs to get attendance and lunch count. Her response to Robin sharing she has a new baby brother is, "we do not have time to talk, we have real work to do"..."I am being observed today teaching math, and we need to catch up...you do not know your multiplication facts"... She frantically takes the roll and calls the office to come get her lunch count and attendance folder, and then gathers up the permission slips for the field trip on Friday, while ignoring many questions about the field trip, with a response, " you should have listened to the principal discuss the trip to the apple orchard last month... there is no time for questions!"...

Robin reluctantly sits down and refuses to get out her math book. "You need to get started on page 67", states Mrs. Pratt. "You can't make me, you are not my mom!" replies Robin. "I don't care about math!", she continues, "And I don't care about you!"...Mrs. Pratt goes to her desk and gets out a bag of M & M's. "Whoever gets out their math book and homework, will receive one M & M"..."AND" she added in a sing-song voice "whoever is goo-ood when the principal arrives, will get TWO!" "Now, get out your book, Robin!" "I know you like M & Ms!"

The day continued with several students getting "into trouble" for not being on task in Mrs. Pratt's classroom. She sent them to the office- after spending at least 30 minutes lecturing the class about behavior and her expectations. She frantically was cleaning the classroom-straightening books and papers, while "teaching" how to multiply...in between straightening the desks, she would offer an insult to a student for not knowing basic math, "Are you kidding?- how do you not know your math facts, yet?- How did you pass your last grade?"...Mrs. Pratt felt out of control when the students offered to help her clean and organize for the visitor- she said, "I will just need to do it myself, you will not do it correctly!"...

Mrs. Pratt's observation time had arrived; the principal entered and sat in the back, taking notes. The lesson began- and the students seemed disinterested and the principal wrote about the non-compliant student behavior and lack of student engagement with the lesson.

Discussion Questions (Complete these before moving on to the descriptions.)
1. What are the teacher behaviors that Mrs. Pratt is exhibiting that are negative?
2. In what ways is Mrs. Pratt communicating that she does not care or support her students?
3. How would you describe Mrs. Pratt's classroom community?
4. How could Mrs. Pratt develop positive relationships with her students?
5. How would you handle this situation?

After you have answered the discussion questions and decided how you would handle the situation, read all three of the choices that follow. Select one that most closely matches your ideas. Or if you read one that you like better than your own ideas, choose it as your own.

Choice A

If I were Mrs. Pratt, I would have explained to the students that I know they have needs and rights in the classroom, and my needs and right to teach without interruption was important that day because I was getting observed. However, I would have not taken the hostile style of teaching as Mrs. Pratt did. I would have been more assertive, where I clearly expressed the expectations for the day, so they would know how to progress through the day. I would probably meet with Robin privately, reminding her of the compliance rule: Do as the teacher asks you to do, immediately. I would have also provided a clear means for the students to share their personal stories during a class meeting. Robin would have known she could write her announcement in our class meeting agenda notebook. If I were Mrs. Pratt, I would have assigned jobs for each of the students in the classroom- where everyone was responsible for some task- each day. There would have been no need to be frantic for a visitor, because our class would run with clear classroom structures. When the students entered my room, they would know we had a visitor scheduled and would have a protocol for the visit. Students would be aware that if they completed their tasks before, during, and after the visitor, they would receive an incentive- such as extra recess time.

Choice B

If I were this teacher, I would first meet the students at the door, with a welcoming smile. The students would enter to find the same routine as the day before. The students who had exciting information, would know they could share in a class meeting on Friday. The students would not have been berated for not knowing multiplication facts, in contrast, they would be told what they were capable of doing, and how proud I was of their progress. My students would have felt connected to me and my observation and would have been asked to contribute in some way to prepare. We would have nothing to "hide" when a visitor comes, we would continue with our usual routine. Robin would have been treated with more dignity and she would have hope that she will eventually be able to share her big news. I would not have used any negative tone- and would have not bribed the students with M & Ms. There would not be nagging of the students to get their math books out- I would state the request clearly, and offer time for compliance. I would speak to the students with respect and look at them when I was speaking to them. I would have planned a lesson that was powerful, so the students would see relevance in the math content. I would have spent as much time on my management plans as I did on my lesson plans.

Choice C

If I were this teacher, I would use the information gathered from the last multiplication facts test to decide how to teach multiplication facts in a more meaningful way. I would take responsibility for planning instruction that would be interesting related to the math they were required to learn. In my classroom community, I do not always want the students to be quiet and compliant at all times. The first thing in the morning is a naturally social time, so I would allow soft chatter in the morning as the students completed a bell-ringer or other tasks in the classroom community, such as the lunch count or the attendance. I know I can share these responsibilities with my students and they can own many tasks in the classroom, since it is their classroom. The rules we would follow would be designed by the students and myself. Robin's announcement would have been a "jubilee moment" of the day. I would have asked how her family was doing and express my shared excitement. The class may even decide to create a card for Robin's new sibling. We would add the birthdate to our class important events timeline. I might have asked the students what they thought we should do to prepare for our visitor, and really the principal's visit would have not been a big deal. He is invited to our classroom anytime and feels part of our learning community. We might have had an impromptu class meeting to discuss any concerns or announcements of the day, in a safe, secure forum. Once this was complete, we could move on to math or other aspects of the curriculum. I would be treating my students in ways that I like to be treated, with respect. You would hear me using I messages that are productive and not demeaning.

SUMMARY

This chapter allowed you to examine your own teacher behaviors that can impact both positive and negative relationships with your students, including verbal and non-verbal skills. The chapter provided a rationale for why this is an important part of managing the learning environment. You were encouraged to reflect on your own teacher behaviors to see if you exhibit barriers or builders to creating positive relationships. You were introduced to methods for getting to know your students, while appreciating differences. The four steps for setting up a classroom community were introduced. Important topics like how to talk to students to show you care and methods for communicating were introduced. Finally, practical ideas for building positive relationships with students were outlined.

Moving On: Reflection Assignments
1. Write a brief introductory letter, introducing yourself to your class. How will you communicate that you care?
2. Who are you as a teacher? Describe yourself and your philosophy for creating positive relationships with students. Use the terms learned in this chapter to describe.
3. Choose one of the practical ideas shared for connecting with your students (classroom economy, greeting at the door, cooperative learning, classroom jobs, etc) and expand on the idea including implementation and details for how you can make it work for you and your students.
4. This chapter introduced Brophy's steps to setting up a classroom community. Describe how you are going to set up a classroom community in your own class? Where will you begin?

Appendix A: Reflect and Act
Think about what you already know about building positive relationships with your own family, friends, and community. What are characteristics of a successful relationship?

Design a T-chart describing positive and negative behaviors that influence caring relationships.

Appendix B: Complete and Share

Think of one child in your classroom whose behavior is challenging you as a teacher. Define his or her behaviors. Create a professional resource list with 5-7 resources related to these behaviors and strategies for discipline and opportunities to teach the child to behave or learn replacement behaviors. This is an annotated bibliography of articles that could be used to create your literature review for your overall evidence.

REFERENCES

Albert, L. (2003). A teacher's guide to cooperative discipline: How to manage your classroom and promote self-esteem (rev. ed.). Circle Pines, MN: American Guidance Service Publishing.

Albert, L., & DeSisto, P. (1996). *Cooperative discipline.* Circle Pines, MN: American Guidance Service Publishing.

Brophy, J., & Alleman, J. (2007). *Powerful social studies for elementary students.* Belmont, CA: Wadsworth.

Canter & Associates. (1998). First-class teacher: Success strategies for new teachers. Bloomington, IN: Solution Tree.

Canter, L.,, & Canter, M. (2002*). Assertive discipline: Positive behavior management for today's schools* (3rd ed.). Bloomington, IN: Solution Tree.

Coloroso, B. (2010). *The Bully, the Bullied, and the Bystander: From Preschool to High School-- How Parents and Teachers Can Help Break the Cycle (Updated Edition).* New York, NY: HarperCollins.

Curwin, R. L., & Mendler, A. N. (1999). *Discipline with dignity.* Alexandria, VA: Association for Supervision and Curriculum Development.

Dreikurs, R., & Soltz, V. (1964). *Children: the challenge.* New York: Hawthorn Books.

Fay, J., & Funk, D. (1995). *Teaching with love & logic.* Golden, CO: Love and logic Press.

Glasser, W. (2011). *Schools Without Fail.* New York, NY: HarperCollins.

Gordon, T. (2008). *Parent effectiveness training: The proven program for raising responsible children.* New York, NY: Three Rivers Press.

Johnson, D. W., & Johnson, R. T. (1990). *Learning together and alone: Cooperative learning.* Allyn & Bacon.

Jones, F. H. (1987). Positive classroom discipline. New York: McGraw-Hill.

Kohn, A. (1996). *Beyond discipline: From compliance to community.* Alexandria, VA: Association for Supervision and Curriculum Development.

National Council for the Social Studies. (n.d.). A vision of powerful teaching and learning in social studies: Building social understanding and civic efficacy. Washington DC, NCSS. Retrieved from http://www.socialstudies.org/positions/powerful

Nelsen, J., Lott, L., & Glenn, H. S. (2000). *Positive Discipline in the Classroom, Revised 3rd Edition: Developing Mutual Respect, Cooperation, and Responsibility in Your Classroom.* New York, NY: Three Rivers Press.

Rhode, G., Jenson, W. R., & Reavis, H. K. (1992). *The tough kid book: Practical classroom management strategies.* Frederick, CO: Sopris West.

Sapon-Shevin, M. (2010). *Because we can change the world: A practical guide to building cooperative, inclusive classroom communities.* Thousand Oaks, CA: Sage Publications.

Skinner, B. F. (1954). *The science of learning and the art of teaching.* Harvard Educational Review, 24, 86-97.

Snyder, J., Cramer, A., Afrank, J., & Patterson, G. R. (2005). The contributions of ineffective discipline and parental hostile attributions of child misbehavior to the development of conduct problems at home and school. *Developmental Psychology, 41*(1), 30.

CHAPTER III

Organizing the Learning Environment

"I never teach my pupils, I only attempt to provide the conditions in which they can learn."
— *Albert Einstein*

"I've come to a frightening conclusion that I am the decisive element in the classroom. It's my personal approach that creates the climate. It's my daily mood that makes the weather. As a teacher, I possess a tremendous power to make a child's life miserable or joyous. I can be a tool of torture or an instrument of inspiration. I can humiliate or heal. In all situations, it is my response that decides whether a crisis will be escalated or de-escalated and a child humanized or dehumanized."
— *Haim G. Ginott*

Teaching is more successful when teachers take time to pre-plan seating, supplies, rules, and procedures (Brophy, 1988). This chapter will introduce the importance and rationale for organizing your classroom. You will read about the importance of rules, standards of conduct, and procedures. The process of organizing the classroom environment starts well before you even meet the children. It starts with reflecting on your own experience with rules, consequences, organization, routines, and expectations. The previous chapter introduced the importance of developing positive relationships with children in your classroom. This chapter will focus on organizing an environment for where these relationships can grow and where learning can happen. It is more likely your students will learn when they are in a positive classroom environment, managed by you, who they trust and respect. This chapter requires you to reflect on your developing philosophy of teaching. Depending on how you feel children should be taught or how the majority of the day should be spent, will require you to think about how to organize the environment. Some may not take this seriously and later, regret not taking time to reflect on the physical environment. Effective teachers take time to reflect on all aspects of managing the learning environment.

Do you want your desk in the front of the room? How will student desks be organized? What will be on the walls of your classroom? What are the rules and procedures for your classroom? What are the consequences for if rules are broken? Who will determine the rules? How will you teach the rules? You will be introduced to ways to organize the physical environment and ways to establish rules and routines. You will learn ways to start the year and ways to prevent misbehavior. The steps and procedures for setting up a classroom will be discussed and you will be asked to stop and reflect on this process. You will read about the importance of student involvement with establishment of rules, consequences, procedures, and routines, including a closer look at preventative measures and the idea of classroom community and holding class meetings. Finally, you will analyze some practical ways to set up your physical and procedural classroom environment for student success.

Guiding Questions

As you read and explore the concepts introduced within this chapter, use the following questions to guide your thinking:

- What are your own needs for a learning environment? Under what conditions do you learn best?
- What are some ways to organize a physical learning environment or classroom?
- How will you establish rules, consequences, and routines?
- Why are procedures important?
- What are some practical ways to prevent misbehavior, including reinforcers, reward, and praise?

Reflect and Act:

Creating a classroom environment requires you to reflect on the type of environment where _you_ learn best. Write a brief description of the atmosphere where you learn best or are most productive. What do you need to have a positive working environment? How much neatness or organization do you require? How do you feel about students assuming responsibilities for tasks in the room, and shared decision-making?

What rules do you think every classroom needs? Why? List the classroom rules you will present, teach, and gain commitment in your classroom. Are they observable, measurable,

---

BACKGROUND

All people need to feel a sense of safety and belonging. This chapter will serve as a guide for your developing position or philosophy of how the learning environment should be organized and managed. A guiding question of this chapter asks that you examine your own personal needs as a learner. How do you study best? What type of environment do you thrive? Do you need natural light, music, cool temperatures? First, we must provide some background and descriptions of learning environments, so that you may examine your own. You will want to design a learning space that is welcoming, safe, and conducive to learning. In general, teachers must be concerned with two aspects for organizing the classroom, 1) the physical environment of the classroom and 2) the guidelines for governing the classroom. It is against human nature to learn in an uncomfortable environment where there is no order. How do you best learn?

According to Evertson, Emmer, and Worsham, (2000), there are three keys to good room arrangement: 1). Keep high traffic areas free of congestion, 2). Be sure students can see and be seen in the classroom, 3). Keep frequently used materials readily accessible. What kind of classroom community do you want to develop? Will there be mostly teacher-led learning or will students be exploring on their own in groups? It is difficult for students to work productively if they do not have guidelines for behavior. When there are not efficient rules and routines, students are not on task and there is a lot of time wasted trying to get students to behave. When there is an orderly environment, there are more opportunities for learning and the critical tasks at hand. A typical elementary classroom consists of approximately 30 students of varying abilities and backgrounds. You will be required to teach these students a set curriculum in a short period of time. The students will be with you for most of the day except lunch, recess, and special classes. Because of this, your class environment must be organized or nothing will get done. There needs to be a flow and routine so that more time can be dedicated to instruction and not management during a regular class day. When there is a "flow" or routine, there can be more emphasis placed on powerful instruction.

In reviewing the literature on rules for learning and teaching, most agree there should be a no nonsense approach with logic and simplicity. Most agree there should be no surprises for the students (Glasser, 2011; Gordon, 2008; Albert,2003; Jones, 1987; Canter, 1989) First, the classroom needs to be analyzed to determine best practices with teaching, learning, safety, and property in mind. Second, experts agree that if you are to have rules, they need to be clearly communicated. There is agreement that students need to show understanding or a commitment to the rules somehow. Finally, there is some agreement of how each rule should be enforced; whether it be punishments, or logical and natural consequences As you continue to create your own philosophy of management, you will determine how you believe rules should be enforced, how misbehavior can be prevented, and if students should be rewarded or punished.

Teachers need to establish routines. This should be a high priority when considering good classroom management. What are necessary routines for children? What were your routines as a child? For example, did your parents set a bedtime, snack time, or nap time? If there are no routines, it may lead to chaos and a moody child, not willing to comply. Likewise, in the classroom, there can be routines for entering and exiting the classroom, lining up for lunch, going to the library, walking down the hall, helping each other, checking out books, gathering on the carpet for calendar time, lunch count, etc. When there are no routines, students might talk out of turn, might not follow directions, and may not be ready to learn. Of course, teachers must review routines that are necessary, list them, establish rules for the routines, and teach the routine explicitly. In other words, this is the "way" of the classroom. Teachers must facilitate the creation of "the way". This is "how we do it in this classroom". When behaviors become routine, there is very little need for instruction of these behaviors each day, they just happen or become "routine". There are certain learning experiences where there is a need for procedures (lab work, group work, presentations, etc). What will be the procedures for certain activities? For example, how will the students behave during a science lab demonstration and experiment? The list of routine procedures a teacher must plan is indefinite, but for starters, a new teacher might want to think about procedures for room use, supplies, large group and small group learning, transitions, emergency procedures, and administrative duties (attendance, lunch count, reports, etc).

In addition to routines, teachers need to establish rules or a "code of conduct". What are the rules and expectations for the class? According to Cangelosi (2000) rules need to be purposefully stated "standards for classroom conduct". When there are few rules, they are more likely to be remembered and understood. Also, when there are few rules (only 4-6), they can be seen as more important then if they were lost in a list of 10 or more rules. When rules are stated with purpose, this appeals to common sense and allows the focus to be on the behavior rather than nonsensical technicalities. For example, a rule that is stated, "All students must remain in their seats" does not answer the question, for what purpose? A better rule might be, "Students must remain in their seats, until they have permission to move". This way the teacher can share the purpose for this rule. It is a small classroom, for safety purposes, we must do it this way. "No talking" does not work as a rule. It does not help the student to learn when they can talk or how to gain permission to talk. A better rule might be, "Raise your hand, wait for permission, and then you may talk". The purpose for this rule can be easily explained, "I want to hear what you say, I care…but if we all talk at once, I will not be able to hear". If your class had a rule, "All students must remain in their seats", there could be some nonsensical technicalities where the student needs to stretch or leans over to pick up a pencil- and is out of their seat- technically. When you design rules, try to avoid technicalities, your daily job is much more sophisticated than spending the day counting how many times student bottoms leave seats.

To further examine the development of your rules, Cangelosi (2000) suggests making sure your rules have purpose. The following questions help you to formulate the standards of conduct: 1) Is the rule's purpose to maximize positive behavior and minimize off task behavior? 2) Does the rule help to secure safety and comfort in the classroom? Is the purpose of the rule to prevent disturbances? and, 3) Is the purpose of the rule to maintain civility and dignity among students, personnel, and visitors?

Finally, what will be the consequence if a student does not follow the routine and breaks a rule? What is a consequence? Or will there be a punishment? What is the difference between a consequence and a punishment? Most of us understand natural consequences. For example, if you touch a hot stove after being told not to do so, and naturally, the consequence is a painful burn. Natural consequences include losing an item when you have been careless, missing a bus when you are late, and being locked out because you forgot your keys. These natural consequences do not always work in the classroom setting, so logic must take over. Logical consequences are those we might be familiar with, such as getting a speeding ticket for speeding, receiving a finance charge when a bill is not paid on time, or a check that bounces when there are not sufficient funds in an account. In a classroom setting, a logical consequence might be, "If you spilled the paint, clean it up" or "If you wrote on the desk, clean the desk" (Rhode, Jenson, & Reavis, 1992).

There are many philosophies on how to organize a learning environment, including democratic, autocratic, or permissive. At the center of most plans for organizing the physical space and deciding on the rules, is the idea of mutual respect, safety, and conducive to learning. The environment and governing rules are a reflection of your philosophy or style of teaching. Rudolf Dreikers (1964) teaches good discipline occurs best in a classroom led by a democratic teacher who shares responsibilities for managing the learning environment. If you are democratic, your physical environment may reflect this by having areas for "choice", bulletin boards created by students, plenty of space for student presentations and projects. In contrast, an autocratic teacher makes all of the decisions and imposes them on students. The autocratic teacher may have the desks in rows all day, every day, this teacher designs and controls all aspects of the physical environment and the rules. They have created the bulletin board displays and are most likely not going to ask for student input on any aspect of organizing the learning environment. The permissive teacher is one who does not have rules, regulations, and the students have no consequences for their behavior. The physical environment of a permissive teacher might have chaos, including no routines, things are often lost, there is no follow through, and often the permissive teacher has "sprouted roots" in one spot of the classroom where they will allow behaviors until they cannot take it anymore and lose their temper in an irrational manner. Again, your philosophy is reflected in the environment and in your expectations of the classroom.

Involving your students in the creation of the classroom environment and rules, consequences, etc may have a positive impact on your students' overall school experience and may impact their learning. In the previous chapter, you read about Albert's cooperative discipline theory (Albert, 2003) and Gordon's (2008) participative classroom management, where students are made to feel as though they are contributing members of the class. Teachers who plan for cooperative learning experiences can set the tone for a more positive relationship with their students, it shows the students they trust them and can share the responsibility of teaching and learning. When teachers share the responsibility for management with their students, teachers can alleviate some of the pressure of having to do it all.

THEORY TO PRACTICE

Reflect and Act:
Think about what you already know about setting up a classroom's physical environment and establishing rules. You have been in an elementary school as a student. What are some things that you know should be included in the classroom? How will you organize the space? What are some ideas you have seen that work? What has changed in classrooms since you were a student? What remains the same? What are the necessary student behaviors that you need in your classroom so that problems will not occur or at least be less likely to happen? Analyze classrooms of the past versus those of the present.

Rationale: Why should you want to create an organized learning environment?

When your classroom environment is organized, structured, and appropriate for learning, the students are more likely to behave in the manner you desire. If your room is unorganized, it sends the message that disorganization is acceptable behavior. When are students most likely to behave? What conditions must be met to ensure students are likely to behave appropriately? Students are more apt to behave when the teacher teaches and models appropriate behavior, while explaining a rationale for behavior and a connection to everyday life. When the students see the relevance of the classroom to their everyday life, they are more likely to behave. They will also behave when there is a clear, mutual, respect for the teacher and student relationship. When setting up your classroom environment, work with your students to set up the goals of the classroom with the rights of the students and the teachers in mind. The students protection and safety are top priority when organizing the classroom environment. The environment must be conducive to learning and mutual respect should be present.

What can potentially enhance appropriate behavior? Teachers who clearly communicate guidelines, gain commitment from students, and model desired behaviors in the classroom, have the potential to enhance the chances for more appropriate behavior (Levin & Nolan, 2000). Behaviors must be taught. Just because they are posted on the wall, does not mean everyone will follow the rules.

relationship are MUST imp.

When teachers take time to genuinely get to know their students, this is time well-spent. Often, there is pressure to get right to instruction of content and no need for "fluffy" "get-to-know-you" experiences. The author disagrees and feels that time spent doing cooperative team building, is valuable and will make instruction even more powerful and relevant.

Practical ways to organize the learning environment
Walls

As mentioned earlier, teachers must be concerned with the physical environment of the classroom and the guidelines for governing the classroom. The physical environment includes the walls, floor, furniture, entry, windows, equipment, etc. Think of the walls and bulletin boards as space for information and visual stimulation. The walls should belong to both you and the students. In the beginning of the year, you will want to have space designated for your rules, assignments, goals, a calendar, etc. It would be nice to have a welcoming bulletin board or "welcome back" sign with the students' names or a class list posted. There could be space reserved for "student of the week" and "in the news". In addition, a nice space to display student work in the future. You will also need to consider where to post emergency routes and procedures for fire/disaster drills.

Also on the walls, you may want to have posters related to content, such as a number line, writing process, graphic organizers, multiplication chart, timelines, etc. The wall can be where you display student jobs or responsibilities. There should be a place for the hall pass or sign-in/sign-out. There are great practical resources for teachers related to decorating the walls, created by teachers, for teachers, such as Mailbox Magazine and Teacher's Helper. But remember, do not feel pressure to decorate your entire room. The walls can belong to the students too. Perhaps allow them to have a "graffiti" area…where they post a topic- and they can write their thoughts freely. For example, should there be school uniforms? What is your favorite movie? Where do you like to go on weekends? Do not over decorate. Most classrooms are small and with 25-30 bodies, they feel cramped. Leave a couple bulletin boards blank. Save some space for the students to showcase work, relevant information, or perhaps some interactive material for an upcoming science or social studies unit.

The purpose of bulletin boards should be to recognize student work, provide opportunities for interaction, share news, and post rules. Students should be involved with deciding what will be displayed on bulletin boards and the walls. Again, share the walls with your students. You are going to be sharing this classroom for a long period of time and it is important for the students to feel some ownership and some part in the décor. Whenever you can share the responsibility with students, do it. The goal of teaching is for students to become life-long learners. The goal of discipline is self-discipline, they need practice with responsibility. Let the walls be their responsibility and their showcase.

32

Floors

First, in regards to the floor, there should be clear paths, open in high-traffic areas, and clear of clutter. When thinking about floor space, how will you want to use it? Will you want students to gather on a carpet near you? Will you have a rocking chair where you can read to the students while they are gathered on the carpet? This is a typical arrangement for grades K-2. On the floor, you might even see "x's" where the students are to sit, "Criss-cross-applesauce". This carpet space could be where the students gather for morning meeting, calendar time, read-alouds, to have space for the teacher input and guided practice part of a lesson. It will be helpful for you to draw a map of your classroom, so you can locate the outlets for your room, decide where technology will be best placed (document cameras, Smart Boards, LCD projectors, overheads, etc). You will need to map windows, entries, closet, your desk, shelving, etc. Once you map out what you have, you can start to add your own personal touches, such as carpet, couch, reading areas, class pets, plants, tables, etc.

Furniture

When arranging students' desks, high traffic areas should be kept clear. Make sure the students have easy access to doors, windows, computers, shelves, lockers, cubbies, centers, etc. Make sure the furnishings are not distractors. For classrooms today, computers should be an integral tool for learning and if you are fortunate, you will be in a school where computers are in every child's hand. You will need to decide, instructionally and philosophically where and how you would like students to access these learning tools. Consider your policy and school policy on smart phones, as they can be valuable tools for learning. Be sure to leave room around the desks so you may assist the students when needed. If you have tables instead of individual desks, you will need to arrange so the students' backs are not toward the "front" of the room, where instruction may take place. When there are tables or "clusters" of desks, they can be seen as "teams" and they can share tools, supplies, etc. These teams can also serve as a great management tactic- group contingency.

Shelves

Your shelving can offer a designated space for bins labeled, "homework", "math", "science", "journals", etc. This will help students to turn in work. You could also have a "To Be graded bin" and a "graded" bin on shelving by your desk. It has been suggested in this book, the importance of teaching the rules and expectations- it would be good to teach the children the layout of the classroom, in other words, you could take them on a "tour" of the classroom. The "tour" is when they would learn about the use of space in the room. First stop, the "Today" chart- to see the schedule, second, the calendar, on to attendance basket, where you will move your name into the basket, next, the homework bin, finally, let's point out the quiet areas of the room. This "tour" could be adapted for your classroom. It may include stops at stations, computer areas, lab areas, and job charts. If you are fortunate to have a "paperless" classroom, where students upload work electronically, then your organization will occur partly in the room and in cyberspace.

Rules, Consequences, and Routines

In general, a rule is a standard for behavior. Rules should communicate expectations for behavior, they should be observable, measurable, and purposeful. Who should determine the rules? You can be an authoritarian and decide on all rules, procedures, and consequences on your own. You can be a democratic teacher and invite the children to create the rules and consequences or you can determine the rules together with the students, or you can be a combination of both, propose a couple rules, and allow the students to have input on the rest. Which style matches your philosophy? Regardless of who determines the rules, you will still be required to teach the rules, routines, and consequences.

You will need to decide on rules and rule-setting that matches your philosophy of teaching and management. You may word them differently, or edit. Perhaps you may find them too general. Remember, each year is different, and your management plan may not work for each class of students. Some of your "toughest customers" may require rules that are purposeful, observable, measurable, and simply stated. Remember to teach the rules, post the rules, model the rules, discuss and earn a commitment from the students to comply and follow the expectations. The students can be given their own copies of the rules, sign them, and review them often. The rules should also be shared with families. Sample Rules:

1. Follow directions
2. Be polite
3. Keep your hands to yourself
4. No talking while the teacher is talking
5. *Compliance Rule* (Rhode, Jenson, & Reavis, 1992) Do as your teacher asks, immediately.

Establishing the rules is only the first step. *Teaching* the rules of the classroom is just as important as teaching the content of the class. The children must first learn the rules before they can follow them, this is why the author believes ownership with regards to rules helps students to learn, accept, and are more likely to commit to them and follow them. Procedures and rules need to be taught though examples and through demonstration. Time spent teaching both rules and procedures is time well spent and considered just as important as time spent on teaching the curriculum (Brophy, 1988). Procedures can become integral to objectives of the lesson. The manner of which rules are phrased is important. Brophy (2000) suggests using the phrase, "We all need to… _____", followed by the rule (behavior expectation) and continue with, "because it is important to _____". This is where you incorporate the principle or purpose for the rule, model the desired behavior, and review often. Be clear of what you expect.

Any rule regarding following directions is a rule that teacher candidates will have the opportunity to teach during their student teaching experiences. Canter (1989) believes this is the most important rule. This needs to be taught and re-taught after long breaks from school. Teach students how to follow the directions. State in a firm, yet friendly, voice: "Please clear your desks of everything except a pencil". "Eyes on me". No talking while I am talking". "Raise your hand and wait to be called on, before speaking". Canter (1989) advocates for a classroom management plan including rules, positive recognition, and consequences. The rules should include observable behavior. Positive recognition should be sincere, genuine, positive attention. For example, send notes home, praise, appreciation, and positive phone calls. Try to call parents when there is good news, not just bad news. Consequences are the results following a behavior choice. Consequences can be both positive (when students behave appropriately) and negative (when students interfere with their own learning or the learning of others). Consequences need to be consistent; students need to be reminded their behavior has chosen the consequence. The Canters (2002) state, " There is nothing more harmful we can do than watch students misbehave without showing we care enough to let them know their behavior is unacceptable.

When planning your levels of consequences, Canter (1989) recommends a hierarchy including, warnings, loss of privilege(s), call home, principal visit, and also recommend there is a severe clause, where depending on the severity of the behavior, the student will go directly to the principal's office. Do reflect on if you can handle the behavior yourself, you do not want to send the message you are not able to handle situations as they arise in your own classroom. You will need to consult the building conduct code to find out what "zero tolerance" behaviors are for your school. You will need to decide what behaviors will send the student directly to the principal or phone call, without a warning or loss of privilege. The author would like to add the importance of trying to handle all situations as best you can without involving the principal, until there is no other option. The author would follow a similar hierarchy but adds a "change of scenery" within the room after the loss of privilege. This can be a change of seats, change of location in the classroom, or even a change of rooms. It is a good idea to have a colleague who you can agree will welcome a misbehaving student for a set period of time. This is a great solution, because sometimes people just need a change. Be sure not to take advantage of your colleague. Offer to do the same for him or her, when needed.

It is important to document behaviors and keep track of misbehaviors on a chart, clipboard, or notebook with every student's name, which is kept private. Do not write student's names on board, in front of all students (unless for positive recognition). It is possible to have cards with the students name on them for them to "flip" when they are on a certain level of consequence. The colored cards could be in folders stapled to the wall, where the students know what each color means. Everyone starts with their green card showing, then as they are warned about behaviors, they need to move the card to a different color, depending on their level of consequence. This will be a way you can remember who needs to lose a privilege, who has already been warned, or who you have moved during the day. There are also plans where clothes clips could be used…where the students "clip up" or "clip down" depending on their behavior.

There is a need for rules because children, in general, are highly sensitive to changing situations and conditions. A long list of "dos and don'ts" sends the message that you are going to focus on minute behaviors and spend little time teaching, more time nagging. You send the message you may be unreasonable, illogical, and somewhat controlling. Rules should be fair, realistic, and rationalized so that the class environment is better and conducive to learning. Rules should not be arbitrary. When considering the rules to govern your classroom, consider your rights as a teacher, the students' right to learn, the emotional and physical safety of the classroom, and the property belonging to all (Evertson, Emmer &Worsham, 2000). If you have children brainstorm possible rules for the classroom, record ideas on the board and discuss. If your rules are logical, rational, and understandable, there will really be no need to vote on them.

Choosing consequences is just as important as designing the rules for your classroom, because when the teacher follows through with consequences will determine if students will follow the rules and learn to behave appropriately. Deciding on a consequence "on the spot" is not a solution or a good idea. This could be perceived as inconsistent, unfair, unreasonable, and unrelated. The students expect to receive consequences for their actions. Your job is to teach them how to behave and teach them to be good citizens. Colorosso (2010) suggests a test for creating the best consequences. You should use RSVP, which stands for the following questions: 1) Is the consequence reasonable? 2) Is the consequence simple? 3) Is it valuable- can the student learn a value?, and finally, 4) Is the consequence practical?

Natural consequences are consequences that occur when a person misbehaves. An example of a natural consequence is no grade on an assignment that did not have a name. Another example is when the lab test has an incorrect outcome when the lab procedure is not followed. Logical consequences are consequences that match the behavior. An example of a logical consequence is when the students lose time from recess because they did not line up correctly. Another example is when the student must replace a textbook that he damaged. Enforcement of expectations through logical and natural consequences allows students to see they can control their own behaviors and are responsible for their actions (Rhode, Jenson & Reavis, 1992).

Reflect and Act:
With a partner, discuss the following questions:
- **Will you let your students know the consequences of breaking rules in advance?**
- **Will you involve the students in deciding on rules and consequences?**
- **What do you think are reasonable consequences for talking out of turn, pushing another student, writing on a desk?**
- **Do you believe in warnings? What about the idea that students should get "two strikes and then they are out"?**
- **Do you believe in the Golden Rule for your classroom- "Do unto others as you would have done to you?" What about Grandma's rule-which is, "If you eat your veggies, you will get a treat". If the student does the less desirable experience, then they receive a reward, "If you do your math problems without whining, you will get to go to recess early". Will you use the Golden Rule and Grandma's Rule?**

Why are procedures important?

What is a procedure? This is a rule applied to a specific activity for ease of completion. The number of procedures and routines teachers and students need to master, so that instruction time is not lost, is infinite (Rhode, Jenson, & Reavis, 1992). For starters, it is important to decide on a routine for money collection, attendance, and hall passes, etc. Deciding on procedures for your classroom may seem trivial at times, but once you reflect on the few procedures mentioned above, you will have the start to a management plan. Various areas of your classroom need procedures, to regulate the use. For example, what are the procedures for keeping student desks orderly? What about your own desk? The author would have a "Clean out your desk time" on

Fridays. What are the procedures for storage areas, checking out materials, procedures for the pencil sharpener? What about entering the room and leaving? How will you gain students' attention during presentations? How will they obtain your help? Will you have a class "quiet sign"?

When you have a solid routine for the beginning of the day and the end, you can set the tone for the class, have a fresh start, and end on a positive note, each day. It is important to establish a positive, welcoming, routine for the start of the day and a similar "wind down" routine for the end of the day. The author would greet her students at the door, the students would enter and follow this routine: move their attendance clip, put away their books and book bag, check the jobs chart (complete any job), find their seat, begin the "bell-ringer" assignment from the board. The "bell-ringer" is a brief assignment which students can complete independently. The students would be aloud to talk quietly with each other and the teacher as they settled in to learn. Following the morning bell, we would say the Pledge of Allegience, listen to announcements, have a morning meeting including going over the schedule for the day. Students would sit in table teams, so they were encouraged to give their team chants to motivate, team quiet signs to signal it is time to work. The end of the day was similar, in that 30 minutes before the closing bell, the author would try to be on the independent practice portion of any lesson, as students finished their work, they would begin packing up their backpacks, checking assignments, and then come one at a time to the "meeting area" and start sharing with the teacher one thing they learned or any questions, they would then give their class cheer or song and say goodbye to one another, as the busses were called.

Classroom rituals and routines can be more like traditions of your classroom. Providing a familiar routine and a common experience can serve to enhance positive relationships with your students. Choosing to honor your students and acknowledging their efforts and individuality can allow for the students to feel more part of the classroom community and more likely to display desired behaviors, and learn. For example, in our morning meetings, I would have "jubilee moments" where the students would have the opportunity to share what is going on in their lives (new baby sister, they are moving, they have a new neighbor, made the basketball team, have a new pet, etc.). Sometimes morning or afternoon meetings involved a "talking stick" where the students who were holding the stick, were able to share something important. We would also feature "students of the week" where the randomly selected student would create a "me poster" and be able to be in the "spotlight" for the week.

Once you establish rules, consequences, and procedures you may consider obtaining the students' commitment or agreement to follow the plan. This could be thought of as a class contract or even a class constitution. Establishing the rules, posting the rules, and explaining the purpose are important parts of organizing your classroom, but without obtaining the students' commitment to follow the rules, the plan will not be successful. For an agreement, sometimes people shake hands or sign a contract to indicate there is a commitment. When presenting rules for the class, it is a good idea to obtain a class contract, where the students sign a poster with the rules, which will be hung in the classroom. They could make a written promise where they state, "I have read and understand the rules. I intend to follow these rules". The students then sign and date the contract.

Reflect and Act:

What is your philosophy of homework? What will be the rules for homework? What about the procedures for checking it? What are the advantages and disadvantages of homework?

Classroom community

Students might be far more likely to respect rules they helped to create than rules handed to them (Koki & Stan, 2000). In Chapter 2, suggestions for setting up a classroom community were shared as a way to nurture positive relationships with students. Brophy and Alleman's (2000) 4 steps for setting up a classroom community were shared : 1) Formulate overall classroom goals specific to a social education learning community, 2) Focus on the physical environment, 3) Establishment of rules, norms, roles, and procedures, and 4) Create a vision for how all of this will function-"What should our classroom look like to us?". When setting up a classroom community, student interest is at the center. Give the students an interest inventory where they can share their personal interests with you. The students should feel safe, secure, respected, valued, and have positive contact with their peers. According to Sapon-Shevin (1999) the five characteristics of a learning community are: security, open communication, mutual liking, shared goals, and connectedness. Students need to feel as an important part of the whole group.

Alphie Kohn (1996) encourages teachers who wish to move beyond threat, reward, and punishment, must do three things: provide an engaging curriculum based on student interests, develop a sense of community, and draw students into meaningful decision-making. Kohn (1996) believes class meetings offer the best forum for addressing questions and problems in the classroom community. Class meetings include a forum for sharing, deciding, planning, reflecting, and he believes they are time well-spent. Often, teachers say there is not enough time for class meetings, but Kohn argues it is necessary to make time for these meetings.

Reflect and Act:

Is it more important to you that students be quiet and compliant, or engaged and motivated? Write a paragraph of your position on this topic? Will you utilize class meetings? Why? Why not? Misbehavior happens during transition times. How will you monitor transitions? Share a way to help children transition smoothly from one

APPLICATION WITH DIVERSE LEARNERS

The definitions of and explanations for appropriate behavior are culturally influenced. Teachers must realize that classrooms are not culturally neutral. Setting up the classroom with the culture of the classroom in mind, is very important. For example, it is important to not impose your personal bias on students. You should not treat a student differently based on clothing, hair color, or any difference. However, ignoring cultural differences is not a wise strategy (Levin & Nolan, 2000). Students come from a variety of cultural backgrounds. Culture is a collection of knowledge, customs, traditions, rituals, emotions, values, and norms shared by members of a population for survival. The white, middle-class culture tends to value mastery and compliance and not so much nurturing and living as one with nature. If you were from a culture that emphasized impulse control over self-expression or encouraged independence versus interconnectedness. If the classroom management plan is based on a "class constitution", similar to the US Constitution, then it is tough to argue with and students feel as though they are learning to live in a society. They are meeting society's expectation, not just the teacher's.

Matching rules, procedures, and guidelines to the culture of the students' home (community) the likelihood students will behave is increased. Classrooms are not culturally neutral communities. When teachers and students are from the same cultural group, it is easier to set classroom rules, routines, and guidelines. Teachers may misinterpret behaviors of students from other cultures. Teachers must take appropriate steps to try and understand their students better. Learn social communications of the minority groups represented in the classroom. It is suggested the teacher will need to modify behavioral expectations and interpret minority behaviors from the minority's point of view (Koki & Stan, 2000). The teacher needs to teach the majority and minority groups of the classroom to appreciate and recognize the value of each other. What one culture might see as "lazy" or "naughty" might not be the same for another culture. They may just be conscientious of their work, take their time, and they do not see this as exhibiting problem behaviors. A student's background needs to be considered when deciding relevant and meaningful involvement in the discipline process.

Misbehavior that occurs because of cultural differences should be handled differently then misbehavior occurring as intentional disruptions and distractions. When a child is misbehaving, consider all of the reasons and consider if it is "misbehavior" or is the child simply behaving in a manner that would be appropriate in his or her culture. Failing to acknowledge differences is not a solution; acting like you do not notice cultural differences is not a solution and may cause more conflict in the classroom. This aversion may make students feel like the teacher does not care and does not appreciate their cultural differences and therefore it becomes not a learning environment where students feel appreciated and there is no trust. Being honest with students is always best (Levin & Nolan, 2000).

When the teacher chooses to avoid the cultural differences in the classroom, it may cause students to "check out" or just "play student" which in any case, they are not being themselves. All students need to be provided with a clear rationale for why rules and procedures are important in the classroom (Ladson-Billings, 1994). Schools are culturally situated institutions influenced by a cultural mindset derived by the culture of the majority or culture of the administration and the teachers. If this is different than the culture of the students, there could be problems, if there is no awareness. Teachers should strive to know all of their students and to learn about the cultural background of the children they teach. One way to do this is by getting involved in the community and participate in events outside the school. When they see their students outside of the classroom, participating in cultural events, sporting events, or plays, the teacher can learn to appreciate what the child is bringing to school each day. Another suggestion is that teachers should intentionally incorporate students' cultural backgrounds into the classroom, through visuals, literature, and instruction. When students feel appreciated and not alienated they are more likely to behave in school (Ladson-Billings, 1995).

As an educator, you will be confronted with more variables to manipulate at the same time than any other profession (Cangelosi, 1992). Children can differ in many areas. Your task as a teacher is to first be aware of these differences, and second adjust or differentiate your planning, instruction, and management with these individual differences in mind. This is not an easy task, considering the students can differ in the following areas (and more): interest in learning, self-confidence, cultural background, attitude toward school, aptitude, anti-social tendencies, home life, prior achievements, and prior experiences. Students are more likely to be cooperative participants in a classroom that is in sync or at least appreciative of his/her background and differences. When students understand, value, and can potentially learn from one another, a cooperative classroom exists. When there is no opportunity for learning from one another and celebrating differences, fear, mistrust, and hostility can arise in the classroom. This is a chaotic scenario where learning can't take place.

Reflect and Act:
Think about the questions below and write responses in your own journal regarding your own discipline experience.
1. **How were you disciplined in school? At home?**
2. **Did your parents have different styles of discipline? Was this a problem? Why? Why not?**
3. **Did your teachers have different styles of discipline?**
4. **Do you recall a time where you were punished and really learned a lesson?**
5. **Is there anything from your past that you will take into the classroom with you? Why or Why not?**

CASE STUDY – Organizing the Learning Environment

The year was starting in one week and Mr. Thompson had just been assigned to teach a 5th grade classroom. It was his first year teaching. He was both excited and anxious to get started. "Where should I begin?" he thought. "Really, by fifth grade, most students know how school "works"...won't the students be ok with everything?", "They will know his expectations; they have been in school for 6 or more years if they were in pre-school".

So, Mr. Thompson proceeded to plan for his first science unit of instruction. He was assigned an old science lab room, which was perfect. It was small but had great, old lab tables, sinks, and plenty of storage space. The room was bare, with nothing on the walls or on the shelves, and he didn't have many materials, so he thought the students would enjoy decorating. They were old enough to handle this responsibility. He decided to make that a first week "activity"...to decorate the room. Mr. Thompson was handed a teacher handbook, school code, and also some school procedures pamphlets. Again, he thought, I am teaching the "big kids", so they will know how it "works". He jumped right into planning an amazing unit for science as he had learned in his teacher training program. He just taught this unit for his student teaching- and he thought it went well…why not try it again? He had some ideas to enhance the lessons, so he began to write his plans.

The first day had arrived and the students entered the room with excitement and nervousness, just as their teacher. They were chatting about the summer, a very social group. Mr. Thompson was not used to this- the classes he had worked with were quiet and did not talk, unless the teacher called on them. He had to come out from the back of the room where he was gathering some science materials, to find the children roaming around the room. The first thing he said to the students was, "Alright, sit down, and be quiet, so we can get started!" He was sort of upset that he had to raise his voice on the first day. He asked the students to get out their pencils and science journals. He told the students to sit wherever they wanted. Some of the students sat on the floor, while others sat with their friends and continued to talk.

There was no mention of rules, expectations, or procedures. He simply said, "Come on now, how long have you all been students?" and continued, "you know the rules by now". He went on to address several students from across the room that were sharpening their pencils. He yelled,

"And now is not the time to do that, it is too loud!" He began his science lesson where he lectured on the seasons of the year, and prepared to show a video, but he was stunned at how many hands were raised during the lecture. He called on one girl, "I need to use the restroom", and then another girl shouted out, "I need to leave early today". "Alright, alright, let's get back to the topic of science!" Mr. Thompson said. Two boys, who had desks that faced the back of the room, began spinning their science journals on their pencils, one child, who was sitting by the wall, turned the lights off and on repeatedly, while another child got on the computer, because he sat at the computer station. Several of the children decided to get their handheld devices, smartphones, and IPads out to play games. Two girls were fussing over a water bottle that had spilled on the floor because they bumped into a table that was between their desks. A young man, named Henry put on his headphones to listen to music and beat out a rhythm on his table, at the front of the room. Henry had an audience and the children were laughing at his rhythmic dance moves. Mr. Thompson tried to redirect the children's attention to him, but the majority of the class was not paying attention. Two boys were doodling on their new notebooks. He gave them a "look" with eye contact, a serious expression, and moved in closer proximity to the boys. They stopped doodling for a while.

Mr. Thompson saw there was a girl who was paying attention, he did not know her name, so he went to her desk, and said, "What is your name?" "Do you like science?" The young girl said, "My name is Cecily." Mr. Thompson announced to the class, "Cecily is the only one in this class who likes science?" Some students responded without raising hands and just shouted out their feelings about science. Because they were all yelling out, Mr. Thompson announced that he was taking away recess from the entire class; they would spend it inside with their heads down. He said, "Wow, this is going to be a long year, if you lost recess on the first day!" "You are all on my 'list!'". "You are acting like a bunch of Kindergartners". "I will not forget this day; you will be sitting inside for many recesses, so you can think about what you have done to me". He went on, "Maybe missing recesses will teach you to listen to my science lessons!". Cecily raised her hand, and asked, "Mr. Thompson, do I have to miss recess?" Meanwhile, the young girl from earlier left for the restroom in a hurry.

Discussion Questions (Complete these before moving on to the descriptions.)

1. Is there anything that Mr. Thompson has done well?
2. What are some potential reasons the students are misbehaving?
3. How would you handle this situation?
4. What advice would you give Mr. Thompson?

After you have answered the discussion questions and decided how you would handle the situation, read all three of the choices that follow. Select one that most closely matches your ideas. Or if you read one that you like better than your own ideas, choose it as your own. Then follow the directions for the activities that follow the explanations of the options.

Choice A

If I were Mr. Thompson, I would have first "taken charge" of the classroom, before the students started the year. Even though Mr. Thompson was hired late, he had a week to organize his room and the learning environment. He could have made some important and simple decisions that would have prevented most of the chaos in the classroom on the first day. He missed the opportunity to map the classroom and decide where furniture and desks should be for the first day. He had time to at least create a "welcome" sign for the door and to post some relevant information for the students, such as emergency and disaster drill procedures, hall passes, and general classroom procedures. When mapping the classroom, he should consider the desks near light switches, computer stations, or high traffic areas. He had desks facing all areas of the room, instead of facing where he lectured. He had enough time to establish a few working rules, including a compliance rule relating to following directions, immediately. He should have had these rules posted, along with a hierarchy of consequences posted for the students to review in the first week. He should have spent the morning of the first day, greeting the students at the door, welcoming them into the classroom, and directing them to a procedure chart, where they will be introduced to the morning routine. Fifth grade is a wonderful grade to establish routines and rituals so the classroom will have mutual respect.

Choice B

If I were this teacher, I would have been more prepared for the first weeks of school, by not focusing so much on the content I was going to teach, and more focused on the learning environment. The old science lab the teacher was assigned, could offer some wonderful space for experiments in the future, but the students need to learn important procedures before learning can occur. I would have posted basic procedures as above, but would have involved the students in the creation of the rules, consequences, and routines. The students could also share responsibility by decorating the classroom with content relevant materials. I would have space for the students to be acknowledged and featured, such as a "student of the week" bulletin board, or students in the news, or place for student work to be spotlighted. The first day is for settling in, learning procedures, perhaps a class meeting to formulate and establish classroom rules. I would begin teaching the rules, along with the students through role-play, and then get their commitment to the rules, by having them sign the "classroom constitution", and post it on the wall. I would have arranged the room in a circle for the first day, so we could have a meeting, to introduce each other, share stories, and also conduct an interest inventory. I would have the students participate in some "icebreakers" and "get to know me" activities, and not too much content for the first day. I would take the students on a tour of the room and building and teach all procedures.

Choice C

If I was this teacher, I would welcome the students into the classroom, ask that they gather on the carpet, and begin with, "Welcome to the classroom community". I would let them know they are an important part of a learning community. I would teach them the definition of community and proceed letting them know that this year, they are going to be involved in engaging curriculum based on their interests and they were going to be involved in the decision-making in the classroom. I would reflect on two questions: 1) How can I work with the students to create this learning environment? And 2) How can I turn this into an opportunity for them to learn? I would have a class meeting where I would identify the student behaviors that will help and those that will hinder an enjoyable learning environment. We would then decide on our class agreements, where the students would create a document listing a summary of behaviors required for a profitable learning community. We would then post the agreements and review them often. We would establish logical and natural consequences that were reasonable, simple, valuable, and practical. I would not treat students in a way, that I would not want to be treated, so I would not make those statements such as "Sit here and think about it, and maybe it will teach you...". I would make sure the students saw my "truth signs" in the classroom. They would read: *Give respect, get respect, We all learn in our own ways, by our own timeclocks, etc.*

Using Tic-Tac-Toe

Choice A

If your response was aligned with the teacher behaviors in Choice A, you may find elements of Lee and Marlene Canter's *Assertive Discipline*, Fred Jones' *Positive Discipline*, along with the philosophies of B.F. Skinner (1954), appealing. These theories fall into the TIC category.

In this scenario, Mr. Thompson does not exhibit any strategies recommended by Canter, Jones or Skinner. If you agreed mostly with Choice A, you believe Mr. Thompson needs to take charge. There are many things Mr. Thompson needs to do, including meet the children at the door, decide on the class layout and room arrangement. Once class started, he did not provide any positive recognition or praise for any of the students. Of course, it was the first day of school, and it is difficult to give personal, genuine, specific, and age appropriate praise to students you have just met. The students who were sharpening the pencils when they weren't supposed to could have been redirected privately, as the Canters suggest. However, the students didn't know the procedures for the pencil sharpener, because they were not taught and not posted. Canter suggests teaching the rules and consequences: 1). Explain why rules are needed, 2). Teach the specific rules, 3). Check for understanding, 4). Explain rewards, 5). Explain consequences, 6). Teach the consequences, and finally, 7). Check again for understanding.

Fred Jones believes that class structure should discourage misbehavior. Jones continues that prevention is key to a successful classroom. Choice A would allow Mr. Thompson to see that prevention begins with setting up the class structure and paying attention to rules, chores, routines, opening, and closing of the day. Teachers also need to design preferred activity time (PAT) for the students. Skinner (1954) adds that punishment has negative effects on children and that reinforcement and rewards need to be consistent, as they will help new learning to be established in the classroom environment.

Choice B

The response emulated by Choice B would fall into the category of the teacher and child (TAC) working together to formulate a solution. Elements included in the response are drawn from Nelson, Lott, and Glenn (2000), Glasser, (2011), Linda Albert's (2003) *Cooperative Discipline,* and Richard Curwin and Allen Mendler's (1999) *Discipline with Dignity.*

Nelson, Lott, and Glenn suggest thinking in terms of solutions instead of consequences. They believe that consequences hurt but solutions help. It is wise to involve students in solutions, focus on the future, not the past. They teach that opportunity comes with responsibility and warn against "piggybacking". For example, "Maybe this will teach you!", "Sit here and think about what you have done!". If you identified with Choice B, you would want the students and teacher to plan solutions together, in advance, or have class meetings, as needed, where the students could brainstorm solutions to problems in the class. William Glasser (2011) believes that every class should have an agreed-upon, printed set of rules. Students would have input in the rules as established, and the consequences would be reasonable. Glasser (2011) warns to never accept excuses from students when breaking rules.

Beginning of the year is a great time to decide on a class motto, classroom code of conduct, and teach problem solving strategies. Linda Albert believes a classroom "code of conduct" is better than "rules", because "rules" imply teachers control students. If you chose Choice B, you would practice Albert's 3 steps to creating a code of conduct, including envisioning the ideal, asking for the students' vision of how they want the room, and finally, asking for parents/families input. Richard Curwin and Allen Mendler feel that responsibility is more important than obedience. If you chose Choice B, you would like to see the students sharing the responsibility for managing the learning environment. Curwin and Mendler encourage teachers to see that student dignity must be preserved. They encourage pro-social behavior, where the students are motivated to learn. This can have lasting results achieved over time.

Choice C

The goal of the TOE teacher is to look for ways for students to move toward ownership of behavior in the classroom and as a citizen. Alphie Kohn (1996), Fay and Funk (1995), Thomas Gordon (2008), and Barbara Colorosso (2010) believe that teachers should encourage students and empower themselves to change their own behavior. Colorosso believes in inner discipline, where there are natural consequences, and you treat children the way you want to be treated. Fay and Funk believe there should be one rule for the classroom, "You can do anything you want in this classroom, as long as it distracts no one". Thomas Gordon would recommend 3 steps to start the beginning of the year. 1). Identify student behaviors that will help, and those that will hinder, learning in the classroom, 2). Discuss your concerns with the class and make a list of the class agreements for making the class enjoyable, and 3). Help the students learn to function in keeping with the class agreements. These tasks will require constant review and are just the initiation of Gordon's (2008) Discipline-as-Self-Control.

SUMMARY

This chapter allowed you to examine how to set up your classroom and make it conducive for learning. The chapter provided a rationale for why organizing the classroom environment is an important part of managing the learning environment. You were encouraged to reflect on your own organization needs and leadership style. You were introduced to methods for organizing the space, walls, furniture, while rules and consequences were introduced. Important topics like procedures, routines, and preventative measures, were introduced. Finally, practical ideas for managing the learning environment were outlined.

Moving On: Reflection Assignments

1. In a paragraph, explain the difference between a routine and a rule of conduct.
2. What will be your classroom rules? List 3-5 classroom rules. Be sure they are observable and measurable.
3. Discuss the advantages and disadvantages of having students democratically decide on the organization of the class, rules, and the standards for conduct.
4. An excellent teacher resource is Teachingtolerance.org. Visit the website and choose an article to write a one paragraph reflection of how the topic will apply to teaching diverse learners.

Appendix A: Reflect and Act

- What rules do you think every classroom needs? Why? List the classroom rules you will present, teach, and gain commitment in your classroom. Are they observable, measurable, and few?
- Sketch a map of your classroom. What is the layout of your current classroom or the classroom you desire to have? How are the desks, chairs, tables, computers, etc. arranged? Offer a brief rationale for why your room is arranged in this manner.

Appendix B: Complete and Share

- Identify a child who is having difficulty in your classroom with one of your rules or perhaps having difficulty with the arrangement of the classroom. Define his or her behaviors and share how you will address this behavior.
- Start to review literature related to helping the child identified above. The Review of Literature serves two purposes: to describe your classroom management philosophies and plan and to explain research-based classroom management interventions for relevant behavioral issues.

REFERENCES

Albert, L. (2003). A teacher's guide to cooperative discipline: How to manage your classroom and promote self-esteem (rev. ed.). Circle Pines, MN: American Guidance Service Publishing.

Brophy, J., & Alleman, J. (2007). *Powerful social studies for elementary students*. Belmont, CA: Wadsworth.

Brophy, J. (1981). On praising effectively. *The elementary school journal, 81*(5), 269-278.

Cangelosi, J. S. (1993). *Classroom management strategies: Gaining and maintaining students' cooperation*. New York, NY: Longman.

Canter & Associates. (1998). First-class teacher: Success strategies for new teachers. Bloomington, IN: Solution Tree.

Canter, L.,, & Canter, M. (2002). Assertive discipline: Positive behavior management for today's schools (3rd ed.). Bloomington, IN: Solution Tree.

Canter, L. (1989). Assertive discipline: a response. *The Teachers College Record, 90*(4), 631-638.

Coloroso, B. (2010). *The Bully, the Bullied, and the Bystander: From Preschool to High School--How Parents and Teachers Can Help Break the Cycle (Updated Edition)*. New York, NY: HarperCollins.

Curwin, R. L., & Mendler, A. N. (1999). Discipline with dignity. Alexandria, VA: Association for Supervision and Curriculum Development.

Dreikurs, R., & Soltz, V. (1964). *Children: the challenge*. New York: Hawthorn Books.

Evertson, C., & Emmer, E., Worsham, M. (2000). *Classroom management for elementary teachers*. Boston, MA.: Allyn & Bacon.

Fay, J., & Funk, D. (1995). *Teaching with love & logic*. Golden, CO: Love and logic Press.

Glasser, W. (2011). *Schools Without Fail*. New York, NY: HarperCollins.

Gordon, T. (2008). *Parent effectiveness training: The proven program for raising responsible children*. New York, NY: Three Rivers Press.

Jones, F. H. (1987). *Positive classroom discipline*. New York: McGraw-Hill.

Kohn, A. (1996). *Beyond discipline: From compliance to community*. Alexandria, VA: Association for Supervision and Curriculum Development.

Ladson-Billings, G. (1995). But that's just good teaching! The case for culturally relevant pedagogy. *Theory into practice, 34*(3), 159-165.

Levin, J., & Nolan, J. F. (1996). *Principles of classroom management*. Boston, MA: Allyn and Bacon.

Nelsen, J., Lott, L., & Glenn, H. (2000). *Positive Discipline in the Classroom, Revised 3rd Edition: Developing Mutual Respect, Cooperation, and Responsibility in Your Classroom*. Roseville, CA: Prima Publishing.

Rhode, G., Jenson, W., & Reavis, H.(1992). *The tough kid book: Practical classroom management strategies*. Frederick, CO: Sopris West.

Sapon-Shevin, M. (2010). *Because we can change the world: A practical guide to building cooperative, inclusive classroom communities*. Thousand Oaks, CA: Corwin, Sage.

Skinner, B. F. (1954). *The science of learning and the art of teaching*. Harvard Educational Review, 24, 86-97.

CHAPTER IV

Collaborating with Families and Stakeholders

Coming together is a beginning; keeping together is progress; working together is success.

Henry Ford

If kids come to us from strong, healthy functioning families, it makes our job easier. If they do not come to us from strong, healthy, functioning families, it makes our job even more important.

Barbara Colorosso

This chapter will introduce you to information related to collaborating with the families of your students and stakeholders in the community. First, we will define families and stakeholders. For this chapter, we will use the term "families" to represent parents, guardians, caregivers, and other people who care for the children in your classroom. We will describe collaborative behaviors for teachers and share how to involve families with a triad approach for student success. A rationale of why we should involve families will be presented. We will present information on how to connect and collaborate with both families and stakeholders so your classroom community can be an enhanced learning environment. Finally, we will share methods for communication with families and stakeholders.

Guiding Questions

As you read and explore the concepts introduced within this chapter, use the following questions to guide your thinking:

- Who are families of elementary children? How should we define "family"?
- Who are stakeholders you should communicate with, regarding your students?
- What is a professional learning community? (PLC)
- What are practical collaborative behaviors for elementary teachers?
- In what ways can you connect and collaborate with both families and stakeholders?

Reflect and Act:

What do you know about communicating, collaborating, and connecting with families and stakeholders? What do you know about families of elementary students? What are their expectations for communication, collaboration with schools? Who are important stakeholders in an elementary student's school experience? List methods for connecting with families and school partners that you may have seen work or are aware are in practice in elementary schools.

BACKGROUND

Who are families of elementary education students?

Parents and families play a critical role in the education of students. Some are actively involved and some relinquish control to the educators. Elementary education students come from a wide variety of backgrounds. Their definition of family may or may not be how you define family. Some children do not have both parents in their lives, some do not have any parent, and some do not have homes. It is important for you, as an educator, and a community leader to know your children and make an effort to make a true home connection, no matter what the definition of family is for your individual students. It is the teacher's responsibility to make every effort to involve parents in the education of their child. For the purposes of this chapter, the author will use the terms "parent" and "family" to denote anyone who cares for the child or who is in charge of the child's well-being.

Who are stakeholders?

There is an African proverb, "It takes a village to raise a child". There are many groups and organizations that have a vested interest in the students in your class. There are internal stakeholders within the school, who care about you and your students. Administrators, support staff, special teachers, parent organizations, and club leaders. There may be a shared mission for the school, a collection of goals, and you and your students are a part of this mission. In this chapter, the authors may use the term "triad". A triad is a term referring to the three groups interested in the success of the child, including: families, teachers, and of course, the students. When educators, parents, and community work together they can be a powerful "triad" for school reform.

There are also external stakeholders who care about your students' success, including tax payers, community members, local business leaders, politicians, department of public instruction, school boards, etc. These people want trained, informed, educated citizens to join the community. Your task as a community leader is to offer and invite external stakeholders into your classroom. Share ideas (set up a classroom economy, speakers, community helpers, job fairs, community history, etc.). If you have never been to a school board meeting, or voted for a school board member, it may be advisable to become more involved politically, at least researching candidates' views on education. What businesses are in the neighborhood of your school? It is a good idea to be familiar with the local churches, organizations, museums, and local figures who understand the history of the community where you are teaching. These organizations want you to be successful because a good school attracts customers and a good school impacts the community.

What is a professional learning community? (PLC)

A professional learning community is any group of people who come together with the goal of improving the school. According to DuFour (2004), a professional learning community should have three goals: a) to ensure the students are learning, b) focus on collaboration, and c) target goals by using results. Any group of people who come together with a shared interest in education can be a committee, PTA, school board, grade-level team of teachers, school improvement committee, or any group with a combination of teachers, staff, parents, community members, and administrators who want to initiate change.

THEORY TO PRACTICE

What are practical collaborative behaviors for elementary teachers?

To begin, teachers must acknowledge that establishing a home connection and recognizing families are an integral part of the education of their students. Creating the classroom community begins with an understanding of where your students are raised and a respect for their home life. If a teacher believes the home connection can help the student's success and sees collaborative opportunities, this can lead to students learning, and the teacher will be well on their way to success.

First, the teacher will need to establish some sort of basic communication plan. There needs to be a consistent method for communicating positive news and information about the classroom. This can be in the form of a website, email, newsletter, or social media (such as edmodo.com). Second, the teacher will need to share how families and stakeholders can communicate with him or her. Will they allow access to home/cell phone, email, the school, or social media? It is important to be consistent with all families here, do not show favorites. If you do choose to give out your phone number, be sure to share hours it is appropriate to call and whether you welcome text messages. The authors caution against giving out a home or cell number. E-mail and other options are less intrusive and even more collaborative. Try to make professional calls from the school phone. Third, the teacher should be inviting to the families and make sure they feel welcome to visit and share in the classroom. They can share culture, professions, hobbies, talents, and volunteer. Teachers need to be aware that what families, parents, and stakeholders say to children about the school, teachers, and the importance of education is central to a successful home school connection.

In what ways can you connect and collaborate with both families and stakeholders? (Home-school connection and home-note program)

Children benefit greatly when a teacher can be the bridge between home and school. Effective teachers reach out and communicate often with families. Surveys indicate that most Americans believe a strong family-school connection is important, but they do not act to support it (Blanchard, 1998). In general, a home-school connection is a connection to be valued, because everyone wins. Students feel supported, teachers feel a part of the team, and parents feel empowered, the local community gains better citizens who feel a sense of belonging. It is important for faculty and administrators to establish their school as an integral part of a community.

What is a home-school connection?

A home- school connection is any collaborative effort where all parties (home and school) have a mutual interest and investment in a project or program. Brophy & Alleman, (2007) suggest that any effort by the teacher to communicate with families, beyond the normal requirements, is a home-school connection. This is substantive communication in addition to a typical newsletter or a note home. Typically, in the past, parents have been able to decide if they want to be involved in the school. Historically family involvement with schools was a one-sided endeavor, where parents and family members volunteer time in the schools. Stereotypically, the parents who help might have been middle-class parents and mostly mothers. This is not the case today. If all families are made to feel welcome at schools, than all families will participate and make more of a connection with their child's education. Everyone benefits when this occurs. Children are able to see their parents and family do value education and they also see their teachers who value family contributions and culture.

What is a home-note program?

When students misbehave in your classroom, it is nice to know you have the support of parents or guardians at home, who will follow through on any powerful reinforcers at home. When the students know you are working together with their families, there tends to be more respect, more compliance, and more potential for academic success. Essentially, you, the student, and the parents agree on something such as a privilege, reward, or even a punishment for the child, if needed. At the end of the day, the child brings home a note relaying whether or not he or she has earned the home privilege or lost it. Be sure to make this a team created program. Be sure students and families buy-in and are committed to the program. It will not be successful if you are the only one initiating the program. Collaboration is key to the success of a home-note program.

What is the best way to communicate with families and stakeholders?

The best way to communicate with families and stakeholders is to take advantage of all forms of communication that students, teachers, and families have access. When it is time to communicate positive information, there are many ways. The newsletter is still important, phone calls, emails, and face to face conferences are also important. Email is convenient and a great way to communicate. Email is also a "paper-trail" and a record of communication. You could keep a folder for each parent on your email account. Always be professional, use correct grammar and spelling. When it is time to communicate negative information, consider a phone call first, to set up a meeting. Sometimes negative information is better received face to face.

Technology can serve the family-school connection in five areas: communication, information, learning, interest, and resources (Blanchard, 1998). There are social-networking options for families and schools, for example, Edmodo (http://www.edmodo.com). Edmodo is a great social networking site for connecting teachers, students, and all learners to resources to meet their full potential. Class Dojo (http://www.classdojo.com/) is an online tool for teachers to collect and share classroom behavior data with families, administrators, and students. It can be used during your school day from your I Pad, IPhone, or PC. Teachers can create free, interactive, professional websites using Weebly or Wix (http://www.weebly.com or http://www.wix.com). The free website templates such as Weebly and Wix.com are great to set up a professional website for communication with your parents and families. Items to include on your website might include: resume, sample lessons, curriculum, relevant lessons, homework help, calendar, pictures, newsletters, field trip information, contact info, etc.

Parents and local communities should be involved in public school education. When parents and families are involved in school children do better. There is no cookie-cutter set of collaborative activities for parents, families, stakeholders, and schools, but there are six general types of experiences that every school should strive to include in their efforts to connect and collaborate (Educational Broadcasting Corporation, 2004). The six areas include: parenting, communicating, volunteering, learning at home, decision-making, and collaborating with the community.

The Educational Broadcasting Corporation (2004) suggest the following ways to improve communication between schools, families, and stakeholders in the community:

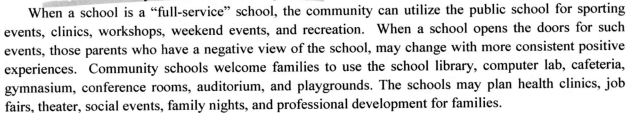

- ✓ Increase the clarity and content of notes home (report cards, etc.)
- ✓ Provide translations for notes and communication in languages of the community
- ✓ Provide ways for parents to ask questions
- ✓ Clarify all work to be completed at home
- ✓ Plan for both informal and formal communication with all
- ✓ Provide a variety of communication options

When a school is a "full-service" school, the community can utilize the public school for sporting events, clinics, workshops, weekend events, and recreation. When a school opens the doors for such events, those parents who have a negative view of the school, may change with more consistent positive experiences. Community schools welcome families to use the school library, computer lab, cafeteria, gymnasium, conference rooms, auditorium, and playgrounds. The schools may plan health clinics, job fairs, theater, social events, family nights, and professional development for families.

Is homework considered a home connection?

Often, a homework folder may be the only communication between the school and home. This is not quality communication. It is one way of communicating, but it is not the only way. If your answer to communication with families is assigning homework, that is one-sided and not a good program for family connections. The author's position on homework is that homework should be an extension or a continuation of what was studied in class, NOT something new. When students complete work at home, not every child has the same environment at home, some have parents or older siblings, who can help. You are not in control of what happens in the home, how are you sure the students are doing all of the work? What is your philosophy? Is it fair to grade a homework project when some students have a quiet place to work, all of their needs met and some students had no help, no guidance, and you are not even sure who completed any of the work. If you want to make a home-connection, you can assign projects where all of the family members can be involved and the project can relate to culture. But this should only be done after you have communicated with families, individually, and offer as a choice assignment.

Reflect and Act:
Why should you involve families with the education of their child? List reasons for why it may be difficult to involve parents and families. When should you involve parents and families in your classroom? Should you expect all parents and families to participate, why or why not? Draft a letter home to families introducing yourself and your classroom.

Why should teachers involve families and stakeholders?

Successful teachers are effective managers, who are also skillful collaborators. Children attending school have social, emotional, and physical needs that create stressors as barriers to teacher success and student learning. By collaborating with agencies, stake-holders, and interested parties, schools and teachers can create what Anderson-Butcher & Ashton (2004) refer to as "wrap –around services and support". Schools cannot do this work alone. Their job is to educate and promote student learning. When there are social issues beyond a teacher's training, schools need to seek social work practices. When there is an effective program for collaboration between families, stakeholders, and schools, there are many benefits, including: increase in student attendance, increase in student achievement, a sense of greater security, fewer behavioral problems, and increase in positive attitude toward school (Educational Broadcasting Corporation, 2004). It is important for schools to make an effort to make connections to both mother-figures and father-figures in the child's life.

What are the challenges with working with families and stakeholders?

Sometimes teachers see parents or families as adversaries- and not as allies. This is a mistake. A truly effective classroom manager knows it is imperative to learn how to best collaborate and communicate with parents and families. There are usually no official means or processes for collaboration between parents and teachers besides the classic "meet the teacher night" and parent-teacher conferences. Public schools need to do a better job of providing an inviting atmosphere where there are opportunities for collaboration and connection.

When children reach adolescence, it is less likely for parents and families to be involved. Some families are just not comfortable in school settings; maybe they had a bad experience in school themselves (Kauffman, Mostert, Trent, Hallahan, 1993; Kyle, & Rogien, 2004). There is often a common contradiction, parents do influence their children but should not be automatically blamed for all problems the child causes. It can be frustrating if there are no formal ways to share responsibility between teacher and parent in public schools. It is sad, that a homework folder can sometimes become the only means of communication. Teachers and Parents can be threatened by each other. Despite this potential for apprehension, parents, teachers, and other stakeholders need each other. Because you are the professional educator, you must make the effort to connect and possibly develop a positive and productive association.

Parents are not always the cause of child misbehavior. Reflective teachers know they cannot always blame parents for students' misbehavior. Children also influence parents. It is possible for educated and well-intentioned parents to display poor parenting skills. When teaching, think about how certain behaviors get "on your nerves" or are annoying, now imagine living with those behaviors 24 hours a day, every day. Just as parents are not always to blame, they can contribute to the behavior problems when they react poorly to their children misbehaving. The authors caution that you should not assume that parents do not care if they are poor at parenting. It is possible that parents who have poor parenting skills want to be good parents, but they lack the knowledge and methods for raising children. When students are behaving the way we want them to in our classroom, we take credit for this, as if we disciplined the students and manage the classroom well. When the students misbehave, we are quick to blame parents or society. Strong parental involvement in a child's education and school environment is essential to the success of the child and the school (Goodwin & King, 2002). There are common misconceptions that school personnel may have about parents, including: a) parents who do not visit schools do not care about their children's education, b) good parental involvement looks a certain way, and c) all parents respond to the same strategies.

When should you involve families and stakeholders?

From the start of the year, and even before, teachers should make every effort to involve families and stakeholders. It is important to not only communicate when something is wrong. You should involve parents and families when there is positive news to share, not just negative. As soon as you know your class list, prepare a brief letter of introduction, such as the one below. The letter should have a positive tone, be welcoming and professional. This is your first impression and you want to show you are competent, prepared, open to communication, and excited to help their child learn. The letter should include about three paragraphs. Paragraph one is your introduction, tell about yourself, your training, education, interests, and experience. The second paragraph should be where you generate enthusiasm for the school year. Share briefly about upcoming projects, events, field trips, or topics of study. The final paragraph is where you welcome communication and share how best to reach you.

Introductory letter sample:

Dear Families and Friends:

My name is Ken Adams and I will be your child's fifth grade teacher. I have a degree in elementary education from University of Virginia. I have experience teaching in grades K-6 and my area of expertise is mathematics. I enjoy football and team sports so I hope to encourage a team atmosphere in the classroom.

This year, we will be studying many integrative units related to science and math. I am most excited about our unit on machines, forces, and motion. We will have a special week of robotics where a professor from UNCC will visit and help our class to build our own robots! We will also be reading several novels together. I was able to earn a grant to purchase class sets of many wonderful books your child will love. Please send a picture of you and your family holding favorite books. With your permission, I will add it to our EVERYONE READS wall.

I look forward to working with you this year and I want your child to experience success in our classroom. My professional website has more information about the year, including interactive forums for projects and assignments. The website is _____. My contact info is on the website- I can be reached by email _____.

Together, we can help your child experience success in fifth grade.

Thank you,

Kenneth Adams

Remember this will set the tone for communication for the year. As with any communication, be honest, professional, positive, and welcoming. At times you will need to contact parents for serious offenses, but those calls can go so much more productive if you have already established a line of communication. If the parent has only heard negative from the school they may even screen the call and you will not get to talk with anyone. So again, it is beneficial to contact the parents of your students early in the year, as soon as you know your class list.

Back to school night

Back to School Night can be the first time you communicate with families face to face. The goal of the night is for the families to meet teachers, learn about the curriculum, learn your goals, philosophy of teaching, and see the room where their child will work for the year. This is not conference time- this is an open house. You are not to get into great details about student's progress. Back to school night is an orientation. You should create a welcoming environment, plan a brief, professional presentation, and perhaps use PowerPoint or Prezi, so you will remember your talking points. You can include brief background on you, your training, and your goals for the year. Tell a little about where you are from, your family, and your hobbies or favorite book. Share the curriculum and your plans for the year, in general. Share your rules and management plan. Explain the roles family members, students, and you will play in the success of their child. Offer ideas for volunteering and share any upcoming events or field trips. This is a good time to share your website or a newsletter, pamphlet, etc. If you are not technologically savvy, a folder with your business card, introductory letter, management plan, and other information could be shared. The author's suggest for you to be prepared. This is when you share how and when there will be communication. Back to School Night can be the beginning of a collaborative connection with the families of your students.

How should teachers communicate with families?

One of the most common methods for communication is the phone call. Foley (2012) states there are three categories for using a phone call for communication with families and parents:

1. Your child is doing really well academically.
2. Your child is not doing well academically.
3. Your child is misbehaving.

No matter why you call a parent, you should document the phone call, including the date, time, and topics for discussion. The authors would keep a phone communication documentation chart. An example of what you might say for a phone conversation where the child is doing well academically:

"Hello Mrs. Moore, I am Ms. Ward, your child's teacher. Is this a good time to talk briefly? I am calling to tell you I am so proud of the work Jonathan has been doing lately in math and reading. His performance has greatly improved since last grading period. He recently scored 100% on his three math tests this week. Thank you for providing such a supportive environment at home to complete his homework assignments and also, thank you for continuing to support his success. If he continues this progress, he may be on the Honor Roll. Thank you."

An example of what you might say if the student is doing poor academically:

"Hello, Mr. Adams, I am Ms. Henderson, your child's teacher. Is this a good time to speak briefly? I am calling because I am concerned about Jeff's science and math grades. I am hoping we can work together with Jeff to help him improve his test scores, participation, and his project scores. Lately, I have noticed he is not as interested or dedicated as usual in school. I truly enjoy having him in class. I miss his

genuine smile and enthusiasm for learning. He seems distracted. Let's find a time that works for all of us to decide on a plan. I want Jeff to be successful again."

An example of what you might say on the phone, if the student has poor behavior habits:

"Hello, Mrs. Lenhof, I am Ms. Estrada, your son's teacher. Is this a good time to speak briefly? I am concerned that Larry's behavior is interfering with his learning and others in the class. For the last week, I have asked Larry to sit close to me, but it doesn't seem to work. I love Larry's personality, but sometimes, in the effort to get other students to laugh, he ends up not able to get his work done. Unfortunately, on our management plan, the next step is detention. Are you available to discuss possible solutions? I want Larry to succeed. I like having him in my class; he just needs to learn when to have fun and when to work. When would be a good time for you to meet and discuss solutions and strategies?"

According to Kyle and Rogien (2004) there are crucial C's of parental support, including: communication, collaboration, and connection. Think of all of the ways you can *communicate* with families and parents. This communication should be on-going. It should begin before the first week of school starts. There are many options for communication including achievement letters, brag notes, happy grams, phone calls, faxes, emails, class websites, "Good Day" notes, etc. Also consider email, fax, phone, and web sites for your positive communication. If you communicate early, there are no surprises and with early communication, you might avoid family members experiencing frustration. Try to avoid surprising families with bad information. As with everything in classroom management-find your method, and realize sometimes it won't be easy.

There are many options for true and substantive *collaboration* with parents and families. Whenever possible, gather family input on what will help solve a problem. Traditionally, parents will volunteer to be chaperones, accept invitations to be guest speakers, and attend parent classes, etc. Be ready for when parents ask, "How can I help?" Have a list of suggested collaborative roles families can assume.

When considering options for creating a family *connection,* there are traditional connections and creative ways to connect. An initial way to make a connection would be to schedule home visits along with another colleague (principal or guidance counselor). The purpose of the home visit is NOT to supervise, evaluate, or judge the home life of the child. It is for the purpose of making a connection where the teacher can appreciate several things (length of bus ride, where the student studies, learn more of the child's culture, meet any siblings, learn of any schedule, and appreciate how education is valued in the home. Teachers and families can make connections when they attend extracurricular activities. The author recalls making a connection with a family at a soccer tournament. The teachers and families can use a camera to document and share family and school events. Family members can make connections when they visit the school as a lunch guest, attend parent nights, and take any school surveys. In order to make a connection, the families should feel welcome to the school (Kyle & Rogien, 2004).

The authors encourage the inviting method for communication, collaboration, and making connections, "Let's work together to meet the needs of your child". As the child's teacher, you can create a feeling of being allies not adversaries, Think in the broadest sense, more than conferences and volunteering. Bring the essential, positive supportive message into our students' homes.

parents should feel welcome!
connect beyond conferences

55

What is important about family conferences?

The authors feel the most important thing about conferences is the teacher should present him/herself in a positive manner, including professional dispositions, body language, promptness, organization, and pleasant smile. It should be obvious the teacher wants to be there, loves teaching, respects students, and is a good person. Even if the conference is about a negative topic, the family member should feel the teacher is inviting, knowledgeable, and willing to work as a team to help the child experience success in the classroom. Following your own attitude check, being prepared is the next important consideration. When you are prepared, you can focus on the concerns, documents, and plan of action needed. Here is a checklist of items to have ready before the conference (Foley, 2012):

- ✓ Portfolios of student work
- ✓ Grades and grading criteria
- ✓ Behavior documentation
- ✓ Seating chart
- ✓ Copies of tests, assignments, projects
- ✓ Textbooks and learning materials
- ✓ Your website up to share, newsletters, etc.

In addition, before the conference, it may be helpful to have the students complete a self-evaluation of their own progress and for the families to complete a survey or questionnaire. During the conference, remain positive, use active listening skills, nurture the partnership, consult the parents as resources, involve the student, identify areas for growth, only deal with the truth, review documented evidence, and always end on a positive note. Jones and Jones (2001) suggest the following agenda for your conference: 1). Open with a positive quality of the student, 2). Share any student self-evaluation, 3). Go over the report card, 4). Review student work, 5). Discuss any behavior (positive and negative), 6). Ask if there are any questions or concerns (review parent survey if completed), and finally, 7). Summarize the conference; go over strengths, areas for growth, and goals. After the conference, plan to follow-up, write this in your plan book, and make a realistic plan for ongoing communication.

The general protocol for a conference might be to meet the parents at the door of your classroom, sit together at a round table with grown-up size chairs. Try not to sit at your desk, when you sit together it symbolizes you are a team and you will work with them to help their child be successful in your classroom. You are not their teacher; you are their child's teacher. Foley (2012) suggests the following guiding questions to use for your conferences:

1) Do you have any questions or concerns about this class?
2) Has your child talked about school or this class?
3) Let me show you some work we have been doing in social studies.
4) How is your child enjoying school?
5) Be sure to comment on something you know about the child outside of class. For example, "I know Derek loves to play soccer, he tells me about the weekend tournaments".
6) Be sure to summarize any main points. For example: " Karen is not paying attention in class, I will move her seat to see if that helps, thank you for telling me she can't see the board"

7) Address any action items. For example: "I will agree to check his book bag each morning, if you agree to check it at night."
8) Always end on a positive note. For example: "I look forward to reading Jonah's book review, please let me know if you would like to visit the class in the future".
9) Again, show you like teaching, enjoy children, and are happy to have their son or daughter in your class.
10) Finally, do not preach to the parents about parenting. If they seem interested or struggling and frustrated, share what you know about adolescent, developing children.

Focus on improving relationships with parents, working together, in a triad, sometimes even with the child present. You will need to decide if you feel the child should be present for conferences. Some experts say the child could become overconfident when the conference is positive and the child could become angst-ridden when present for a negative conference. If you decide to have student-led conferences, avoid such topics as teaching methods, relationships with other students, and comparing other students (Foley, 2012).

What is advice for telling unpleasant information?

The best advice we have for telling unpleasant information, is to be honest, be sincere, and to listen. If you choose to write a letter to share unpleasant information, this may be too formal. When you are on the phone, it can be difficult to build a rapport, especially if this is the first communication. Try to be sure; your first communication with a family member is not negative. Make it a point to schedule positive phone calls each grading period just to check in with the family.

The best way to communicate unpleasant information would be to make an initial phone call to schedule a meeting, meet with the family member, and then write a letter to reiterate time/place, and a conference or to follow-up on the plan for solutions discussed at the face to face meeting. Even though you may be sharing information about the child's behavior, be an advocate for the child, be objective, and do not make it obvious you are angry with the child. It is the behavior, not the child, that is frustrating.

During the meeting, highlight student's progress, and do not convey only good or only bad. Here is a checklist of reflective questions to ask yourself before the meeting:

- ✓ Am I able to avoid blame?
- ✓ Am I willing to admit when I am wrong?
- ✓ Am I aware of cultural differences?
- ✓ Can I find a positive about the child? For every one negative, try to find two positives.

What is a home-note program?

Parents have control over powerful reinforcers, for example: television, video games, telephone, and other privileges. Home-note programs require that you evaluate student behavior and the parents evoke punishment, deliver consequence, or loss of privilege. This can be mutual, where if the student misbehaves at home, the student can lose a privilege or reward at school. The basic guidelines of a home-note program include: a) meet with parents to set up features of the home- note program, b) involve the student in the development of the program, c) when there is more input from the student, the program is more likely to be consistent and more likely to be carried out successfully, d) use reinforcers-not punishments, it should be a positive program, e) clearly define the target behaviors that need to change or the positive behaviors that need to be exhibited, f) If the student loses the note? = Negative report, g) the note should not be lengthy or detailed. It might be good to use email- or other reporting software or tools.

For example, a card could go home with red light, green light, or yellow light. If there was a red colored in by the child, he would not get to play his video game (or lose a pre-determined privilege). If the yellow light was colored in, the parent would determine if he was able to play his favorite game (or lose a privilege), and if the green light was colored in, the child could have an evening where he had all privileges.

How do you communicate with angry and hostile family members?

The best advice we can give to you regarding angry parents, is to hear them out if you are in a safe place. If it becomes out of your control and is no longer safe, leave immediately. As the parent talks, be empathetic ("I understand you are upset right now"). If you can, hear them out, listen to their concerns, see if you can separate the genuine concern from perhaps this might be the "straw the broke the camel's back" and there are bigger issues not related to you or the student. If you are able to speak in between their anger, ask questions, "Who? What? How? And Where?" Get the details. Remain pleasant and fight the urge to yell back, if they are yelling. Never interrupt someone who is ranting and raving, let them go as long as they are not hurting anyone. Speak in a calm voice, maintain eye contact, and try not to show your nerves. When they are calmer or at any point, ask if they would like to set up a meeting to resolve the issue, especially if they have just shown up at your door.

Foley (2012) reminds us, the goal is always to resolve any issues and maintain or establish positive relationships. If you are wrong in a situation offer an apology, simply and quickly. This will present that you would expect the same from them if they are ever wrong about something in the future. When you have the urge to attack, do not act on this; but do not give- in either. Never let another adult berate you, admit any mistakes, speak slowly, be careful what you say, and keep it simple. Say something like, "I would be happy to speak to you when things have settled down, you can make an appointment in the office". Stay calm, speak with an even tone, without emotion, and remember the best defense is a good offense. When you have your room organized and the class is set up with clear expectations, rules, and policies are known; there is no room for argument. If you know an upcoming conference is going to be difficult, arrange for another professional to be with you (administrator, school counselor, or colleague).

- Do not take things personally; you may have families who have a negative attitude toward school, in general.
- Get your reaction under control.
- Respond professionally and realize that a parent's angry reaction usually has nothing to do with you.
- Active listening until calm and let them know they are heard, "I can tell you are angry"…"I hear what you are saying, you are frustrated that Sarah has failed science".
- Give Respect and focus on solutions.
- Remain calm, allow the parents to feel angry and acknowledge the feelings.

In a hostile situation, you have no obligation to stay or remain in the conference. You have no obligation to remain in a room if a person is violent. Seek immediate safety. If there are any future conferences planned with hostile individuals, ask to have a colleague present (Kauffman, et.al, 1993).

> *"It seems as if you are a little too upset for us to work on solving this problem today...Let's schedule a time to meet when we can both approach from a reasoned position".*

It is not ok to stop in the middle of teaching to address parent concerns. Be welcoming, but indicate a better time to schedule a meeting. During class time, your students are your priority.

APPLICATION WITH DIVERSE LEARNERS

There are more non-traditional families than ever before. The role of the teacher in relation to the role of the parent is shaped by changes in society. Public schools are a window into society. Teachers must have the ability to work with culturally and linguistically diverse students and parents. This starts with getting to know your families, where they are from, where they live, and who they are. Being culturally responsive is essential to a strong home-school connection.

One-fourth of all children in the United States live in poverty. It is thought that only middle-class and upper-class families are involved with the school experience-and that research about successful school and community partnerships are those in upper-class neighborhoods. However, in contrast, research shows that families of low-income children will attend school events and will make efforts to become involved when they are made to feel welcome (Educational Broadcasting Corporation, 2004).

When the culture of the classroom is incongruent with the culture of the child's home, there can be problems. Historically, school norms and structures have been, and continue to be, most responsive to middle class, able-bodied, U.S. born, English-speaking individuals. There is an urgent need for schools to include a more diverse population, as the nation's demographics change (Goodwin, A. L., & King, S. H, 2002).

Home-school collaboration is important to all children, particularly significant for students whose backgrounds include economic disadvantage, incomplete parent education, stressful home-life, or where there are cultural differences between home and school (Raffaele & Knoff, 1999). Raffaele and Knoff (1999) suggest a five phase plan, involving a shift from, "what parents are doing wrong" to, "what can be done differently in schools". They suggest the school faculty and staff must:

1) Be proactive, rather than reactive;
2) Involve sensitivity and respect for cultural backgrounds;
3) Recognize and value important contributions parents make and see parents as having skills to impart; and
4) Encourage parent empowerment through positive, meaningful two-way communication, based on respect and trust.

Raffaele and Knoff (1999), suggest schools look at the levels of involvement they offer for families and parents to become more engaged with the schools. Level 1: "Parent Awareness" includes sharing any school documents, handbook, handouts, perhaps going on home-visits, etc. Level 2: "Parent Cooperation" is where there are invitations to events, parents are surveyed, telephone conversations, home-school reading, home-school notes, and (homework folders). Level 3: "Parent Collaboration" is participation in town meetings, school-improvement plans, parent representatives on boards and meetings, full-service schools where it is thought of as a community center, self-help parent groups, forums, and neighborhood involvement. There is risk for disengagement when there are only Level 1 awareness activities in the school.

CASE STUDY – Communicating with Parents

It was early January and Mrs. Iden was coming in from a cold recess duty with her 5th grade students. Even though she had reviewed the classroom rules often, the children had a long winter break, and must have been "out of routine". They were uncharacteristically chatty and not able to settle in for a science lesson. Mrs. Iden was excited because she had prepared the children for a "Physics Day" where they were going to conduct several experiments in the classroom related to basic physics, simple machines, forces, and motion. As the children came in from recess, and a brief locker stop, Mrs. Iden, let them know not to bother the experiment tables, where there were many items- tennis balls, marbles, rubber bands, plywood, Matchbox cars, dominoes, etc.

"Attention, boys and girls, eyes on me, please. We are going to get ready for Physics Day. Please bring your science journals and come to the front lab table", said Ms. Iden in a firm, yet friendly tone.

The children moved to the lab table, unfortunately, Donnie was interested in the plywood and tennis ball on the back table. He swung the wood and hit the tennis ball, like a baseball, in the classroom- toward the wall. Luckily, nothing, and no one was hurt. It bounced against the wall, and rolled out the classroom door, down the hall. This surprises Mrs. Iden because Donnie has never had difficulty following directions, but lately, he is easily distracted. Donnie was due for a phone call home because he was already warned earlier in the day for behavior, the class was warned not to mess with the science materials, and he had already been moved today for misbehavior.

"Please go get the ball, Donnie and meet me in the hall outside of the class door". Mrs. Iden asked the students to copy down the problems for investigation in their science journals.

"No, you can't make me. You are not my mom and I do not care about any stupid Physics Day..." mumbled Donnie. Recently, Donnie has also been showing a negative attitude in art class, physical education, music, and on the bus. He has been disrespectful today, and Mrs. Iden would like to elicit the help of his father in trying to discipline Donnie. Mrs. Iden requests for Donnie to go to his desk and lets him know privately, that she understands he is angry about something, but that his behavior is not acceptable for their classroom. She lets him know she is going to teach science and he is welcome to join after he calms down. She shared with him she would be calling his father after class. Donnie slowly works his way to a desk, slumps down and says, "I don't care".

Mrs. Iden calls the family members of her class often and has a set routine of positive phone calls, so when there is a negative call, it is usually well-received. Mrs. Iden calls Donnie's father after science class. She keeps it brief, does not go into too many details, and uses the time to set up a face to face meeting. She knows there is no need to get into details. Donnie's father is a single father who works 2 shifts at the local factory and has a stressful job. She knows to value his time. They are able to find time to meet later in the week. In the meeting, Mrs. Iden learns there is a family crisis. Donnie's dad has lost his job and has to find part time work that is making his schedule very difficult. Donnie has been staying with neighbors and an elderly grandmother lately and does not understand why his mother (an alcoholic) is not able to watch him.

Mrs. Iden shows empathy and asks how she can help. She asks if his grandmother still has the video games and lets Donnie play and she does. Mrs. Iden and Donnie's father come up with a plan. They will try a home-note program where Mrs. Iden, Donnie, and Donnie's father will share back and forth, by email, whether Donnie has earned certain rewards for the day and at home. He loves his video games and right now, with all of the stress, the games are a nice distraction. Mrs. Iden sees an opportunity to work in the TRIAD with Donnie's father to help, not add stress to a tough situation. The home-note program can help Donnie take more responsibility, as a 10 year-old. Donnie will be an important part of the triad...Mrs. Iden has also suggested Donnie see the school guidance counselor on a regular basis to help him learn coping skills for stress and anger.

Reflect on the following questions before moving on:

1. What do you think about Mrs. Iden's way of handling the situation with Donnie?
2. What should happen when students respond to a request with, "No, you can't make me, you are not my mom!"?
3. If you were Mrs. Iden, how would you have approached and prepared for the conversation with Donnie's father?
4. How should Mrs. Iden respond to Donnie's misbehaviors, now that she knows the situation? Should she think his father is just making excuses?
5. Do you feel that Mrs. Iden should have punished Donnie or reacted differently? If you were Mrs. Iden, how would you handle this situation? Why is it important to care about what a child is experiencing at home?
6. As a teacher, should you stay out of the child's personal business and just punish or reward based on his behavior, no matter what?
7. Has someone ever cut you a break because they knew you were going through a tough time? Should we just have the idea that everyone goes through tough times? Why? Why not?

After you have answered the discussion questions and decided how you would handle the situation, we encourage you to participate in a discussion with your peers in class to facilitate an understanding of the various factors that impact how Mrs. Iden might address the situation. Next, within the description that references TIC-TAC-TOE that follows, we will not address the scenario. Instead we will establish how various elements of the theories highlighted across the continuum can be considered simultaneously to provide a multifaceted approach to communicating with families.

Case Study: Using TIC TAC TOE

Throughout the book, we've focused your attention on various ways to consider your philosophy within the context of a Case Study that exemplified a particular situation relevant to the topic of the chapter. However, we feel that communicating with parents and families necessitates an intersection of each of the philosophies. We acknowledge that sometimes it is challenging to step outside your chosen philosophy, but to be an effective communicator; you must make additional considerations relevant to the parties involved as well as have multiple strategies at your disposal.

Perhaps most consistent with the TIC approach is the necessity of clearly communicating consequences as part of your management plan. Did Mrs. Iden's conversation with Donnie's father show she was in charge? What does "in charge" look like? Should Mrs. Iden have been visibly angry and yell back at Donnie when he broke the rule? Was calling his father the best reaction?

When considering TAC, in previous chapters, we've examined information relevant to Curwin and Mendler (2008) on multiple occasions. We will do so once again in regard to family communication. In this case, Mrs. Iden could have invited Donnie to the conference. Donnie is in 5th grade, developmentally, he could handle this conference, and it may be good that he sees and hears how his father and teacher are his advocate.

Finally, teachers whose views most align with the TOE philosophy, which is focused on the empowerment of students, can utilize elements consistent with Ginott (1972) and Coloroso (2002), as well as Kohn, Fay and Funk, and Gordon. We recommend considering actions associated with the TIC and TAC philosophy in conjunction with tenets of the TOE philosophy as a long-term solution. When communicating with families, teachers need to share they are organized, have "withitness", and are "in control" of their own learning environment. They need to involve the students in the management plan, teach respect, respect the child, while expecting respect in return. Mrs. Iden has an opportunity to empower Donnie in a very powerless time in his life. Mrs. Iden invited family members and other professionals to help with her student. She could have just yelled at the student, punished him, and went on with the day. But Mrs. Iden cares and wants to help Donnie be a better person in spite of his tough situation.

SUMMARY

In this chapter you were introduced to methods for collaboration with families and stakeholders in the community. In review, we presented how to communicate with families and stakeholders. Sample letters, phone conversation dialogue, and protocols for conferences were shared. We also presented ways to improve communication and methods for conferences. Methods for communicating with hostile parents were discussed along with shared consideration for diverse learners. Finally, a rationale for involving families and stakeholders was presented.

MOVING ON: Reflection Assignments

1. Describe the methods you (or your school) implement currently or would like to in the future to help with families who resist involvement at school.
2. What strategies or forms have you used to communicate with parents/guardians? What strategies do you plan to adopt or adapt that might help with future encounters? Share your experiences and resources and include tips—specific things to do or say and specific things to avoid. Solicit ideas from classmates to help with difficult parent/guardian relationships.
3. A comprehensive approach to classroom management, the teacher considers every aspect of the student's life: the student's needs, family system, cultural background, values, socio-economic status, etc. When a student's family and cultural factors produce negative dynamics, what strategies and skills do you need to help you deal effectively with the student and achieve positive results?
4. You are speaking with a parent who is angry about a grade his or her son earned, in what way(s) would you respond to this parent?

5. Visit http://www.edmodo.com/ and http://www.classdojo.com/
   Sign-in and see what these management tools have to offer you. Share how you could utilize them in your class to enhance family and stakeholder communication.

Appendix A: Reflect and Act

Draft an introductory letter to families regarding you and your classroom. What would you include on a professional website? Visit http://www.weebly.com/ or http://www.wix.com/ and design your own free professional website. You can decide what you will include (resume, philosophy statement, picture, biography, relevant websites, sample lessons, and videos of you teaching). Draft items to include.

Appendix B: Complete and Share

When helping a child to behave, it requires collaboration with families and stakeholders. Write a reflection of your collaborative efforts to help an identified student in your classroom.

REFERENCES

Aeby, V. G., Manning, B. H., Thyer, B. A., & Carpenter-Aeby, T. (1999). Comparing outcomes of an alternative school program offered with and without intensive family involvement. *School Community Journal, 9*(1), 17-32.

Anderson-Butcher, D., & Ashton, D. (2004). Innovative models of collaboration to serve children, youths, families, and communities. *Children & Schools, 26*(1), 39-53.

Blanchard, J. (1998). *The family-school connection and technology*. ERIC Clearinghouse.

Brooks, A. (2012). Examining Support That Exists for Social and Emotional Program Implementation in Elementary Charter Schools. Dissertations. Paper 333. Retrieved from http://ecommons.luc.edu/luc_diss/333.

Brophy, J. & Alleman, J. (2007) Powerful Social Studies for Elementary Students Thomson, Belmont, CA: Wadsworth.

Brotman, L., Calzada, E., Huang, K., Kingston, S., Dawson-McClure, S., Kamboukos, D., & Petkova, E. (2011). Promoting effective parenting practices and preventing child behavior problems in school among ethnically diverse families from underserved, urban communities. *Child development,82*(1), 258-276.

Bryan, J. (2005). Fostering educational resilience and achievement in urban schools through school-family-community partnerships. *Professional School Counseling, 8*(3), 219-227.

Canter, L.,, & Canter, M. (2002). *Assertive discipline: Positive behavior management for today's schools* (3rd ed.). Bloomington, IN: Solution Tree.

Caspe, M., Lopez, M. E., Chu, A., & Weiss, H. B. (2011). *Teaching the teachers: Preparing educators to engage families for student achievement*. Cambridge, MA: Harvard Family Research Project and Alexandria, VA: National PTA.

DuFour, R. (2004). What is a "professional learning community"? *Educational leadership, 61*(8).

Educational Broadcasting Corporation. (2004). Concept to classroom. Retrieved from Concept to classroom. (n.d.). Retrieved from http://www.thirteen.org

Fay, J., & Funk, D. (1995). *Teaching With Love and Logic: Taking Control of the Classroom*. Golden, CO: The Love and Logic Press, Inc.

Finders, M., & Lewis, C. (1994). Why some parents don't come to school.*Educational Leadership, 51*, 50-50.

Fridell, M. E., & Alexander, K. (2011). A framework for principals: Promoting student success through leadership and collaboration. *Journal of College Teaching & Learning (TLC), 2*(9).

Foley, D. (2012). Ultimate classroom management. (2nd ed.). St.Paul, MN: JistWorks.

George, C. Y. S. (2009). How Can Elementary Teachers Collaborate More Effectively with Parents to Support Student Literacy Learning?. *The Delta Kappa Gamma Bulletin, 32*.

Ginott, H. (1972). *Teacher and child*. New York: Macmillan.

Goodwin, A. L., & King, S. H. (2002). *Culturally Responsive Parental Involvement: Concrete understandings and basic strategies*. Washington, DC: AACTE Publications.

Grothaus, T., & Cole, R. (2010). Meeting the challenges together: School counselors collaborating with students and families with low income. *Journal of School Counseling, 8*(27), n27.

Hoover-Dempsey, K., Battiato, A., Walker, J, Reed, R., DeJong, J. , & Jones, K. (2001). Parental involvement in homework. *Educational Psychologist, 36*(3), 195-209.

Kauffman, J. M., Mostert, M. P., Trent, S. C., & Hallahan, D. P. (1993).*Managing classroom behavior*. Upper Saddle River, NJ: Pearson/Allyn and Bacon.

Kyle, P. B., & Rogien, L. R. (2004). *Opportunities and options in classroom management*. Boston, MA: Allyn & Bacon.

Meadan, H., Shelden, D. L., Appel, K., & DeGrazia, R. (2010). Developing a Long-Term Vision: A Road Map for Students' Futures. *TEACHING Exceptional Children, 43*(2), 8-14.

Minke, K. M., & Anderson, K. J. (2005). Family-school collaboration and positive behavior support. *Journal of Positive Behavior Interventions, 7*(3), 181.

Moll, L. Amanti, C., Neff, D., & Gonzalez, N. (1992). Funds of knowledge for teaching: Using a qualitative approach to connect homes and classrooms. *Theory into practice, 31*(2), 132-141.

Raffaele, L. M., & Knoff, H. M. (1999). Improving home-school collaboration with disadvantaged families: Organizational principles, perspectives, and approaches. School Psychology Review, 28, 448-466.

Smit, A. G., & Liebenberg, L. (2003). Understanding the dynamics of parent involvement in schooling within the poverty context. *South African Journal of Education, 23*(1), 1-5.

Suárez-Orozco, C., Onaga, M., & Lardemelle, C. D. (2010). Promoting academic engagement among immigrant adolescents through school-family-community collaboration. *Professional School Counseling, 14*(1), 15-26.

Sugawara, C. ,Hermoso, J. , Delale, E., Hoffman, K., & Lupšić, D. (2012). Parental Involvement in an Emerging Democracy: The Case of Croatia.*Advances in Social Work, 13*(2), 451-470.

Wohlstetter, P., Malloy, C., Chau, D., & Polhemus, J. L. (2003). Improving schools through networks: A new approach to urban school reform. *Educational Policy, 17*(4), 399-430.

Weinstein, C., Curran, M., & Tomlinson-Clarke, S. (2003). Culturally responsive classroom management: Awareness into action. *Theory into Practice, 42*(4), 269-276.

CHAPTER V

Responding Effectively

When another person makes you suffer, it is because he suffers deeply within himself, and his suffering is spilling over. He does not need punishment; he needs help. That's the message he is sending.

Thich Nhat Hanh

This chapter will introduce you to information related to responding effectively to student behavior. First, we will establish the purpose of discipline and define discipline. Next, we will describe characteristics and effective skills for culturally responsive teachers, when responding to both positive and negative behaviors. A rationale for reflecting and considering responses to positive and negative behaviors in the classroom will be provided. We will also present information related to punishments, rewards, and consequences and a case study will be examined for TIC, TAC, TOE. Finally, we will share practical methods for responding to students in an effective manner. We will examine ways to respond to positive and negative behaviors in your classroom.

Guiding Questions

As you read and explore the concepts introduced within this chapter, use the following questions to guide your thinking:

- What is the definition and purpose of discipline?
- What are the characteristics and skills of a teacher who responds effectively?
- What is punishment? What are the pros and cons of punishment?
- What is reward? What are the pros and cons of reward?
- What are consequences for students? (reasonable and natural)
- What are practical methods for responding to negative and positive behaviors in the classroom? In what ways can you respond effectively to students?
- How should you respond to aggressive or violent behavior?

Reflect and Act:
What is the definition of discipline? How would you define it? Find a dictionary definition…read all entries. After reading the definition, what do you think is the purpose of discipline? What do you know about punishment? What do you know about rewards? Have you ever been punished? Have you ever been rewarded? Should children be rewarded? If so, how? How often? Why? Should students be punished? If so, why?

BACKGROUND

What is the purpose of discipline?

The purpose of discipline is self-discipline (Charles, Senter & Barr, 1989). In the classroom, the teacher should not feel like they have to do everything, the students should be able to contribute and share responsibility. This is where the purpose of discipline comes in. It is not possible to follow someone around for their entire life, doing everything for them. As a teacher, can you imagine following around your 28 students for the rest of their lives, doing everything for them? If we do not have discipline in the classroom, we are not helping to create future citizens who will be responsible for their own lives. When someone has self-discipline or is disciplined in their lives, this could mean they take responsibility, follow rules, and are consistent with their own behavior. It may mean they are able to eat healthy and avoid foods that are fattening. It may mean they are disciplined in that they consistently workout every morning, no matter what. It may mean they are disciplined in that they are able to maintain a clean, organized home where work is done well and on time. With this in mind, discipline with young children can be thought of an opportunity to teach children how to live a healthy, consistent, responsible life. As you teach, you have the opportunity to help children on their path to wisdom and self-discipline.

Discipline can be defined as an opportunity to teach (Charles, 1983). The purpose of teaching someone appropriate behavior is so we can all be more productive and more accomplished. The purpose of helping someone to learn how to behave in school is to give them a more intrinsically rewarding experience. When people are disciplined, goals can be achieved, projects can be accomplished, and learning can take place. It is the teacher's challenge to encourage and facilitate discipline, often, in the classroom. This can be exhausting, considering all of the curriculum that is already required to teach. If teachers see the purpose of discipline as the opportunity to teach, then students should be instructed that discipline is the opportunity to learn how to be better people.

What are the characteristics and skills of a teacher who responds effectively?

A teacher who responds effectively to student behavior is one who is patient, rational, caring, and reflective. A teacher who responds effectively is one who is comfortable being the adult, in any situation. They are not going to respond by trying to earn the student's friendship. The effective teacher knows to respond in a firm, but friendly manner. It is not the concern of the effective teacher that all students like them, and they are not always pleasing the students. Sometimes teachers have the opportunity to teach (discipline) when it is not easy or received well by the students- when teachers respond honestly, swiftly, and with fairness, the students will be more likely to respect the teacher. The authors' best advice is to be an effective adult role model. Respond with natural authority.

A teacher, who is skilled in responding effectively to negative behaviors, allows the child to "save face" and shows respect for the child, even though the behavior is not acceptable. A skillful response is one that is "a matter-of-fact" or calm. A skilled teacher who knows how to respond to a misbehaving child is able to take time, breathe, and not react with anger, especially, if there is no one hurt. Every day, teachers are given the opportunity to teach knowledge and skills for proper behaviors. An awareness of this helps in the skillful response. A teacher may say, "I see coats are on the floor and not where they should be, thank you for this opportunity to remind you of our rules". Or "Can anyone tell me one thing we are doing wrong right now?" "Yes, you are right, we are not raising our hands to ask a question, let me take this opportunity to review the procedures for classroom discussion, listening, and why it is important to wait our turns to speak".

An effective teacher is one who is disciplined. It is much easier to lead by example and actions do speak louder than words. When a teacher responds with confidence and assurance to the students misbehavior, the student feels safe and that he or she will learn how to be successful. For example, you want to send the message you are there to help them, not there to embarrass or demean them. They need your help and support; they are learning the ways of society and the school. A skillful teacher projects a trust-worthy attitude where the students know if they make a mistake; the teacher will correct and help them to not make the mistake again. The positive teacher will stay focused on the student by constantly encouraging them to behave in the desired manner, not giving up on them.

The authors advise you to work *with* your students and realize you can NOT *control* anyone. Stop trying to do so. Once you realize you are not the authoritarian "know-it-all", you will feel a huge sense of relief. Share responsibility with your students. It is incredibly too difficult to maintain an authoritarian style. One possible reason for high teacher "turn-over" could be because most teachers think they have to be "in control" at all times. This is not possible. Be a facilitator. Be a leader in the classroom and delegate. Effective teacher leaders respond by giving students choices. "If you choose to tip your chair, you will lose your chair". "If you choose to cut in line, you will need to go to the back of the line". Beginning teachers have enough to worry about with planning, instructing, and managing the learning environment. If teachers see discipline as positive opportunities to teach, instead of negative conflicts, perhaps the "burn-out" rate for teachers would decrease.

Effective teacher leaders model and teach the desired behaviors. They know these behaviors do not just happen, they state expectations clearly, and show the students how it is done. Finally, effective teacher leaders do not respond with lengthy lectures about behavior, they may simply ask, "How can I help you" as Glasser (2011) suggests. Posing this question to two students who are misbehaving is an opportunity for the children to redirect their own behavior. Often the students will check themselves to see if they need help and then realize they can behave in the appropriate manner. Again, the idea is you want to encourage self-discipline.

What is punishment? What are the pros and cons of punishment?

I have never been a fan of the phrase, "in the real world" because the students you are teaching are currently in the real world, are they not? So, why not have realistic or natural punishments. When adults misbehave (speed, do not pay a bill, or talk on their cell phone while driving) they must face a penalty or retribution for their reckless driving or neglecting to pay a bill. Punishment can be defined as the infliction of a penalty as retribution for an offense. Punishment is usually in the form of a ticket, higher interest, or a fee of some sort. These realistic punishments might work in your classroom, if you set up a classroom economy- where the students have "salaries" and are given a budget where they can earn the "bucks" for good behavior, completing work, etc. Then they can "pay" or lose bucks when they misbehave or do not follow the rules, just as adults do in the "real world". This is a great practice for becoming a citizen.

The best scenario is when a teacher can provide opportunities for students to be involved with deciding on the penalty to be received, although this takes coaching. Sometimes children can be too harsh on themselves. Fairness is important part of punishment- and when this is missing, the opportunity to teach is shaded by the phrase, "That's not fair!" But if your instruction and management are linked, where fairness is taught and an understanding of the concept is sought, the students can participate democratically, in deciding penalties or consequences. Students who are given responsibilities and opportunities to practice deciding on their own consequences are more likely to become more self-disciplined.

A possible negative aspect of punishment is that it can be one-sided and often, students do not decide on the punishment or are not asked to be part of the decision process. Other possible negative aspects to using punishment, is when students can only get attention from the teacher by receiving a punishment. A negative scenario might be when teachers do not take the opportunity to teach how to behave in the classroom and only punishments are handed out for misbehavior. Remember- the goal of discipline? What is the point if the teacher is always handing out punishments- and never sees the opportunity for reward or the opportunity to teach how to behave appropriately? Consequently, too much reward is also poor response to behavior.

Colorosso (1984) describes the difference between discipline and punishment. Discipline is defined as an "opportunity to teach", so this opportunity allows you to leave the dignity of the child intact, allowing the child to "save face". When a teacher sees discipline as an opportunity to teach, the teacher can help a student to become more responsible, resourceful, and resilient. Whereas, punishment may cause students to make excuses, blame others, deny misbehavior, student may feel powerless, manipulated, and out of control. The goal of discipline is self-discipline, so the student may learn how to solve problems encountered in life. So what should you do? When a student misbehaves, Colorosso (2010) suggests you follow 4 guidelines: 1). Make the student fully aware of what they have done, 2). Students must own the problem, as they are able to handle, 3). Provide options for the students to solve the problem, 4). Leave the student's dignity intact.

What is reward? What are the pros and cons of reward?

Typically, there are two types of rewards: intrinsic and extrinsic. Just as the goal of discipline is self-discipline, the goal of rewarding is for people to do the right thing because of intrinsic reasons, not just because they are paid, rewarded, or recognized in some way. Teaching intrinsic motivation is tough.

As it is with punishment, when there is too much reward, it is not an effective response to behavior of students. If we are constantly giving students rewards for every little task or behavior, then people may become over saturated with rewards and might only function with extrinsic rewards. There is nothing worse than requesting a child open his or her book and he replies back, "what are you going to give me if I do?"…you do not want a class full of students reliant only on rewards.

The pros of rewarding students include: positive behavior is acknowledged, rewards give attention to individuals, and rewards can show appreciation. However, if they are not associated with tapering off— the student will become dependent. Some believe it is better and easier to work up to a reward, then to taper off. Would you work at a job without a raise? Would you eventually just do the job because it felt good? When rewarding, be sure to consider first, asking the child, "How does it feel to finish this project?" "Did you work hard?" Just as you would involve students in ideas for consequences, involve students in what they can work toward. This is good practice in goal-setting. The pros of rewards are that students should feel a variety of positive rewards, such as intrinsic (feeling good about themselves, pride, telling families about their success, etc) and extrinsic (certificates, pat on the back, candy, etc). There are many ways to reward, we just want to make sure we avoid the extremes (never acknowledging or too much).

There is a negative side to rewarding students. Think of the scenario in a classroom where "everyone wins" or everyone gets a trophy...is that the way it is outside of school? Do you want your children in your class to feel what it feels like to work hard and then be rewarded for their efforts? OR do you want them to just feel like everyone gets to go to the treasure box if they put their coat where it should be? Do you want a class of students who are "working for peanuts" or working because they want to be, should be, and know how to be? Teaching students to be independent is tough but again, the goal of discipline is self-discipline.

Also, if you choose to reward students often, this can get expensive. Rhode, Jenson & Reavis (1992) encourage using non-material rewards as often as possible. Consider cheers, chants, applause, high-fives, feature student's work, brag about your students in front of other teachers, and principal. But if you need to have rewards, think about treasure chests where you have a selection of items individuals may earn the right to select one item after good behavior...or perhaps a lottery where the individuals hold on to their ticket if they behave- lose it if they misbehave- those lottery ticket holders will participate in a drawing for one prize. The prizes do not need to be expensive, it is all in the "hype" or how you "sell" the reward.

Prevention and Intervention: Praising, Rewarding, Redirecting, Reinforcing *Practical ways to prevent misbehavior or intervene*

Positive behavior is increased if it is reinforced. Teachers must be careful not to "reward" negative behavior by punishing or giving time to a student who might be attention-seeking. Even a reprimand can be a reward for inappropriate behavior. You can redirect inappropriate behavior by giving students a replacement behavior, changing the subject, changing scenery, or tabling the matter. A warning is usually enough to help redirect the student when misbehavior occurs. At times, teachers may find involving the students with the instruction or experience in the class, can help. Assigning the student a role, where they can accept responsibility for something is a great way to redirect.

Prevention

Ben Franklin is quoted as saying, "An ounce of prevention is worth a pound of cure". What do you think he meant? When planning for your classroom, thinking of preventative measures is important. This is where you might consider how you will plan for meaningful learning experience and how your powerful lessons will be engaging- where there will *not* be time for misbehavior. Your instruction and management will be "linked". For example, if you are teaching geography, you could have the students assume the role of a Pirate to use a "treasure map" and secretly look for treasure around the school, while they are using their geography and map-reading skills. They can assume roles, work in cooperative teams, and your lessons can be experiential exercises where the students are placed in situations where they must behave. What if they assumed the role of an astronaut, lost in space, are attending a "museum" learning about significant people from history, or they are riding a "train" or "bus"(room arrangement) to take a "tour" through PPT or the Internet. Their "tour guide" (you) would need them to be quiet or they will have to get off the ride.

Ten ideas for creating a preventive environment include (Charles, 2008):

1. Make the learning relevant, meaningful, and integrative.

2. Foster positive relationships with peers and adults in the classroom. Get to know your students. Have one-on-one meetings with them as often as possible.
3. You will TEACH behavior management skills. Remember, discipline is an opportunity to teach. It means to teach by definition and origin.
4. Consider your room arrangement. Make sure the seating matches the experience.
5. Model appropriate behavior.
6. Conflict resolution, empathy, tolerance, respect will be a part of your preventative strategies…they can be the foundation of your class.
7. Preventive atmospheres are inclusive and strengthen self-confidence and self-efficacy.
8. You will help students have a low stress environment when you learn what triggers their misbehavior.
9. Prevention includes hope. Instill hope and a positive attitude.
10. Again, you should keep the goal of discipline in mind, self-discipline, and, of course, trust and support your students.

Plan your lessons well, have variety and interest in your lessons, keep the momentum going, call on students regularly. Use name cards, multitask, utilize the "ripple effect" (good behavior can spread- so can poor) have smooth transitions, clarify expectations, and decide how you will manage student work (Charles, 2008). Fred Jones (2007) encourages you to "work" your room and consider the room arrangement, so you may move freely around the room to access each student's desk or work station.

Five things you can do to prevent misbehavior:
1. You can make sure your materials are ready.
2. You can pace your lessons properly.
3. You can plan an interesting way to launch the lessons, what will you do for focus and review?
4. You can be sure you manage your time, so as to not have students with down time. This is when students misbehave.
5. You can display "withitness" you will prevent behavior problems (Kounin, 1970).

Effective teachers take the time to consider prevention. Working on ways to prevent misbehavior is a valuable use of time. Remember, you can't control the children, but you can control yourself. You can control the amount of prevention you would like to have…even if it is just an ounce, it will be worth it.

Praise

In Chapter 2, you read about building positive relationships. Positive interactions between teacher and student can increase students' social skills, emotional regulation and motivation, engagement, and abidance to rules. Negative interactions and relationships put children at-risk for school failure. Praise is a practical preventative measure. If you increase the frequency with which students are recognized and receive positive reinforcement for appropriate behavior. Praise should exceed reprimands. Perhaps there can be a ratio of three positive statements for every one corrective statement? What do you think?

Is praise overused? Teachers can often be heard saying, "good job". Can we get carried away with extrinsic rewards in the classroom? Is it bribery or best practice to offer up positives all of the time? What do you think of candy and treats as rewards? Will you use them in your class? Will you have a treasure box? Do you know other ways to praise a child? Does a sticker really motivate? Rhode, Jenson, & Reavis (1992) warn against creating classrooms full of "praise junkies" with the idea that overuse of "good job" can undermine independence, interest, and pleasure. What motivates you? Do you seek praise?

Here is a thought- we want to nourish interest...why not talk less, and ask more. For example, Rhode, Jenson, & Reavis (1992) suggest asking the child questions such as, "Why have you chosen to make the clown's feet purple and large?" or "What was the most difficult thing about creating this picture?" or "What are you feeling now that you are done with this huge project?" instead of just walking past the student with a flippant, "Good job". If we place the focus on us, "*I* like the clown's big feet-fun!" or "Good job on the picture"...the focus is on *our* feelings *not* the child.

Rewards

Various rewards should be available in the classroom. They include adult approval, praise, recognition, special privileges, points, or other reinforcers. Teachers must gradually reduce and eliminate rewards. By fading the reinforcement, the students can move toward self-discipline and behaving appropriately because they know to do so, not just because they will receive something (Rhode, Jenson, & Reavis, 1992). Teachers can contract for a reward with the students and the reinforcer (reward) needs to be immediate. Reinforcers can be consumables, tangible, tokens, activities, or privileges. Alphie Kohn (1999) and Thomas Gordon (1989) share there can be several types of reinforcers, including, natural, edible, and social. Natural reinforcers are free and they are obvious rewards for behavior. When the teacher can offer a smile, praise, contact, or proximity, these are positive and natural. A social reinforcer could be allowing the student to work with a friend. Edible is pretty self-explanatory but always check for allergies. Interest inventories can be used to find out what motivates students and for what they might be willing to work. There are several interest inventories available, we found and those in the Tough Kid Toolbox to be worthwhile (Rhode, Jenson, & Reavis, 1992).

Redirecting

When a child is misbehaving, there should be a warning (this is an opportunity for the teacher to redirect the behavior), if there is no change then- the child will have a loss of privilege or a negative reinforcer. The student needs to be redirected when misbehavior occurs. If the redirection does not work, the student needs to feel there is hope to earn the privilege back. Make sure that when you state a punishment, you use a calm, matter-of-fact tone. Be sure the punishment is relevant to the behavior. When you are redirecting or issuing a consequence, be clear, it is the behavior to be rejected, not the student.

What are consequences for students? (reasonable and natural)

Responding effectively with consequences involves the skills and characteristics mentioned earlier in the chapter. Consequences should be reasonable and the students should have a part in the decision-making process toward what the consequence might be. For example, you may consider consequences by level: A warning first, a change of seat or scenery, loss of privilege, a phone call home, and finally a referral to the office with potential for detention. Deciding on consequences is a philosophical exercise. As an adult, if you make a mistake, you would appreciate reasonable consequences for your actions, correct? We all want to be treated fairly. Also, in life, we encounter natural consequences, where there are ramifications to our own behaviors, such as touching a hot stove- the consequence comes naturally, you are burned. When organizing your classroom and deciding on a philosophy to guide your instruction and management, you will decide on consequences for misbehavior, levels of consequences, and if they should be natural, reasonable, and/or natural.

Reflect and Act:

Think about your own elementary school experience. Were students rewarded with tangible items? In what ways were students rewarded in your elementary school? Was it effective? Were the same students getting the rewards each grading period? What do you think about "catching students being good"? In your elementary school classroom were there punishments?

What about violent behavior?

For the most part 99% of your students will not be violent, but, in the case of violent behavior, it is good to be prepared with some simple steps. You are teaching people and people have strange behaviors sometimes. Children have needs to express themselves; unfortunately, sometimes they express their anger with violence, which should not be tolerated in the schools. The following steps may not work in all situations, but for the most part, if you remember to remain calm, you will make the best choices in a tough situation, thinking of your own safety and the safety of the other children in the classroom. Five suggested thoughts for dealing with violent behavior:

1. Send for assistance if you can. What is your school procedure for this? Do you have an intercom? Are you aloud to send a student to the office with the name of the violent child on a red card- with URGENT on it. Ask for another adult to be present in your room immediately.
2. Remain calm. Do not confront a violent individual. If you need to say something, validate the child's behavior. "I know you are very angry, I can see that, but we can work this out"- use the child's name.
3. Continue to be calm, non-confrontational, non-threatening. Be gentle, yet firm. "Stay in your own space".
4. Ask the other students to leave (they can go to a previously designated classroom or area).
5. Remind the child of policies and rules—but only after the child has calmed down.
6. After the incident, record notes of what was said and done.

Reflect and Act:
Is there ever a time to "not respond" as your response to negative or positive behavior?
How do you feel about praise? Is it overused? Do we not do it enough? Developmentally, can elementary school age children be intrinsically motivated to behave the way they should, without reward, praise, or punishment? Would you work without reward?

How do you respond to angry, hostile children?

According to Fay and Funk (1995), it is important to stay calm when responding to children. It is best to respond with something like, "I understand you are angry, but we have other ways to solve problems in this school". Be aware of your body stance; Fred Jones (2007) suggests facing the student from a distance and speaking in a clear, firm tone. Jones and Jones (2001) suggest there are three phases of handling violent behavior: Phase 1: Validating, Phase 2: Choices, and Phase 3: Invitation. We will examine these phases closer, as you consider how to handle these tough situations.

Phase 1: Validating (Jones and Jones, 2001 pp311)

1. Validate the feelings of the child.
    a. *It is ok to be frustrated.*
    b. *How else can you express that in this class, given our class rules?*
2. Help them to understand impact of their behaviors.
    a. *When you _____, I get concerned because I care. I want this classroom to be a safe place.*
    b. *You deserve a nice place to learn and so do the other children.*
3. Help them to understand the behavior violates the class rule.
    a. *When you_____, which one of our rules, we all agreed on, are you violating?*
    b. *I am so glad you know our rules. I am going to help you go from here.*

Phase 2: Choices/Options/Teaching Opportunity

1. *What was the initial problem?*
2. *What would be a better way you could have solved the problem?*
3. *What is a better choice?*
4. *Would you like to take a few minutes in the quiet area to calm down or would you rather just have relaxation at your desk?*
5. *If you continue to violate this rule, you are choosing to work this problem out with the principal. I would prefer to help you. How can I help you to not make this transgression again?*
6. Teach them the difference between a mistake and a transgression.

Phase 3: An Invitation

1. *I am sure we can work this out*
2. *You have been making such good choices lately, so I know we can come up with a way to solve this.*
3. *I really want you to stay here in the classroom, and solve the problem, because I would miss you if you left.*

What are your thoughts on time-out or problem-solving time? Also called Resolution time?

Time out is one of the most common management techniques in schools and homes. This is a period of time in which students are asked to leave the activity due to their behavior. The length of time out is often debated, as well as the appropriate age of the child. Some state time-out should be time related to the child's age, so if you are six, you will have six minutes of time out. Some experts say that time out increases maladaptive behaviors such as withdrawal, avoidance, and passive-aggressive behavior. Others feel that time-out causes feelings of rejection, aggression, and humiliation. Some feel it causes anxiety (what is going to happen to me after time out?) and feel that it does not offer a replacement behavior-therefore it is dead-end. Should time out be replaced with social skills modeling and instruction? What do you think? Will you use time out? Can it be abused? Is it effective in the home and classroom? Why? Why not?

APPLICATION WITH DIVERSE LEARNERS

Effective teachers are able to respond to all children in their classroom, with differentiation in mind. They need to consider the needs of every child and respond to misbehavior and positive behaviors with attention to the individual. Just as we differentiate instruction, we must differentiate responses to our students. One student may only need a redirect or warning and will be back on track, whereas another student may need a redirect, extra time for compliance, and another redirect. When working with all students, be sure to face the student, allow plenty of space between you and the student when addressing them, do not yell, just speak in a firm, but friendly tone. Always keep in mind the goal of discipline-which is for all children in your classroom to achieve self-discipline.

Offer behavior choices, options for students who need. For example, a child with ADHD- HDD, may need two desks, where he or she has the option to redirect himself and move to the new seat when needed (of course not every 5 minutes). The author would set up centers for individuals, where they could listen to books, music, etc to have some much needed down time. Not every student needed this. I have found that non-verbals are great for responding to individuals. I had a student where he and I shared a private sign for when he needed help or I needed him to be quiet or to behave.

The author has found contracts to be a beneficial way to respond to individuals in the classroom. First, respond to the student's misbehavior by defining the misbehaviors, in clear observable and measurable terms. For example, the student will not stay in his seat or the student will call out and not raise his hand. I can observe these behaviors and count how often they occur. The best part is the teacher can respond positively when the student has reduced the number of times the negative behavior occurs. Find out what the student is interested in through an interest inventory, and create a contract, where if the number of misbehaviors is reduced or diminished greatly, the student will earn a privilege or reward-personal to him or her.

When working with learners who are different than you, please consider the cultural norms of their home. How are they rewarded and punished at home, if at all? What is the tone of the home? How is it different from the classroom? Being aware of these differences will help you to understand and allow for the differences.

CASE STUDY – Responding Effectively

Ms. Adams was a new First Grade teacher who often felt "out of control" when it came to what was happening in her classroom. She had identified three students who would just call out answers without raising their hands. She would yell at them for doing this and made them sit in the back of the classroom. The same students would not stay in their seats, or leave others alone. These three students often had their names written on the board for misbehavior, and never were able to participate in fun activities with the class; they were "regulars" in the principal's office. Ms. Adams would often take the students out in the hall and yell at them, sometimes she would yell at them in front of the class and call them names, like "Lazy" and "Dopey"... The students were not "bad" they just did not comply with Ms. Adams' three rules: a) Please raise your hand, wait for me to call on you, and then share your answer, b) Stay in your assigned seat, unless your teacher asks you to move, and c) Keep your hands to yourself: Stay in your own space.

Ms. Adams responds to children not following the rules by placing their names on the board. One of the students will actually let the teacher know he needs to be placed on the board, because, "he is sure he is going to make a mistake again today". Once the students have their name placed on the board, they just proceed with breaking the rules, and eventually are sent to the principal's office. Ms. Adams does not take the opportunity to teach the children what she would like them to do. She gives up on them so easily. Ms. Adams posted her rules, laminated the poster with her rules and consequences. Her consequences are warning, name on board, loss of privilege, family phone call, and finally, a visit to the principal's office. Even though her consequence levels are posted on the wall, she often skips to level 5, a trip to the principal's office.

She often complains about these "bad" children to her class, to her colleagues, and to her family. She even calls them names, insulting them in front of other students and teachers. These are her trouble students and she has resolved there is nothing to do, she is frustrated. She has given up on them and states, they are just "that way". She yells at the children, they do not listen, so she writes their name on the board, to save her voice. They continue to misbehave, so she sends them to the principal. Her response to the children not following the rules is not surprising, considering this is what she experienced when she went to school. She remembered teachers writing names on the board, placing checkmarks after names, and then so many checkmarks were different levels of punishment. She is just doing what she knows and feels no one will help her.

This week, the principal is very busy and does not have time to have his weekly "meetings" with Ms. Adams' students. So he has sent the students back and has asked to observe her teaching very soon.

Reflect on the following questions before moving on:

1. What do you think about how Ms. Adams has responded to the misbehavior?
2. What should happen when a student doesn't comply with the rules?
3. If you were Ms. Adams, how will you prepare for the principal's observation?
4. How should Ms. Adams respond to the three rule breakers?
5. Do you feel that writing names on the board is effective? If you were Ms. Adams, how would you handle this situation?

After you have answered the discussion questions and decided how you would handle the situation, we encourage you to participate in a discussion with your peers in class to facilitate an understanding of the various factors that impact how Ms. Adams might address the situation. Within the description that references TIC-TAC-TOE that follows, we will address the scenario. We will establish how various elements of the theories highlighted across the continuum can be considered simultaneously when considering how to respond effectively to student behavior.

Case Study: Response Choices
Choice A

If I were Ms. Adams, I would clearly present the rules and consequences in my classroom and would review this often. I would continue placing the names of students who misbehave on the board or a clipboard. I would remind the students who was in charge and continue to follow the levels of consequences I had set in the beginning of the year. I would not change this, just because of a "bad class" of students. Every year is different. If you chose this option, then turn to page 79 and read the underlying ideas of this response from recognized classroom management theorists.

Choice B

If I were Ms. Adams, I would speak with each student to find out what is causing their behavior. Maybe have a one- on- one conference with each of the so-called "bad" children. Ms. Adams should review her rules with the children and ask for their input, perhaps in a class meeting setting. It is never ok to yell at the students and call them names. If you chose this option, then turn to page 79 and read the underlying ideas of this response from recognized classroom management theorists.

Choice C

In this situation, I believe Ms. Adams should definitely have a class meeting. This should already be an established-integral part of her class. She would be present for the meeting but she would request that the students work together to review and refine the class rules and consequences. She needs to share the responsibility with the children and facilitate this meeting. Once the rules are reviewed and revised, she needs to invite students to decide on responsibilities for the classroom tasks. It could be, the "bad" children just need more responsibility. If you chose this option, then turn to page 79 and read the underlying ideas of this response from recognized classroom management theorists.

Case Study: Using TIC TAC TOE
Choice A

Throughout the book, we've focused your attention on various ways to consider your philosophy within the context of a Case Study that exemplified a particular situation relevant to the topic of the chapter. Perhaps most consistent with the TIC approach is the necessity of clearly communicating rules and consequences. (Skinner; Canter, 1989; Jones, 2007). The actions described in this choice are well-aligned with the "Teacher-In-Charge" philosophy of classroom management. Generally, you believe in administering consequences, and sticking to your management plan. While we feel that levels of consequences should be followed, we would recommend considering elements of the TAC theory for the potential long-term benefits of such approaches. It may be more effective when the students are involved in the process.

This scenario, shares a frustrated teacher who is refusing to look at her own behaviors. She is not considering the children and why they may be "always in trouble". Perhaps there is something she can change? Perhaps she could talk to the students, observe them and find out what are the triggers. In addition, the researchers stress teaching students methods to deal with their own self-discipline. Perhaps

Ms. Adams could teach the children to behave. When creating your rules and consequences, it is advisable to allow the students an active voice in the process, increasing buy-in from all stakeholders.

Choice B

When considering TAC, in previous chapters, we've examined information relevant to Curwin and Mendler (2008) on multiple occasions. We will do so once again in regard to responding the student behavior. Ms. Adams was not helping children to make better choices. In this choice, we see elements of teachers and students coming together to reflect upon the events that occurred as well as to develop a potential plan of action for going forth. An essential piece of any response that falls within the TAC philosophy is behavioral support. When the latter is present, acceptable behaviors are not simply expected, they are modeled, taught, and reinforced. When not emulated by a student, such approaches advocate providing specific instruction to that student or, as necessary, developing (with the student) individualized plans that include partnerships between the stakeholders (teachers, student, and family) to ensure behavioral success (Frankland, Edmonson, & Turnbull, 2001; Sugai, Horner, & Gresham, 2002).

In this case, sitting down with "the bad children" will allow Ms. Adams to gain a greater understanding of the context for their misbehavior. Ms. Adams could focus on the children's current behavior and helps them develop a judgment upon the effectiveness of their actions (e.g. Did it help you or others? Is your behavior distracting?). Once this context is established, Ms. Adams can help them to reflect on behaviors and discuss what is acceptable in the classroom and what is not.

Choice C

Finally, teachers whose views most align with the TOE philosophy, which is focused on the empowerment of students, can utilize elements consistent with Ginott (1972) and Coloroso (2002), as well as Kohn, Fay and Funk, and Gordon. The goal of a teacher whose philosophy aligns with the actions described in Choice C would be to empower students to develop their own solutions. We recommend considering actions associated with the TAC philosophy in conjunction with tenets of the TOE philosophy as a long-term solution. Your classroom is shared with your students, so you AND the children should have a voice in the management of the learning environment. It is ok for you to have some rules in mind, but be sure to have the student's voice so there is "buy in"...as well as communicate and involve the families with the creation of the rules and consequences. There needs to be commitment from all parts of the "triad" (student, families, and teacher). It is also advisable to involve the principal with your plan. Please make sure it is relevant to the building plan and that you are respectful to the principal's time and role. It is NOT a solution to send every problem to the principal's office. This sends the message to the students that you do not trust them and you are not capable to work together toward solutions. As the goal of the TOE teacher is to look for ways for students to empower themselves, the teacher, Ms. Adams had no opportunity for this.

SUMMARY

In this chapter you were introduced to methods for responding effectively to behaviors in the classroom. In review, effective teachers respond with giving students choices, reflect on their own behavior, and involve the students in the methods for responding. We established the purpose of discipline and defined discipline. We described characteristics and effective skills for culturally responsive teachers, when responding to both positive and negative behaviors. A rationale for reflecting and considering responses to positive and negative behaviors in the classroom was provided. Information was presented related to preventative measures, punishments, rewards, and consequences. A case study was examined for TIC, TAC, TOE. Finally, practical methods for responding to students in an effective manner were shared and ways to respond to positive and negative behaviors in your classroom were examined, including responding to aggressive and violent behaviors.

MOVING ON: Reflection Assignments

1. Write your own definitions of the following: Reprimand, Reinforcer, Redirect, Reward
2. A student in your class breaks a rule. How would you respond to this? What do you do first?
3. Think about any incentive program. What are the pros and cons of an incentive program, for example where students earn points?
4. How do you feel about peer mediation or conflict resolution? Is it ok for peers to respond to other students' behaviors?

Appendix A: Reflect and Act

Create your own protocol for misbehavior. What will you do if…? What happens when your students misbehave? How will you respond effectively to misbehavior? Create an IF/THEN chart. For example, IF a student is fighting in my classroom, THEN….IF a student breaks a rule, THEN… IF a student is disrespectful to me, THEN… You could review your own list of classroom rules and decided on what happens when students do not follow the rules. **Create an IF/THEN chart for how you will respond to students' positive and negative behaviors.**

REFERENCES

Brophy, J. (1981). On praising effectively. *The elementary school journal, 81*(5), 269-278.

Canter, L.,, & Canter, M. (2002). *Assertive discipline: Positive behavior management for today's schools* (3rd ed.). Bloomington, IN: Solution Tree.

Canter, L. (1989). Assertive discipline: a response. *The Teachers College Record, 90*(4), 631-638.

Charles, C. M. (2008). *Today's best classroom management strategies: paths to positive discipline.* Boston, MA: Pearson/Allyn Bacon.

Charles, C. M., Senter, G. W., & Barr, K. B. (1989). *Building classroom discipline* (pp. 143-148). New York: Longman, Inc..

Charles, C. M. (1983). *Elementary Classroom Management. A Handbook of Excellence in Teaching.* New York, NY: Longman, Inc.

Coloroso, B. (1984). *Discipline: Winning at teaching.* Ontario, Canada: Professional Development Committee of the Ontario Secondary School Teachers' Federation.

Curwin, R. L., Mendler, A. N., & Mendler, B. D. (2008). *Discipline with dignity* (3rd ed.). Alexandria, VA: Association for Supervision and Curriculum Development.

Fay, J., & Funk, D. (1995). *Teaching With Love and Logic: Taking Control of the Classroom.* Golden, CO: The Love and Logic Press, Inc.

Ginott, H. (1972). *Teacher and child.* New York, NY: Macmillan.

Glasser, W. (2011). *Schools Without Fail.* New York, NY: HarperCollins.

Gordon, T. (1989). *Teaching children self-discipline... at home and at school: New ways for parents and teachers to build self-control, self-esteem, and self-reliance.* New York, NY: Times Books/Henry Holt and Co.

Grant, T. (1993). Motivation in the classroom: Reciprocal effects of teacher behavior and student engagement across the school year. *Journal of educational psychology, 85*(4), 571-581.

Jones, F. H. (2007). *Fred Jones Tools for Teaching: Discipline-Instruction-Motivation.* Santa Cruz, CA: Fred H. Jones and Associates, Inc.

Kohn, A. (1999). *Punished by rewards: The trouble with gold stars, incentive plans, A's, praise, and other bribes.* Boston, MA: Houghton Mifflin Co.

Kounin, J. (1970). Discipline and group management in classrooms. Austin, TX: Holt, Rinehart, & Winston.

Kyle, P. B., & Rogien, L. R. (2004). *Opportunities and options in classroom management.* Upper Saddle River, NJ: Pearson.

Lewis, R. (2006). Classroom discipline in Australia. *Handbook of classroom management: Research, practice and contemporary issues,* 1193-1214.

Madsen Jr, C. H., Becker, W. C., & Thomas, D. R. (1968). Rules, praise, and ignoring: Elements of elementary classroom control. *Journal of applied behavior analysis, 1*(2), 139.

Partin, T. C. M., Robertson, R. E., Maggin, D. M., Oliver, R. M., & Wehby, J. H. (2009). Using teacher praise and opportunities to respond to promote appropriate student behavior. *Preventing School Failure: Alternative Education for Children and Youth, 54*(3), 172-178.

Rhode, G., Jenson, W. R., & Reavis, H. K. (1992). *The tough kid book: Practical classroom management strategies.* Frederick, CO: Sopris West.

Sherman, T. M., & Cormier, W. H. (1974). An investigation of the influence of student behavior on teacher behavior. *Journal of Applied Behavior Analysis, 7*(1), 11-21.

Smith, S. W., & Daunic, A. P. (2004). Research on preventing behavior problems using a cognitive-behavioral intervention: Preliminary findings, challenges, and future directions. *Behavioral Disorders*, 30(1), 72-76.

CHAPTER VI

Handling Misbehaviors Beyond the Behavior Plan

Behavior is what a man does, not what he thinks, feels, or believes.

Emily Dickinson (n.d.)

People's behavior makes sense if you think about it in terms of their goals, needs, and motives.

Thomas Mann (n.d.)

In this chapter we will focus on discussing methods that will be helpful in working with students who may exhibit behaviors that necessitate actions beyond those addressed in the behavior plan that was discussed in Chapter 4. It will also describe successful interventions that can be used specifically with children who exhibit violent behaviors or tendencies toward violence, including fighting. Finally, the chapter briefly discusses office referrals as well as zero tolerance policies.

Guiding Questions

As you read and explore the concepts introduced within this chapter, use the following questions to guide your thinking:

- What are some common, chronic misbehaviors seen in the classroom?
- How can these chronic misbehaviors be addressed?
- What characteristics are associated with students who may exhibit disruptive or violent behaviors?
- How can you prepare for and respond to defiant behavior?
- What management strategies can used to handle extreme behaviors and diffuse situations?
- When are office referrals an appropriate course of action?

Reflect and Act:
Think about the methods for responding to misbehavior that were discussed within Chapter 4. While these are designed to work with all students, what do you do in situations where the student continuously exhibits misbehaviors? What other methods could you consider to help that child become behaviorally successful?

BACKGROUND

The majority of classrooms are orderly, containing students who follow the classroom management plan, allowing learning to proceed without major disruption. In fact, researchers have characterized most classrooms as adhering to a 70-20-10 principle in regard to student misbehavior in the classroom (see Curwin, Mendler, and Mendler, 2008). That is, 70% of the students in the classroom rarely break the rules, 20% break the rules on a fairly regular basis, and 10% break the rules on a regular basis. Curwin et al. further characterize students in the latter group as "chronic rule breakers [who are] generally out of control most of the time" (p. 33). Using this information, in a class of 25, you could reasonably expect 2-3 students to be represented as part of this 10%.

While having only a few students with whom you have to have regular disciplinary-focused interactions may seem minor and within your capabilities as a teacher, it actually represents a serious challenge to a teacher's ability to teach and, subsequently students' ability to learn. To put this in some context, let's examine this situation from the perspective of the amount of instructional time lost. Consider the following:

Let's say that you have two students in your class that you'd label as chronic "misbehavers". If each of these students exhibits a misbehavior that warrants your attention 5 times per day and each misbehavior requires an average of two minutes to take care of, you've now spent around 20 minutes per day solely on the misbehaviors of these two students. Compound this over an entire school year of 180 days and you could lose somewhere in the neighborhood of **60 HOURS** of instructional time. Think about that total for a second – it represents nearly two full weeks of school.

Furthermore, our conversations with teachers reveal that in many of the cases that involve students who chronically exhibit misbehavior, it is necessary to constantly revisit management methods used to limit misbehaviors with varying levels of success. Thus, not only are you losing instructional time, but you are losing planning time that could be focused on planning effective lessons.

As we have advocated throughout the book, successful classroom management involves thinking proactively and implementing various strategies based on the needs of the students. As a result, we've focused a significant portion of the chapter on helping you to begin to think in advance about how you might handle a few of the more common forms of behavior exhibited by the students represented in Curwin and colleagues' 10% statistic. In doing so, we recognize the misbehavior may still happen, but having thought about it previously, you may limit the loss of instructional time associated with developing various strategies to work with these students.

THEORY TO PRACTICE

Reflect and Act:
Before continuing, take a moment and reflect on the behaviors that you think might be most associated with those students who would be characterized as "chronic rule breakers". Using p. 161, write a list of 3-5 of these behaviors and share them with a colleague.

Chronic Misbehaviors

Burden (2010) defines chronic misbehaviors as "troublesome behaviors that students repeatedly or compulsively perform" (p. 234). He goes on to list a number of these behaviors, including clowning, lying, defiance, and failure to complete assignments. For these behaviors, which are likely to be exhibited by the 10% group, teachers may need to reflect on a variety of actions to minimize both the prevalence of the behaviors as well as their impact in the classroom. The challenge is that as teachers, we're sometimes focused on what we do after misbehavior occurs (reactionary). Yet, when a student's disruptive behaviors persist, it is critical to think about the factors that might be contributing to the student's misbehavior. For example, you may need to consider the problem from the student's perspective and determine what needs are not being met as opposed to solely how to stop the behavior in the immediate context. You will also need to think about and become familiar with the warning signs that precede disruptions associated with the misbehaviors. The key, as you explore responsive actions, is to remember that the proactive steps you learned earlier in the book and the suggestions in this chapter form the foundation for preventing and handling behavior problems. The proactive steps you take prior to the actual misbehaviors play an essential role in establishing the climate for effective responses to violations because you've taken the steps necessary to diminish their likelihood in the first place.

As we discuss specific misbehaviors that will have a significant impact on the classroom, we've chosen to focus on those that we feel are less characterized as being aligned with curriculum or instruction, e.g. cheating. Instead, we describe actions that may impede student learning due to the disruptions they cause in the learning environment. These include, among others, clowning, profanity, rudeness, and defiance or hostility towards the teacher

Clowning. Burden (2010) uses the term clowning to describe actions that are meant to be humorous or silly, but ultimately disrupt class due to their impact on others. Comedic relief is acceptable in the proper circumstances, but it is not always exhibited in such situations by students who may fall with the 10% group. In many of these cases, clowning is ultimately about getting attention, which several classroom theorists (e.g. Albert, 2003; Dreikurs, 1968) note as being one of the primary functions of behaviors. Albert (2003) helps us distinguish between moments of levity and clowning specifically for attention as she notes that attention under the "wrong" circumstances is likely to cause the teacher to experience feelings of irritation (especially if the behavior is repetitious) and annoyance. She also mentions that when attention is provided to the student who is exhibiting the clowning, the student stops because he has received the reward (attention) he was seeking. While there are a variety of reasons students may need attention, clowning may be precipitated by a lack of attention at home or a lack of knowledge on the part of the student on how to appropriately gain the attention being sought. In general, the student is seeking to fulfill the need to belong or be accepted (Albert, 2002).

To prevent or stop attention-seeking behaviors, such as clowning, focus should be on providing attention for appropriate behavior. This is often referred to as "catch 'em being good". However, especially during the early stages of trying to do this, other strategies may need to be enacted simultaneously. For example, instead of directly responding to the behavior verbally, proximity or a "teacher look" with direct eye contact can be used as it is non-disruptive to the rest of the class, but lets the student know that you are aware of the behavior and would like it to cease. If this initial reaction is not enough to stop the clowning, Albert (2003) advocates using the "Target-Stop-Do" method. To do this, the teacher states the student's name, explicitly states the behavior that must be stopped, and provides an alternative action. For example, the teacher might say, "Mark, stop making the funny face towards Clara, and complete problem #4 on the paper in front of you." When praise is used to encourage the appropriate behavior, be sure to be explicit, e.g. "Thank you for refraining from making a comment or mimicking Clara when she fell out of her chair." Success is demonstrated within the diminishment of the clowning behaviors, but, in truth, it may be an extended period of time before true change is seen.

Profanity. Little explanation is needed for this term, yet it could represent a significant disruption in the classroom, especially if the behavior is a common one and exhibited in front of other students. As with clowning, there is likely an element of the need for attention present, especially considering the "shock" value that such language could produce among students and teachers. However, for young children, it's important to note that they may have little knowledge of the meanings of words and may be repeating something that was overheard in another context. Each of these situations should be handled differently because there are differences of intent within each. For a situation with a younger student, it is more appropriate for the teacher to engage the student in a conversation that informs the student that profanity is not appropriate for school. It will become quickly clear to you whether it was a lack of knowledge that precipitated the use of the profanity within such conversations. However, you may consider asking the child if she knows the meaning of profanity (but be prepared if you ask them to share it with you!). In either case, intentional or because of a lack of knowledge, we suggest that you engage in a follow-up conversation with the parent.

In situations where students knowingly and intentionally use profanity, we have to consider two reasons for this behavior. The first is to gain attention. In that case, we recommend that teachers have a private conversation with the student to stress to the students that the language will not be tolerated as well as describe to them what is appropriate for the particular context. While the latter may seem to be obvious, clarifying the expected behavior is likely to strengthen your position. Depending on your management philosophy, you may consider a logical consequence, including potentially having the students call their parents to explain the situation. On the other hand, the use of profanity may also represent a power-seeking behavior (Albert, 2002). Generally, in these instances, the student wants to have a sense of control of a situation, or at least try to present the impression of control. As a teacher in this type of situation, we may begin to feel angry or frustrated, especially if the student persists in using the profanity after repeated warnings or consequences. The key is to not retaliate in such a way as to create a power struggle with the student. These instances call for private conversations with the student, engaging them to determine the reasons for the use of the profanity. Many teachers will still likely administer consequences in some form, but as power-seeking is a form of assertiveness, conversations can describe methods to display more socially acceptable practices for the school context. It may also be necessary to discuss appropriate outlets for this language. For example, there are a variety of creative endeavors that include language that might not be deemed appropriate for verbal interactions, including poetry or song-writing. This would likely have to be something to discuss with an administrator, but if an appropriate outlet can be mutually defined, it is likely to diminish the potential for this to happen verbally in the classroom, especially in conjunction with conversations about contexts.

Peer Harassment/Rudeness. On occasion, as a teacher, you will observe students to be discourteous towards one another. This may consist of verbal remarks, ignoring the other student, or name-calling. Sometimes this may be playful banter between friends; however, when there is a perceived status differential, e.g. popular/unpopular, the action is more likely to be seen as teasing (Hoover & Oliver, 1996). While initially, it may not be perceived as harassment, if repeated, it can quickly be construed as such and could eventually escalate to bullying, which will be discussed in Chapter 9. Perceived differences appear to be an especially compelling reason among students for peer harassment or rudeness (Froschl & Gropper, 1999). After interviewing more than 1,000 students, Shakeshaft and colleagues (1997) came to the conclusion that "kids made fun of other kids" (p. 22), especially girls who were deemed unattractive or males that did not exhibit typical male traits.

A noteworthy result that appears constant among the research studies examining peer harassment is the lack of response from the teacher. Within our view, the teacher should intervene immediately when such behavior is observed. However, the intervention should be part of comprehensive set of principles and actions, especially if the problem is pervasive. Shakeshaft et al. (1997) recommend a multifaceted approach for diminishing this behavior and suggested activities that provoke students to reflect on the prevalence of the behavior, and, as a result, raising awareness. Students and teachers should work together to jointly define acceptable and unacceptable behaviors. By engaging in this process, all students take ownership of the situation, diminishing the likelihood that it will continue (or begin). For younger children, this could involve conversations about differences, helping them to develop the understanding that differences are natural and acceptable. Work with all students should include active modeling and practice of how to intervene when harassment occurs. Similarly, the teacher should maintain vigilance for and take an active role in making it clear that such behavior and speech are unacceptable as the students are gradually accepting more responsibility within the process. Doing so enables students to see a clear example of active intervention.

Aggression. Some students, especially boys, may engage in physical play where they behave aggressively towards other students. This may involve bumping, shoving, or slapping. Often, this represents mischievous or harmless "fun" without intent to harm. However, while generally noting that such behavior should be stopped because it can quickly escalate, regardless of the intent, the aggression we are addressing here goes beyond simply being playful. It represents a consistent pattern of aggression with the intent to hurt or unduly influence (bully) other students. In these cases, it is important to put an immediate stop to the behavior, using the classroom rules/guidelines as a starting point. For example, you may have the guideline, "Keep hands and feet to ourselves at all times", which could be used to begin a conversation with the student regarding the behavior. In the event an initial conversation does not diminish or eliminate the situation, a more in-depth follow-up conference may be necessary to discover the underlying reason for the behavior. In some instances, students may be seeking to "fit in" and are thus seeking peer acceptance through gaining attention using aggression. When this is the case, the teacher may need to specifically focus on teaching positive replacement skills as alternatives to the aggressive behaviors. In addition, there should be a focus on facilitating the development of skills necessary to self-monitor and maintain control. Often, school counselors are an excellent resource to determine various courses of action that could be pursued to help the student with self-control.

While discussing the aggressive behavior or teaching replacement skills, it is important to maintain a focus on the behavior and not the student. In discussing the situation, describe the behavior using non-evaluative terms (e.g. wrong). Instead say what you saw and its relationship to the expectations. For example, you can say, "When you hit Julio, it did not match our expectation that states we will keep all parts of our body to ourselves." Follow-up questions may focus on why the behavior was exhibited and what a better decision might be in the future. When evaluative terms are used or when you accuse the student of misbehaving, it may actually escalate the situation as the student can adopt a "me versus you" mentality. Furthermore, it's important to avoid trying to prevent aggression with further aggression on your part. This presents the double standard of "Do as I say, not as I do."

Fighting. Fighting has special significance as a behavior. It is physically dangerous to all participants as well as a teacher who may try to intervene. Generally, fighting will not occur in the classroom where an adult is present, but will take place in the hallway or playground where supervision is limited. The classic scenario where students agree to "meet behind the school at 3:00" is more of a reality than perhaps many adults think.

Lee Canter (as cited in Cangelosi, 2004) describes three stages associated with fighting. These include posturing and provocation, intense physical aggression, and lull. In the first stage, the students engage in threats and verbal taunting as a means of demonstrating their readiness to engage in the second stage, which is characterized by physical violence. Fighting is more likely to reach this second stage only when an adult has not successfully intervened while the students were verbally threatening each other. Finally, the brief, but intense physical actions exhibited in stage 2 may lead to a period where the students rest briefly or try and disengage from the fight.

The teacher's role in stopping a fight is actually dependent on a number of factors. Foremost is the stage of the fight as described in the preceding paragraph. Fighting is likely to be averted or cease if the teacher is able to effectively address the students in stage 1 or 3. If the students have begun to physically assault each other, the teacher must consider the context. If she is the sole adult on the scene, one of the first actions, if possible, would be to send a student to summon another adult or administrator. If a crowd has gathered during the fight, the teacher should immediately attempt to disperse the crowd as removal of the audience may significantly increase the likelihood that participants will cease fighting. There is no longer a need to "save face" when no one else is around. Due to the potential for injury to the teacher, intentional or not, physical restraint should be used only in a last resort. Professional judgment should be the overriding factor in a teacher's decision. For younger students, the risk of injury is diminished; however, with students who are approaching middle school, the chances significantly increase that inadvertent physical contact could result in injury. In most cases, physical intervention should not be attempted unless another adult is present in case the intervening teacher is injured. Once the fight ends or reaches the lull stage, school policy must be followed to ensure any follow-up activities that must be completed per the policy are adhered to. School policy or the administrator will dictate the individual to conduct any follow-up actions, which may include calling the students' parents, arranging a conference, and, potentially, phoning the police.

Defiance, Hostility, or Violence towards the Teacher

At some point in your career in education, you will likely encounter a situation where a student refuses to follow an explicit direction or directly confronts you in the classroom. The student may be excessively non-compliant; to the point the student demonstrates actions that are defiant or hostile towards you. As a teacher, this behavior is very threatening, especially when it occurs in front of other students. Not only are we understandably feeling threatened by the student's actions, but, furthermore, we fear losing control of the rest of our students if we do not successfully and effectively react to the student exhibiting the behavior.

Before describing the actions that can be taken in this type of situation, it's important to consider things that we can look for prior to these situations to limit (or eliminate) the likelihood of it happening. In other words, the early warning signals that a child may exhibit any of the behaviors listed in the heading. These include:

1. Declines in school achievement
2. Social withdrawal
3. Diminished attention towards physical appearance
4. Decreases in activities
5. Personality changes (Burden, 2010)

These may manifest themselves in different ways, but they represent a pattern of behaviors, especially in combination, that may indicate a child may be on his way to displaying more challenging behaviors.

While the previous list represents a number of early indicators, according to Burden (2010), challenging or potentially violent students may display behaviors that could be categorized as "behavior excesses" and "behavior deficits" (p. 241). Burden notes students who exhibit excesses are likely to break rules, argue, make excuses, throw tantrums, or demonstrate aggression. On the other hand, when a student cannot demonstrate a behavior, such as the case with behavior deficits, she is likely to show poor social skills, be impulsive, show a lack of awareness of consequences for actions, and may be struggling academically. In both categories, students who exhibit these misbehaviors are subsequently at risk for additional behavior and academic problems. Thus, as with the early warning signs, noting a pattern of several of these behaviors demonstrated concurrently should represent a significant red flag that requires action.

As we consider how to react in these situations, it is natural as an adult and authority figure that our first response in either situation is primarily directed towards gaining control over the student. This comes in the form of raising our voice, administering consequences, or ordering the student from the classroom. However, none of these responses is likely to be effective because they will likely lead you to engage in a power struggle with the student. Statements such as "you will do as I say in the classroom" or "Billy, when are you going to get a clue that I'm the boss here" are likely to escalate the situation, especially considering the student may try to get the last word. In these instances, one of the most important actions by the teacher is to remain calm (Faye & Funk, 1995). In the view of Faye and Funk (1995), when calm is not exhibited and especially when "the teacher displays anger, the child gets caught up in the anger… [and] there is little thought about the mistake or new plan of behavior" (p. 36). When this is the case, especially with older students, it becomes increasingly unlikely that the student will back down from the confrontation.

While interacting with a child who is demonstrating hostility, the focus should be on defusing the situation. To help with your own feelings, it may be necessary to count to ten or take deep calming breaths before reacting. The teacher should utilize non-threatening language and nonverbal signals. The former can include acknowledging the student's feelings and perspectives, while confirming that the actions are unacceptable and reminding the student of the consequences of his action. As advocated by multiple classroom management theorists (e.g. Albert, 2002), any verbal interaction should not be personal and should be directed towards the action, not the student. For example, you could state, "To help the other students learn this content, I need to finish this lesson. We can talk immediately after I finish." Nonverbal signals include an open posture, leaving the student plenty of space, and speaking in a low and calm, but firm, voice. In some cases, if the student is left alone once the desist is given, it may allow him to calm down, creating effective conditions for a follow-up discussion. This discussion can then focus on finding out what caused the situation, reinforcement of expectations, and a mutually satisfactory understanding. All of this should be documented by the teacher to ensure a proper record of the event and resolution.

If a confrontation does escalate to the point of violence, one of the first actions by the teacher should be to seek assistance. In the event the teacher cannot immediately access another adult, she should send a student to ensure a rapid response. In fact, it is best to send all students away from the immediate situation, if possible. The individual who arrives to provide assistance can remove all remaining children to a safe location if they are still in the same locale as the student exhibiting the violence. They can also act as a witness to ensure events are portrayed accurately and in a non-biased manner. Both adults should continue to demonstrate the behaviors included in the preceding paragraph, in turn trying to calm the student and end any violent acts.

Office Referrals

Office referrals represent an avenue of last resort that many teachers are hesitant to use, unless the circumstance is extreme, because they do not want to be perceived as not being able to "handle" their students. Sometimes schools have policies that are written into their discipline plans that explicitly state specific behaviors that warrant an immediate referral to the office. These can include such actions as fighting or defacing school property. Office referrals also generally require some form of documentation to ensure the administrator or school representative in charge of discipline can adequately address the situation as well as keep a record of the infractions committed by the student. Generally speaking, schools will use a hierarchy of consequences based on the number of referrals, with each additional referral warranting an increasingly punitive consequence, from detention to suspensions. However, more serious infractions, such as fighting or violence may result in consequences at the highest level of the hierarchy, per guidelines published in the school's disciplinary code.

According to Emmer and Evertson (2009), teachers should carefully consider their office referrals and, in fact, use them sparingly. A proactive classroom management plan and positive relationships with your students may help with this, but, in general, only the most severe cases of conduct should necessitate a referral – severe disruptions or physical violence (threats or actions). Accordingly, you must be sure to document the referral in your own records as well as provide the necessary information as required by your school administrator and the school's discipline policy. It is helpful to follow up with the administrator to ensure that the situation has been adequately addressed and a resolution is or will be forthcoming. Ultimately, when an office referral is made, it's important to realize that the authority for decision-making is no longer yours. The principal or individual responsible for discipline will now make certain decisions, sometimes with your input, but not always. As a result, you should be aware that the decision made by the individual may not align with what you would have done or what you would like to see done.

Zero Tolerance Policies

One approach to diminishing the most serious behaviors that has received a great deal of attention within the last few years is the use of zero tolerance policies. Within these policies, a strict set of guidelines mandates the consequences associated with a behavior that falls within a given category. For example, a student may face a mandatory suspension or expulsion if caught with a weapon on school grounds. In general, researchers have found this policy to be very limited in its effectiveness and it may be associated with increasing the prevalence of serious behaviors problems (American Psychological Association Zero Tolerance Task Force, 2008). Researchers (see Green, 2008) have noted that such policies do not account for situations that involve children with developmental (e.g. social or emotional) deficiencies that prevent them from critically reflecting upon their actions or the consequences associated with them. Instead, the members of the American Psychological Task Force cite research (e.g. Elliott, Hatot, Sirovatka, & Potter, 2001) and advocate a three tier system of support and intervention such as might be associated with Positive Behavioral Intervention and Supports (PBIS). While the full list of the Task Force's recommendations are beyond the scope of this chapter, suggestions include training for faculty and staff on the appropriate methods to handle specific infractions, using a set of consequences that are aligned with the severity of the infraction, and increased communication and coordination among schools, parents, and agencies that come into contact with students who are behaviorally at-risk.

APPLICATION WITH DIVERSE LEARNERS

Regardless of the school you teach, there is likely to be a great deal of diversity in your classroom, especially when you account for achievement, abilities, background, and attitudes. Each of these represents a factor in determining the characteristics of the learners in your classroom. When we examine and become knowledgeable about the characteristics of the learners in our classrooms, we can more effectively plan for and implement a system of management that is effective for all learners. In short, we've written about it in previous chapters, but to enable your students to feel safe, secure, and accepted, we need to create an environment that is structured and predictable, yet is supportive to students' unique needs. Sometimes this means overlooking behaviors that are minor to avoid escalation and demonstrations of the behaviors that we have outlined in previous sections of this chapter. We also need to become familiar with precursors and stressors that may precede or intensify aggression, hostility, or other chronic misbehaviors. Unless a student's IEP specifies conditions that would alter your discipline system, this allows you to utilize these best-accepted, research-based methods with any student in your class who needs assistance in behaving in a more responsible manner.

Kottler and Kottler (1993) recommend a series of reflective questions that you should ask yourself when you observe behavior that may not be "typical". These questions include:

1. What is unusual about the child's behavior?
2. Is there a pattern associated with the behavior?
3. What additional information would be necessary to further inform my thinking?
4. Where would this information come from?
5. Who can I consult with to help me with a decision about this case?

While these questions can be asked within any case of misbehavior, we feel that they are especially important when working with children from diverse backgrounds because of the potential for mismatch between a teacher's expectations and behaviors due to differences in background or a lack of knowledge about the learner on the part of the teacher. Researchers (see Skiba & Rausch, 2006) have proposed that disparities between behaviors and expectations contribute to a disproportionate number of disciplinary referrals to minority students, especially in comparison to Caucasian students.

CASE STUDY – Developing Your Philosophy

As the bell sounded to end 4th period, Ms. Hammond's sixth grade science quickly exits the classroom with more than the usual pre-lunch buzz. Curious to see what the situation is that caused everyone to hurry towards the end of the hall, Ms. Hammond looks in the direction most of her students are heading. She is alarmed to notice most of her class as well as students from other homerooms congregating around two boys, one from her class (Alex) and another from Ms. Harrison's class (Marcus), who appear to be confronting each other. Ms. Hammond quickly begins to move down the hall towards the boys.

"Let's go," said Marcus to Alex. "You took my stuff and I now I'm going to make you pay for it."

89

"I told you I didn't take it, but if you really want to get your butt kicked in front of everybody, that's fine with me," responds Alex. As Alex steps forward, towards Marcus, he bumps Marcus with his chest. In the background, several students shout encouragement for both boys to fight. Ms. Hammond is trying to move quickly toward the situation, but is not close enough to be heard over the crowd yet.

Reflect, Part 1, on the following questions before moving on and reading more in the scenario:

1. What is the context for the confrontation? At this point, have the boys broken any rules?
2. In thinking back to Canter's stages of fighting, what stage is being exhibited at this point?
3. What should Ms. Hammond do?

"Get off me," says Marcus, who pushes Alex. Without hesitation, Alex pushes Marcus back very hard. The students around them continue to encourage the two boys to fight. Without further comment, Marcus swings his arm wildly, connecting with Alex's shoulder. Alex is taken aback for a second and then charges at Marcus in an attempt to tackle him.

At this point, Ms. Hammond has reached the crowd, which begins to quickly disperse when they see her enter the circle they had made around the boys. Alex is on top of Marcus on the floor, but it appears that the boys are primarily wrestling and no further punches have been thrown.

"Marcus, Alex, release each other immediately," states Ms. Hammond in a very firm authoritative voice. When the boys do not respond and continue to wrestle, Ms. Hammond tells one of her students who is at a nearby locker to go to Ms. McAlpine, the assistant principal, and ask her to come immediately. She also tells the students who are continuing to watch to go to the class or location they are supposed to be at for that period of the day or risk disciplinary action. Ms. Hammond then returns her attention towards Alex and Marcus.

"Alex and Marcus, if you do not stop this immediately, you will face suspension," states Ms. Hammond. "As soon as you stop, we can go somewhere to calm down and talk about this."

Reflect, Part 2, on the following questions before moving on to the final portion of the scenario and further questions associated with the content of the chapter.

1. What stage of fighting is being exhibited?
2. Should Ms. Hammond try to separate the boys since they are just wresting on the ground? Describe the rationale for your thinking.
3. If Ms. Hammond chooses to not try and separate the boys, what should she do next?

Ms. Hammond continues to monitor the boys' activities, but, as both are larger than her, she chooses not to attempt to physically intervene. Instead, she repeats her previous requests for the boys to disengage from each other. Marcus appears to be getting the worst of the fight as he has hit his head on the floor several times as the boys have wrestled around. Within a minute, Ms. McAlpine arrives, providing the support of another adult. Immediately, she requests the boys to stop fighting in a loud, authoritative voice.

When this was not successful, she moves closer to the boys and says, "Marcus and Alex, stop fighting now."

This time the command causes both boys to look up and Alex releases Marcus. Ms. McAlpine immediately steps between the two boys and asks Ms. Hammond to take Marcus to the nurse to have her look at a spot on his head where he has hit it on the floor. She then asks her to bring him by her office when the visit to the nurse is complete. She requests that Alex come with her directly to her office. Consider how you would handle the situation at that point if you were Ms. McAlpine. For example, what actions would you take with each boy individually? Would you conference with them together in the same room? Should the boys' parents be notified? Once you've considered your responses to these questions and others that you may have thought of on your own, examine the responses below and choose the one that best matches your own.

Case Study: Response Choices
Choice A

If I were Ms. McAlpine, I would administer the consequence for fighting to each boy, as described in the school handbook. I do not think it would be necessary to conference with the boys together because they both engaged in the fighting, which is strictly prohibited, and should be punished accordingly, regardless of the preceding events. I would ask Ms. Hammond to file documentation describing what she observed, but would not involve her in any further conversations regarding the fight. The family of each student would be called and they should be immediately sent home for the day.

If you chose this option, then read the underlying ideas from recognized classroom management theorists associated within the Choice A response below.

Choice B

Ms. McAlpine should speak individually with each student to obtain their versions of the events that preceded the altercation. After a period of time has elapsed, allowing the students to calm down, she should bring them together, with Ms. Hammond and Ms. Harrison, to discuss the situation and to develop a plan for handling situations in the future.

If you chose this option, then turn to page 94 and read the underlying ideas of this response from recognized classroom management theorists.

Choice C

In this situation, Ms. McAlpine should have the students meet in her office and discuss the situation. Ms. McAlpine would be present, but she would request that the students work together to develop a report detailing the events that lead to the situation, a method of handling the situation more appropriately, and a contract that describes future behaviors that will be taken should a similar situation arise. If the boys were unable to do this on their own, another student would act as a peer mediator to facilitate a resolution.

If you chose this option, then turn to page 95 and read the underlying ideas of this response from recognized classroom management theorists.

Case Study: Using TIC-TAC-TOE
Choice A

The actions described in this choice are well-aligned with the "Teacher-In-Charge" philosophy of classroom management. Generally, you believe in administering consequences, and, if an especially severe behavior is exhibited, an established severity clause prescribes the consequence that should be used. While we feel that there are certainly instances when consequences should be administered, we would recommend considering elements of the TAC theory for the potential long-term benefits of such approaches.

Fighting that has already occurred is subject to the policies described in the student handbook for the school. As a teacher or administrator, you would need to be careful to follow the provisions outlined, documenting the events as necessary, and administering any consequences described. However, we feel it's also important to engage the students in conversations regarding the incident. There may be underlying causes to the behaviors that are not immediately clear if we simply note the action of fighting. For example, perhaps Marcus received the item in question from his grandmother, who is now sick, making him react in a manner that might be more aggressive than usual. On the other hand, a conversation with Alex may reveal his parents are going through a divorce and he is experiencing feelings of despondency that he is not sure how to deal with. Of course, these types of situations may not be the case every time fighting occurs, but it's important that, even if consequences are administered, conversations occur to provide you with all information necessary to make an informed decision about the actions that were exhibited.

This scenario, by administering the same consequence to both students, does represent an instance of what could also be deemed a zero-tolerance policy. While Curwin and Mendler (1999), who are associated with the TAC philosophy, note this type of policy may be warranted in non-traditional environments, in most cases they feel it is not the most effective manner in which to handle cases that occur in a "traditional" school context. Instead, they advocate working with students to teach the students how to successfully manage conflict through effective choices and how to choose alternatives to violent behavior. In addition, the researchers stress teaching methods to deal with such feelings as anger and frustration directly to students. To increase the likelihood of the successful implementation of teaching strategies, there should be a school-level focus on building a climate through Curwin and Mendler's principles associated with an "As Tough as Necessary" policy. In essence, within this policy, a set of guidelines implicating everyone's role in establishing a safe environment are created in addition to a series of rules focused on maintaining the safe environment. This assures students have an active voice in the process, increasing buy-in from all stakeholders.

Choice B

In this choice, we see elements of teachers and students coming together to reflect upon the events that occurred as well as to develop a potential plan of action for going forth. An essential piece of any response that falls within the TAC philosophy is behavioral support. When the latter is present, socially acceptable behaviors are not simply expected, they are modeled, taught, and reinforced. When not emulated by a student, such approaches advocate providing specific instruction to that student or, as necessary, developing (with the student) individualized plans that include partnerships between the stakeholders (teachers, student, and family) to ensure behavioral success (Frankland, Edmonson, & Turnbull, 2001; Sugai, Horner, & Gresham, 2002).

In this case, sitting down with Marcus and Alex will allow the teachers and Ms. McAlpine to gain a greater understanding of the context for the altercation. Multiple elements of William Glasser's (1988) model for problem-solving could be employed as Ms. McAlpine focuses on the boys' current behavior and helps them develop a judgment upon the effectiveness of their actions (e.g. Did it help you or others?). Once this context is established, all of the adults present can help the boys reflect upon their actions within the situation, discussing what was acceptable and what was not, and engaging them in conversations about more appropriate ways to respond. These conversations could function as teaching episodes, especially if either boy was unclear about the behavioral expectations. Should it be necessary, a plan could be developed that would enable monitoring and/or alternative behaviors. For example, a series of "If-Then" statements could be created describing how the boys would respond when presented with specific situations similar to what occurred, subsequently causing the altercation. To ensure success of the plan, however, a commitment from the students must be obtained to maintain their accountability and responsibility.

Choice C

The goal of a teacher whose philosophy aligns with the actions described in Choice C would be to empower students to develop their own solutions. That written, there are some circumstances that may not lend themselves well, at least initially, towards a focus solely on empowering the student. We feel this represents one situation. We believe that there are elements of the TOE approach that are applicable, but note these elements would take time to develop and would therefore have to be in place prior to their use in this situation. As a result, we recommend considering actions associated with the TAC philosophy in conjunction with tenets of the TOE philosophy as a long-term solution.

As the goal of the TOE teacher is to look for ways for students to empower themselves, the teacher in choice C chose to initially have the students engage in a discussion; however, we believe that, even with the principal present, an agreement may not be forthcoming due to lingering feelings of distrust and anger. As a result, unless the school has an established record of peer mediation, engaging in a conference such as that described in Choice B (TAC philosophy) may be more productive for generating a solution. Adhering towards a gradual release of responsibility, which might be more aligned with the TOE philosophy, the teachers or administrator could focus on suggestions or simply facilitate a conversation. The key, however, is that they do take an active role. This fact alone differentiates the actions that are more aligned with TAC than TOE.

The suggestion for a peer mediation conference is certainly an element that would be associated with empowering students to formulate their own solutions. As we discuss problem-solving approaches, including peer mediation and conflict resolution, extensively within Chapter 7, we will refer you to that chapter for the specific steps involved in such a process. However, we must point out that the approach is one that must represent a paradigm shift at the school level as the children become more and more involved in the process and the adults have a diminished role, which is the opposite of what most teachers are used to. The faculty and staff must be committed and recognize that this is a gradual process as all components within such programs are taught, practiced, and reinforced.

SUMMARY

In this chapter we have explored information related to chronic misbehaviors as well as those that might necessitate specific and immediate actions from the teacher. We've tried to reinforce the importance of maintaining a focus on the underlying causes of the behaviors, while still reacting in a manner consistent with your own classroom management plan and the school's policies. As you consider how you might react in various situations, it's important to maintain a focus on proactively considering situations and reflecting on methods that you would use to successfully intervene should it be warranted.

MOVING ON: Reflection Assignments

1. Discuss the advantages and disadvantages of providing positive attention towards a student who may exhibit behaviors associated with clowning, disrupting the learning of other students.

2. In the school you are teaching or observing, interview the principal, assistant principal, or guidance counselor to determine the school's policy for fighting.

3. Use page 162 to write a scenario in which a student (or students) engages in one of the behaviors listed at the beginning of the chapter (e.g. profanity, aggressions towards another student or teacher). Act out the scenario and have peers discuss how to effectively handle the situation.

REFERENCES

Albert, L. (2002). *Cooperative Discipline* (2nd ed.). Circle Pines, MN: American Guidance Service Publishing.

Albert, L. (2003). *A teacher's guide to cooperative discipline: How to manage your classroom and promote self-esteem.* Circle Pines, MN: American Guidance Service Publishing.

American Psychological Association Zero Tolerance Task Force. (2008). Are zero tolerance policies effective in schools? An evidentiary review and recommendations. *American Psychologist, 63,* 852-862. DOI: 10.1037/0003-066X.63.9.852

Burden, P. R. (2010). *Classroom management: Creating a successful K-12 learning community* (4th ed.). Hoboken, NJ. John Wiley & Sons, Inc.

Cangelosi, J. S. (2004) *Classroom management strategies: Gaining and maintaining students' cooperation* (5th ed.). Hoboken, NJ: John Wiley & Sons, Inc.

Curwin, R. L., & Mendler, A. N. (1999). Zero tolerance for zero tolerance. *Phi Delta Kappan, 81,* 119-120.

Curwin, R. L., Mendler, A. N., & Mendler, B. D. (2008). *Discipline with dignity* (3rd ed.). Alexandria, VA: Association for Supervision and Curriculum Development.

Dreikurs, R. (1968). *Psychology in the classroom* (2nd ed.). New York: Harper & Row.

Elliott, D., Hatot, N. J., Sirovatka, P., & Potter, B. B. (2001). *Youth violence: A report of the Surgeon General.* Washington, DC: Office of the U.S. Surgeon General.

Emmer, E. T., & Evertson, C. M. (2009). *Classroom management for middle and high school teachers* (8th ed.). Upper Saddle River, NJ: Pearson.

Fay, J., & Funk, D. (1995). *Teaching With Love and Logic: Taking Control of the Classroom.* Golden, CO: The Love and Logic Press, Inc.

Frankland, C., Edmonson, H., & Turnbull, A. (2001). Positive behavioral support: Family, school, and community partnerships. *Beyond Behavior, 11,* 7-9.

Froschl, M., & Gropper, N. (1999). Fostering friendships, curbing bullying. *Educational Leadership, 56,* 72-75.

Glasser, W. (1988). *Choice theory in the classroom.* New York: Harper.

Greene, M. B. (2008). Reducing school violence: School-based curricular programs and school climate. *The Prevention Researcher, 15,* 12-16.

Hoover, J., & Oliver, R. (1996). *The bullying prevention handbook: A guide for teachers, principals and counselors.* Bloomington, IN: National Educational Service.

Kottler, J. A., & Kottler, E. (1993). *Teacher as counselor: Developing the helping skills you need.* Newbury Park, CA: Corwin Press, Inc.

Shakeshaft, C., Mandel, L., Johnson, Y. M., Sawyer, J., Hergenroter, M. A., & Barber, E. (1997). Boys call me cow. *Educational Leadership, 55,* 22-25.

Skiba, R., & Rausch, M. K. (2006). Zero tolerance, suspension, and expulsion: Questions of equity and effectiveness. In C. M. Evertson & C. S. Weinstein (Eds.), *Handbook of African American Male Discipline Patterns classroom management: Research, practice, and contemporary issues* (pp. 1063-1092). Mahwah, NJ: Lawrence Erlbaum.

Sugai, G., Horner, R., & Gresham, F. (2002). Behaviorally effective school environments. In M. R. Shinn, G. Stoner, & H. M. Walker (Eds.), *Interventions for academic and behavior problems: Preventive and remedial approaches* (pp. 315-350). Silver Springs, MD: National Association of School Psychologists.

CHAPTER VII

Individual Behavior Plans

The most effective approaches to school-based prevention of antisocial behavior are proactive and instructive—planning ways to avoid failure and ...actively teaching students more adaptive, competent ways of behaving.

James Kauffman (2001) *Characteristics of Emotional and Behavioral Disorders of Children and Youth*

Regardless of how well we manage our classroom there will come a point in time where one of our students may need additional, individualized support to be successful. This chapter will introduce the individual behavior plan as one method to help us meet the needs of a student who requires scaffolds to help him exhibit appropriate behaviors in our classroom. In doing so, we will describe functional behavior assessments, their use in designing a plan for behavioral change, and the importance of effectively monitoring and modifying the plan as necessary. Within the Case Study you will be introduced to Mr. Cooper and Ms. Elliot, two classroom teachers, as well as Bradley and Martha, two students in their classes that have had behavioral difficulties and would benefit from individualized assistance. In turn, you will help Mr. Cooper and Ms. Elliot develop plans to help Bradley and Martha become successful in their classrooms.

Guiding Questions

As you read and explore the concepts introduced within this chapter, use the following questions to guide your thinking:

- How can I determine the necessity of a behavioral intervention?
- What is an individual behavior plan?
- How do individual behavior plans differ from regular classroom management plans?
- Why is data an important element within the development of an individual behavior plan?
- What steps need to be taken to implement a successful individual behavior plan?

Reflect and Act:
Think about all the misbehaviors that can be observed in a classroom. At what point does a misbehavior become excessive? Write a list of behaviors that you think would necessitate a specific intervention, beyond the regular classroom management plan for an individual student.

what/who defines misbehavior?

BACKGROUND

As the amount of diversity in our classrooms continues to expand, so do the various academic and behavioral needs of our students. As a result, teachers are increasingly required to use a variety of management and instructional strategies to ensure that students are consistently and actively engaged in activities and misbehavior remains low. Within our instruction, it is common for teachers to differentiate our processes or content to meet the various academic needs of students; yet there is a similar, perhaps greater, need to engage in a related process with students who are exhibiting limited capabilities in demonstrating acceptable classroom behavior. Research has revealed as many as 5 percent of students may need some form of individualized intervention for behavior (McIntosh, Campbell, Carter, & Dickey, 2009). Thus, it's important to consider steps that can be taken to actively ensure the students who fit into the aforementioned category have the support and assistance necessary to become behaviorally successful, which has a high likelihood of improving academic success.

As is often the case when implementing any form of intervention, the key in such situations is to examine and incorporate strategies that have proven to be effective. What has made this process difficult, however, is that there is no single behavioral model or strategy that will work with all students. In many cases, teachers may have to try multiple methods before finding one that is successful, and, even then, they may have to make several modifications as effectiveness diminishes. Short-term success may not translate into long-term behavior change. As a result, we recommend teachers do not focus solely on a given misbehavior, but expand their analyses to include the multiple factors present when the misbehavior is exhibited, including time, place, and severity (Gathercoal, 2001). In essence, they assess a context and situation, not just a behavior. This data gathering process can be instrumental in helping teachers arrive at conclusions that move beyond simply focusing on "what" behavior is being exhibited and instead address the underlying "why" for the exhibited behavior. Furthermore, incorporating multiple sources of information that address the cause of the behavior allows teachers to use the behavioral "assessment" data to develop more comprehensive, multi-faceted plans, increasing the likelihood of preventing (or significantly diminishing) the behavior in the future.

THEORY TO PRACTICE

> **Reflect and Act:**
> **Think about assessing behavior. Write down your answers to the following questions: What format would the assessment take? What processes would you use that would be similar to academic assessment? What would be different?**

Why is Assessing Behavior Important?

Competence in classroom management requires a number of skills, including responding to inappropriate behavior. Often, teachers respond in a reactionary manner – they seek to end the disruption through a verbal reprimand, loss of privilege, or other more severe consequence. The challenge in this approach is that the underlying "need" or "cause" of the misbehavior is never addressed. The student may respond to the initial reprimand, but the lack of attention towards determining "why" the misbehavior occurs increases the likelihood that it will be observed again in the future. Similarly, responsive techniques do not provide a student with replacement behaviors that are acceptable behaviors within the context of the classroom.

In attempting to make all children successful, it is critical that we assess and reflect on behavior, just like we would assess and reflect the learning and instruction that occurs within our classroom. For example, if my students are demonstrating some misbehavior, is it because the lesson is not interesting? Could it also be in response to the lack of understanding of a task, concept, or skill? The challenge in any of these situations is determining the underlying reason for the misbehavior. Extending these situations, at what point do behaviors indicate an individual problem that is more significant than that exhibited by the class collectively?

To answer these questions, it's important that we begin to gather information to help us in our decisions. For example, we may begin to collect anecdotal notes within informal observations to help us reflect on situations that occurred during the school day. During my (Mike's) career, I carried a clipboard with a manila folder throughout the day. Inside the folder were sticky notes where I could quickly write down my observations, indicating the date, time, and the student's initials to ensure I remembered the context as well as who I was referring to when I looked at the notes later. What I learned, and research has confirmed, is that it was important to concentrate on observable behaviors because it allowed me to look for patterns (Jones & Jones, 2009). For example, in one case, I noticed that a particular student was often off-task when students were given the opportunity to begin writing in their reflective journals after my science lessons. Using this information, I was able to confirm that the misbehavior resulted from a consistent lack of understanding of the concepts being taught. Often, such informal observations were enough to develop modest interventions that paralleled my primary management plan. However, that will not be the case for all children. At that point it becomes necessary to progress to a more formalized approach to examining behavior.

Functional Behavior Assessment

Primarily associated with a behaviorist (TIC) ideology, functional analysis was a term used to describe the relationship between a behavior and the environment (Skinner, 1953). While the use of the term has varied since it was first introduced, we subscribe to the idea that the term *function* conveys the purpose the behavior serves for an individual, i.e. the underlying, internal "reward" the individual receives as a result of engaging in a particular behavior. For example, if a student consistently called out during math instruction and each time the teacher responded by sending the child to the hall, the function may be related to the reward of escaping math class and/or challenging instruction.

A functional behavior assessment is a formal observation protocol that is focused upon examining and identifying the conditions which cause or increase the likelihood of a particular behavior being observed. Identification of the environmental conditions is proposed to allow the teacher or other stakeholder to modify the conditions, resulting in a subsequent decrease in the observed, problematic behavior. In general, a functional behavior assessment involves conducting observations of the subject within the environment and direct measurement of the instances of the problem behavior. The intent of such observations is to form conclusions about the antecedent – the event or conditions that are likely to immediately precede the behavior that has been noted as problematic – as well as the consequences when the behavior is exhibited. The latter can refer to the actions from the teacher as well as the apparent reward to the student.

Some versions of a functional behavior assessment, referred to as the experimental analysis of behavior by educational psychologists and researchers (e.g. Carr & Durand, 1985; Gresham, Watson, &

Skinner, 2001), include the active manipulation of conditions, using an experimental approach to facilitate treatment of the problem behavior. While this may be applicable in a clinical setting working with specific populations of participants, e.g. persons with developmental disabilities (Hanley, Iwata, & McCord, 2003), this approach is not always possible or recommendable within the general education classroom. As a result, we advocate a less formalized approach, called applied behavior analysis, which involves observations of behavior in naturalistic settings. Examples of our approach are encompassed within practices that advocate antecedent-behavior-consequence recording (see Groden, 1989). This approach maintains the necessity of a focus on data collection and analysis, yet data is likely to consist of researcher/teacher recorded notes in a short-hand or narrative format, as opposed to frequency counts. Once the antecedent and consequence events are noted, the focus shifts to effectively planning and implementing interventions that result in acceptable behavior (Witt, Daly, & Noell, 2000; Wolf, 1978).

Within our process there is a focus on diagnosing the function of the behavior. There are several theories regarding the categories for behavioral functions. For example, Albert (2003) describes four functions of misbehavior: attention-seeking, power, revenge, and avoidance of failure. Carr (1994), on the other hand, lists five categories:

- social attention/communication;
- access to tangibles or preferred activities;
- escape, delay, reduction, or avoidance of aversive activities;
- escape or avoidance of other individuals; and
- internal stimulation.

reasons behind behaviors

The key is not necessarily the theory you subscribe to or the label that is used, but arriving at the specific reason your student is engaging in the behavior.

Acknowledging that most teachers do not have a formal school psychology background nor do they necessarily have time to engage in in-depth searches for observation protocols, we have developed and included a template that will allow you to conduct a functional behavior assessment (see Figure 1). Of note, should you wish to find your own, researchers sometimes refer to similar forms as an A-B-C recording form (Gresham, et al., 2001), so using this term may help in you're the search. There are a variety of such forms available and several websites are included in the **MOVING ON: Reflection Assignments** that may be of interest. Such forms not only help you analyze the behaviors, but they function as a form of document should you decide to implement an individual behavior plan as a result of your observations.

Individual Behavior Plans

We've acknowledged that there comes a point in a teacher's interactions with a student where it becomes clear that the general management plan is not working. This is usually established by a string of "red flags" within interactions with the student. For example, the student doesn't change her behavior after multiple reminders of the expected behaviors as well as efforts to redirect her actions. Perhaps the teacher has also held individual conferences with the student to engage her in efforts to problem-solve and develop plans and replacement behaviors to help her act acceptably in challenging situations. All this occurs with no discernible change, significantly impacting the student's ability to learn and be successful

key to all!

Figure 1. Functional Behavior Assessment Tool

Functional Behavior Assessment

Student_____

Step 1 – Describe the behavior.

What does the behavior look like?

How often does the behavior occur? How long does it last?

What is the setting where the behavior is most likely to occur?

Step 2 – Describe the antecedents.

Date	Location	Activity	Behavior	Intensity
				Low High 1 2 3 4 5
				Low High 1 2 3 4 5
				Low High 1 2 3 4 5
				Low High 1 2 3 4 5
				Low High 1 2 3 4 5
				Low High 1 2 3 4 5
				Low High 1 2 3 4 5

Step 3 – Describe the consequence.

What happens as a result of the problem behavior? (Include the subject's, teacher's, and other students' reactions as well as the specific events, e.g. removal to the school office)

Step 4 – Summarize the information.

Antecedent (Predictor)	Behavior (of concern)	Consequence (of adult, peers, etc)

Step 5 – Propose a function for the behavior in each of the ABC sequences listed above.

1.
2.
3.

in the classroom. Subsequently, the teacher conducts the previously described functional behavior assessment.

Using the results of an assessment, e.g. applied behavior analysis, teachers will likely wish to create an individual behavior plan (see Figure 2). The key to such a plan is to establish and teach a series of behavior goals that provide the student with alternatives to engaging in the behavior or behaviors that have caused the necessity of the plan. These should be developed specifically in relation to the function of the behavior, as determined by the behavioral assessment. For example, if the student is exhibiting power-seeking behaviors, such as throwing tantrums to gain control of a situation, it may be necessary to determine methods to involve the student in decision-making (TOE strategy).

Individual behavior plans are formal documents that establish the behaviors to be targeted by within the plan, the goals for the plan, including any potential replacement behaviors, and the progress-monitoring procedures that will allow successes to be noted or changes to be determined. In Step 1, the teacher should describe or include a list of the behaviors that are the target of the plan. These should be specific and observable to ensure that all stakeholders, including administrators and other teachers (where necessary), can accurately assess and identify the behaviors. Generally, this section should be completed solely by the teacher who is creating the plan, but the accuracy of the behavioral descriptions should be shared and confirmed with the student. Within Step 2, the behavioral goals for the plan are established. Ideally, this should parallel and directly correspond with the behaviors identified as part of Step 1. To increase ownership, we recommend that the student is an active participant within the process of establishing the goals. This can also be done in collaboration with any other stakeholders, including parents or other teachers. The primary benefit of these conversations is that they allow the parties to discuss mutually acceptable alternatives as well as the specific actions that will be taken, ensuring "buy-in" by all parties. We include several elements consistent with a coaching model (Fournies, 2000) in our model, including increased situational awareness and the use of problem-solving strategies, as they have proven beneficial in behavior change. It is important to note, however, that the teacher initiating the process should be comfortable with any specific plans that are created, thus there is a level of negotiation that may be necessary. Steps 3 and 4 are focused on progress-monitoring and review. In Step 3, individual goals are aligned with data collection procedures, including the identification of the individual responsible for the collection. Clarity is important at this step to ensure that responsibilities are clearly noted and a timeline is provided as a framework within which to operate. Similarly, all parties must be aware of the dates for review, both concerning the progress-monitoring as well as the primary plan (Step 4). Setting specific dates ensures the process can stay on target and provides accountability for the teacher or individual responsible for implementation and monitoring. Finally, acknowledgement of the plan comes in the form of signatures by all involved parties.

Using TIC-TAC-TOE

We feel that it's important to establish the continued relevance of TIC-TAC-TOE within a discussion of individual behavior contracts, even when the apparent use of a behavioral assessment is associated primarily with the ideas of B. F. Skinner, who was included within the TIC category. As you'll note, we've provided and will continue to provide specific references to strategies that are consistent to the categories within the continuum. While we cannot change the underlying theory for the development of the functional behavior assessments, we can recommend that you use the most applicable, relevant strategies that match your management orientation within the continuum as well as effectively meet the needs of the individual student.

Figure 2. Individual Behavior Plan Template

Individual Behavior Plan

Student_____   Date _____

Step 1 – Describe the behaviors to be targeted.

Step 2 – Establish behavioral goals (observable and measurable).

Step 3 - Determine progress-monitoring procedures.

Goal	Data Collection Procedures	Person Responsible	Dates

Step 4 – Establish a review date.

This plan will be reviewed on _____.

Step 5 – Collect signatures of responsible parties.

_____
Student

_____
Parent (when applicable)

_____
Teacher

_____
(Responsible party #1 – when applicable)

_____
(Responsible party #2 – when applicable)

> **Reflect and Act:**
> **Re-examine the list of functions of misbehavior associated with Albert (2003) and Carr (1994). Think about what actions or strategies a teacher could use to effectively provide appropriate, alternative behaviors that would address the student's needs. Develop a list and share it with colleagues.**

APPLICATION WITH DIVERSE LEARNERS

Chapter 1 briefly introduced the principles of culturally responsive classroom management, but in light of developing individual plans for students, it's important to revisit the information. We've noted previously that teachers' concerns about classroom management are heightened when working with students who may be culturally, linguistically, or ethnically different from themselves (Milner, 2006). This is especially salient when we consider that students of color are disproportionately referred to the office, often for infractions that may be based on a "more subjective ... interpretation" (Skiba, Michael, Nardo, & Peterson, 2002, p. 317) of their misbehavior. Researchers (e.g. Skiba et al., 2002) have proposed that this may be the result of a cultural disconnect between the teachers and students or a general lack of knowledge about cultural norms and mores on the part of the teacher. For example, Thompson (2004) noted that when an African-American student speaks in a loud voice, it may be viewed as an act of defiance as opposed to a cultural characteristic. The potential result is a conflict between the teacher and student as the teacher feels the need to administer a consequence or subsequently teach an alternative behavior that may match expectations consistent with the dominant cultural paradigm.

As a result, it is recommended that teachers prepare themselves to demonstrate culturally responsive classroom management principles. This includes:

- developing an understanding of students' cultural backgrounds (Weinstein, Curran, & Tomlinson-Clarke, 2003);
- acknowledging that the teacher's own beliefs about what constitutes appropriate classroom behavior are culturally based (Weinstein et al., 2003);
- establishing positive, authentic relationships with students (Ladson-Billings, 1995; Ware, 2006); and
- establishing and clearly communicating high expectations for all students (Brown, 2003)

Furthermore, the teacher should exhibit behaviors associated with an authoritative stance such as setting limits, avoiding power struggles, and a focus on earning respect as opposed to demanding it (Delpit, 1995). Many of these characteristics are what we would associate with our Teacher-and-Child (TAC) philosophy.

How does this relate to an individual behavior plan? First, teachers who are aware of cultural norms and characteristics and who know their students may be less likely to identify the necessity of this type of plan because they can accurately assess functions of behavior. However, when the need is present for this type of plan, the teacher works hand-in-hand with the student to find a solution that is acceptable to all parties and meets the needs of all parties, including the greater school community where applicable. This may mean the inclusion of teaching cooperation or conflict resolution or teaching using a culturally responsive pedagogy, but the focus is on the development of the plan collaboratively, as opposed to by

104

mandate. There is certainly not a fixation on using coercive or controlling means to modify behavior, as might be present when the teacher acts as the sole authority (Teacher-in-Charge).

In working with teachers, we feel it is critical to have them reflect upon their emerging ideas about culturally response classroom management to help their proficiency in the process. One shared the following anecdote in working with her students:

> To be an effective classroom manager in a culturally diverse classroom, a teacher must ensure that all of her students understand what the norms are for each specific behavior ... I have been making more effort to determine whether a child's misbehavior is truly inappropriate, or if it seems inappropriate to me because of my own cultural norms. This may mean allowing students from other cultures to respond during lessons in the way they are most comfortable, such as letting my African-American students have a chance to "call and respond" on occasion.

Engaging in such self-reflections will allow a teacher to be more responsive to her students and, ultimately, limit the necessity of the implementation of an individual behavior plan.

CASE STUDY – Developing an Individual Behavior Plan

Case #1 - Bradley

Bradley was informally introduced to Mr. Cooper's attention as a potential behavioral issue at a teacher work day two days before the start of school. Bradley's second grade teacher made it a point to pull Mr. Cooper aside and let him know that Bradley had some behavior problems last year, but had made some improvements over the last two school years. She mentioned that Bradley seemed to struggle with making friends as well as consistently following the behavioral expectations for the classroom While Mr. Bradley thanked the teacher for the information and made a mental note of the conversation, he also wanted to approach the school year and each child with an open mind, thus he didn't follow up any further prior to the first day of school.

The first week began smoothly and Mr. Cooper thought that perhaps Bradley had made strides over the summer break. However, the following week, two parents of students in Mr. Bradley's class asked that their children not be seated near Bradley because of incidents of name calling and insults. Two other parents expressed concern that Bradley could be a "bad influence" on their children, with one parent even blaming him for her child's use of bad language the prior year.

As a result of these conversations, Mr. Cooper began to watch Bradley more closely. During the second and third week, there were a few incidents of name calling. When they occurred, Bradley was generally apologetic. However, after another week of observations, Mr. Cooper deduced that Bradley was verbally impulsive. He often began conversations with the students in his cluster about any topic that struck him as interesting at the moment. He also began to regularly call out in class. His "call outs" differed from those of other students, though, as he was not necessarily responding to questions from Mr. Bradley. Instead, he would speak out in response to others, sometimes insulting the other students in the process. For example, one day after a student requested information about an assignment that Mr. Cooper had just covered in great detail, Bradley called out, "That was a stupid question!" While Mr. Cooper asked him to apologize, what was noteworthy about the comment was that it was not delivered in a tone meant to be insulting; instead it seemed that Bradley verbalized his inner speech without thinking through the consequences and effects on others.

After moving Bradley to the front of the room to curtail needless talking and to try and use proximity control to limit call outs, Bradley began talking to Mr. Cooper while he was teaching. His comments ranged from answering questions posed to the class, to asking questions out of turn, or even "adding on" to Mr. Cooper's instruction by telling what he knew about the subject. These behaviors not only interrupted instruction, but Mr. Cooper also noticed that the verbal barbs often hurt the feelings of others. Mr. Cooper did have some success as Bradley generally remained engaged in the lesson, but knew that he was not completely successful yet as Bradley still forgot to raise his hand most days before speaking, regardless of Mr. Cooper's location.

Mr. Cooper also noticed that Bradley was having a difficult time following other procedural norms. He frequently talked while the students were supposed to be lining up; however, he easily corrected his behavior when asked to do so. Bradley was also easily excited and sometimes had a difficult time beginning a task for independent seatwork. This often caused a delay in the start of instruction, reducing Mr. Cooper's already limited instructional time. Conversations with the two special areas teachers revealed similar behavior patterns. Consistent with becoming overly excited, the physical education teacher reported that Bradley was "almost out of control" in PE one day. The art teacher complained that he never stopped talking out, even when asked to stop.

Mr. Cooper has chosen to implement a behavioral intervention with Bradley, primarily due to the previously described behaviors. However, foremost in Mr. Cooper's mind is that Bradley is often able to correct himself when asked and appears to understand why it is important to make behavioral corrections. Bradley also shared with Mr. Cooper that he has a reputation for bad behavior. He specifically said that in prior years, students expressed their disappointment when he would return to school after an absence. He told Mr. Cooper that this made him feel bad. Bradley is very bright, and Mr. Cooper would like to see his impulsiveness channeled so that he can shed his bad reputation and gain a reputation as a student leader with high academic potential.

Reflect on the following questions:

1. What are some of the behaviors being exhibited by Bradley?
2. Are any of these behaviors disrupting other students?
3. What actions has Mr. Cooper taken to help Bradley? Were any successful?
4. What are some potential reasons Bradley may be exhibiting the behaviors he is?
5. Think about what Mr. Cooper could include within his behavioral intervention plan. Use the document in Figure 2 to begin a plan to help Bradley be more successful.

After you have answered the reflection questions and decided how what should be completed to help Bradley be more successful in the classroom, move on to Case #2 - Martha.

Case #2 - Martha

Martha is a student in Carol Elliot's 2nd grade classroom. It is the third week of the school year and Ms. Elliot has already begun to note that while she is providing directions, Martha has a difficult time staying on task and easily becomes distracted. When distracted, Martha will often seek out other students in the classroom and then mimic the behavior she observes from the other student, seemingly unaware that Mrs. Elliot is talking or that the other children are trying to listen. In an effort to maintain the attention of the rest of the class, Ms. Elliot initially used proximity to redirect Martha, sometimes gently touching her on the shoulder. In most cases, this would "bring Martha back" and she would return to her seat. However, it did not resolve the underlying issue. In fact, on several occasions, as soon as Ms. Elliot moved away from Martha, she was off task again, watching or moving toward another student. In these situations, Ms. Elliot used a verbal cue, calling Martha's name to gain her attention, with some success, but only for a short period of time.

Ms. Elliot is in her third year and considers herself knowledgeable about effective management strategies, but, the truth is, even though she has tried a number of strategies, most end similarly. After reading some additional literature on classroom management, she attempted to engage Martha in choice-making. When Martha was off-task while the rest of the class was completing independent work, Ms. Elliot would offer statements like the following: "You can choose to start your recess now by playing during seatwork and sit out for part of recess, or you can choose to begin your work now and still have the full amount of time to play at recess." This worked the first few times it was used, but, recently, when choices were provided, Martha complied for only a short amount of time. When Martha did not comply, Ms. Elliot responded, "I see that you are choosing to begin your recess, you will sit out for 5 minutes and reflect on your behavior." In each case, this resulted in an immediate tantrum, with Martha throwing herself on the floor and crying uncontrollably, to the point where she would find it visibly difficult to breath.

Adding to Ms. Elliot's challenges is that Martha constantly calls out during the day. Ms. Elliot can usually ignore the behavior or use proximity-control, but sometimes these strategies are also ineffective. When that is the case, Ms. Elliot usually describes the appropriate behavior exhibited by other students aloud. However, in sum, these strategies have not decreased the number of times Martha calls out during the day. In fact, the episodes of calling out have reached the point where they happen often throughout the day, at least four to six times per instructional period.

Ms. Elliot is unsure what to do at this point. The class becomes entirely distracted when the Martha throws a tantrum and it is hard to get them back on track, especially as Mrs. Elliot makes an effort to console Martha. There have been regular conversations with the Martha's mother about her behavior and she has been very supportive of Ms. Elliot; however, little has changed/progressed.

Reflect on the following questions before proceeding:

1. What are some of the behaviors being exhibited by Martha?
2. What is happening in the classroom when these behaviors are observed? Is there a consistent pattern for the misbehaviors?
3. What actions has Ms. Elliot taken to resolve the problems? Were any successful?
4. What are some potential reasons Martha may be exhibiting the behaviors she is?
5. How would you handle this situation?

Now that you've had the opportunity to examine both cases, we feel it's important to inform you that we have purposely chosen to not provide "solutions" to the preceding cases. Our rationale for doing so is that solutions can vary greatly when individualized behavior plans are created. They are often unique to the individual student as well as the teacher and/or intervention team involved in the development. Our goal in creating the cases was to help you begin to think more holistically about causes of misbehavior, seeking to consider the "why" behind it, and use the data obtained through the use of the templates to facilitate reflection. In addition, we also wanted to create an opportunity for collaboration within discussions about various methods that could be utilized to help Bradley and Martha experience greater success in their behavior.

SUMMARY

In this chapter you were introduced to the individual behavior plans. These plans are primarily for individuals who continue to experience behavioral challenges that have disrupted their learning and that of the other students in the classroom. To ensure the development of the plan is effective, the concept of the functional behavior assessment was presented as a means to collect data. The intent of the assessment was to note the antecedent for the behavior as well as the consequences. This facilitated the identification of the probable function of the behavior for the student. In turn, the teacher, student, and other relevant stakeholders collaboratively develop an individual behavior plan that is designed to limit the demonstration of the inappropriate behaviors, while focusing on alternative behaviors that are acceptable within the classroom, help the student become successful.

MOVING ON: Reflection Assignments

1. Use the Functional Behavior Assessment form provide on p. 163 in Appendix A to complete several observations of a student in a classroom. Develop a list of potential causes for the behavior, choosing one to address within an individual behavior plan.
2. Examine the Functional Behavior Assessments found at the following links below and compare them to the one found in Figure 1. Create a chart noting similarities and differences between the tools and discuss the strengths and weaknesses of each with a peer
   a. http://www.pbis.org/common/pbisresources/tools/EfficientFBA_FACTS.pdf
   b. http://www.pbisnetwork.org/wp-content/uploads/2010/10/NWPBS-Conference-Handouts1.pdf
   c. http://lcps.k12.nm.us/Departments/SPED/Addressingstudentbehavior.pdf (beginning on p. 24)
3. Use the steps noted in Figure 2 to develop a script that demonstrates the dialogue that may occur during the development an individual behavior plan. Collaborate with a colleague to act the dialogue

REFERENCES

Albert, L. (2003). *A teacher's guide to cooperative discipline: How to manage your classroom and promote self-esteem.* Circle Pines, MN: American Guidance Service Publishing.

Brown, D. F. (2003). Urban teachers' use of culturally responsive management strategies. *Theory Into Practice, 42,* 277-282.

Carr, E. (1994). Emerging themes in functional analysis of problem behavior. *Journal of Applied Analysis, 27,* 393-400.

Carr, E. G., & Durand, V. M. (1985). Reducing behavior problems through functional communication training. *Journal of Applied Behavior Analysis, 18,* 111–126.

Delpit, L. (1995). *Other people's children.* New York: New Press.

Fournies, F. (2000). *Coaching for improved work performance.* New York: McGraw Hill.

Gathercoal, F. (2001). *Judicious discipline* (6th Edition). San Francisco, CA: Caddo Gap Press.

Gresham, F. M., Watson, T. S., & Skinner, C. (2001). Functional behavioral assessment: Principles, procedures, and future directions. *School Psychology Review, 30,* 156-172.

Groden, G. (1989). A guide for conducting a comprehensive behavioral analysis of a target behavior. *Journal of Behavior Therapy and Experimental Psychiatry, 20,* 163–169.

Hanley, G .P., Iwata, B. A., & McCord, B. E. (2003). Functional analysis of problem behavior: A review. *Journal of Applied Behavior Analysis, 36,* 147-185.

Jones, V., & Jones, L. (2009). *Comprehensive Classroom Management: Creating Communities of Support and Solving Problems* (9th Edition). Englewood Cliffs, NJ: Prentice Hall.

Ladson-Billings, G. (1995). Toward a theory of culturally relevant pedagogy. *American Educational Research Journal, 32*(3), 465-491.

McIntosh, K., Campbell, A. L., Carter, D. R., & Dickey, C. R. (2009). Differential effects of a tier two behavior intervention based on function of behavior problem. Journal of Positive Behavior Intervention, 11, 82-93. doi: 10.1177/1098300708319127

Milner, H. R. (2006). Classroom management in urban classrooms. In C. M. Evertson & C. S. Weinstein (Eds.), *The handbook of classroom management: Research, practice & contemporary issues* (pp. 491-522). Mahwah, NJ: Lawrence Erlbaum.

Skiba, R. J., Michael, R. S., Nardo, A. C., & Peterson, R. L. (2002). The color of discipline: Sources of racial and gender disproportionality in school punishment. *Urban Review, 34,* 317-342.

Skinner, B. F. (1953). *Science and human behavior.* New York: Macmillan.

Thompson, G. L. (2004). *Through ebony eyes: What teachers need to know but are afraid to ask about African American students.* San Francisco: Jossey-Bass.

Ware, F. (2006). Warm demander pedagogy: Culturally responsive teaching that supports a culture of achievement for African American students. *Urban Education, 41,* 427-456.

Weinstein, C., Curran, M., & Tomlinson-Clarke, S. (2003). Culturally responsive classroom management: Awareness into action. *Theory Into Practice, 42,* 269-276.

Witt, J. C., Daly, E., & Noell, G. H. (2000). *Functional assessments: A step-by-step guide to solving academic and behavior problems.* Longmont, CO: Sopris West.

Wolf, M. (1978). Social validity: The case for subjective measurement of how applied behavior analysis is finding its heart. *Journal of Applied Behavior Analysis, 11,* 203-214.

CHAPTER VIII

Problem Solving in the Learning Environment

Children learn how to make good decisions by making decisions, not by following directions.

Alfie Kohn (2006) *The Homework Myth*

This chapter will serve as an introduction to problem-solving and the related strategies and techniques for its implementation within your classroom or school. As you read this chapter, think about the value of these skills for students. Their application has immediate benefit in the school setting and extended benefits for life, including learning skills that will help with conflict in the workplace and in relationships. As follow-up to problem-solving at the individual and classroom level, we will also briefly present how problem-solving can be expanded to enhance school-wide behavioral outcomes.

Guiding Questions

As you read and explore the concepts introduced within this chapter, use the following questions to guide your thinking:

- What are problem-solving approaches?
- How can students be taught to self-monitor their behavior and resolve conflicts through positive interactions?
- How can I incorporate problem-solving into my classroom management plan?
- How can problem-solving strategies be developed and implemented school-wide to enhance positive learning environments?

Reflect and Act:

How do you solve problems in your own life? Do you engage in a fairly regular set of steps that allow you to not only consider various alternatives for action, but to also actively reflect upon your choices? Do you choose a course of action and analyze the impact of the choice later?

BACKGROUND

I think we would all agree that there will be times in school that children demonstrate less than desirable behavior. If we are to enable them to diminish these behaviors, we must implement methods that cause them to examine and reflect on how the behaviors affect them personally, but also the impact of their behavior on others. In extension, sometimes the behaviors of individual students will also lead to conflict between students. In these cases, regardless of where the conflict occurs, these disagreements may be brought into the classroom and interrupt the learning for all students. While the outward exhibition of the conflict may vary from verbal to physical, ultimately it is critical that whatever caused the conflict be resolved, preferably to the satisfaction of both parties, to ensure learning can occur. Our goal as a teacher in either of these types of situations is to potentially diminish their impact and prevalence. In essence, we should seek to establish and environment where students experience positive relationships with each other, enhancing their overall feelings of safety and connectedness in the classroom (McCluskey, et al., 2008).

To ensure our students' behavioral requirements are addressed in a climate that allows them to experience the aforementioned feelings, we advise considering the implementation of a problem-solving approach. Many such approaches exist and several notable classroom management theorists, including William Glasser, Jim Fay and David Funk, and Richard Curwin and Allen Mendler, have proposed approaches to problem-solving with students. Research has proven various types of problem-solving approaches to be effective for diminishing up to 90% of classroom management related events (Meyer & Evans, 2012). The specific steps within each model may differ within the process of implementation, but, overall, there is a focus on actively involving the student or students in developing a plan to change an undesirable behavior. We will spend most of the chapter examining and describing the general approach to problem-solving and what this might look like in practice.

THEORY TO PRACTICE

> **Reflect and Act:**
> Think about a time that you have observed two or more children come into conflict with one another. What caused the conflict? How was it resolved? Were the children able to resolve the problem without adult assistance or was the adult the primary factor in alleviating the conflict?

What is a problem-solving model?

In the purest sense, a problem-solving approach is a procedure. It generally features a set of discrete steps that are completed in order to help students engage in self-reflection and analysis regarding a specific problem that occurred. Several commonalities exist amongst problem-solving approaches, including:

- problem recognition;
- solution generation;
- examination of consequences;
- decision making; and
- reviewing the outcome (see Greenwood, Walker, Carta, & Higgins, 2006; Joseph & Strain, 2010; Palmer & Wehmeyer, 2003)

Regardless of the actual method chosen by a teacher, the first step may be the most critical in the process as the student is asked to consider the context and recognize the behavior that initiated the sequence. Without recognition that an unacceptable behavior has occurred, progress within all subsequent steps may be diminished. Upon recognition of and reflection about the unacceptable behavior, the student then produces a list of potential solutions that would diminish or alleviate the behavior in question. This is followed by active consideration of the solutions as well as the consequences associated with each. It is

requires self-awareness & empathy 112

important for this reflective process to also encompass the consequences on others for each of the proposed solutions. The student then selects one of the solutions based on his examination. Finally, the results of the implementation of the solution are examined in light of the identified consequences to note if the desired results were achieved.

Problem-solving has been proposed as a mechanism to help students develop a more positive, outlook towards various capabilities that would be considered life skills (Stark, et al., 2005). Benefits to using problem-solving approaches in the classroom include helping students build the capacity to:

- consider consequences that will result from actions;
- reflect on and generate alternate solutions to problems or conflicts;
- respect and acknowledge the perspectives of others; and
- develop means-end thinking (Zirpoli, 2005)

thinking beyond themselves

Students who are competent problem-solvers have been shown to display fewer incidents of aggressive behavior and be less likely to demonstrate an inability to empathize with others in comparison to poor problem-solvers (Shure, Spivack, & Jaeger, 1971). The persistent challenge, however, is one that seems to challenge teachers in multiple facets of their chosen career - finding time to teach and implement the procedures within the multitude of demands on instructional time.

While problem-solving approach is often focused on individual behavior, other forms exist that can be used to solve conflicts between students. These approaches are sometimes referred to as conflict resolution or peer mediation. Each of these programs offers a variation on the traditional approach to problem-solving, encompassing a slightly different focus within the development of a positive outcome. For example, within conflict resolution approaches, the intent is to eliminate problem behaviors that occur between two or more individuals with a significant emphasis placed on effective communication skills and the ability to see others' perspectives. Participation in a conflict resolution program has been shown to improve the atmosphere within a school, reduce violence, develop deeper self-reflective capacity in students, and improve decision-making ability (Crawford & Bodine, 1996). Peer mediation, on the other hand, involves settling conflict among students through the use of a neutral third party (student) within the development of a solution. It is focused on the development of skills that will allow students to navigate their own disagreements, including understanding conflict, communication, listening, and confidentiality. Figure 1 contains a list of questions that are associated with the approach. It is important to note that within peer mediation and conflict resolution, the role of the teacher is significantly diminished, allowing students to develop a sense of independence and power.

Figure 1. *Peer Mediation Questions*

1. Can you tell us what's happening here?
2. How does this make you feel?
3. What upsets you most about this situation?
4. What would you like to see happen?
5. What ideas do you have to help with this?
6. Is there anything you could do to make this situation better?
7. What would you like _____ to understand about this situation?
8. Do you feel this conflict is resolved?

Implementation of a Problem-Solving Approach

Since the problem-solving approaches are analogous to a procedure, implementation should follow the process that would be engaged in when teaching students any procedure. To ensure students know and understand the procedure, the steps must be taught, discussed, modeled, and practiced before full-scale implementation. Jones and Jones (2012) advocate the following steps in this process:

1. Show the students the steps using some visual or written cue;
2. Discuss the steps in the procedure, providing examples to ensure understanding;
3. Use role-plays followed by discussions to reinforce the steps in the process;
4. Provide additional reinforcement through continued practice as well as opportunities to problem-solve scenarios that include behavioral infractions; and
5. Evaluate students' knowledge of the procedures by asking them questions related to the steps and the sequence.

A key component within this implementation, which also fosters student buy-in, is modeling and use of the procedures within "regular" classroom situations as opposed to solely within disciplinary events. In other words, problem-solving should be seen as an integral process within the classroom as opposed to something that only applies to students when particular situations arise.

To help students articulate their thoughts and ideas, problem-solving approaches can be enhanced through the completion of a form, similar to what is shown in Figure 2. As students gain familiarity and comfort as result of multiple opportunities to use the steps, it is common for teachers to have an area of the classroom where students can go to complete the problem-solving form or to hold a problem-solving, i.e. peer mediation, conference. This allows the students to solve the problem away from their peers, limiting distractions, and away from the teacher's help, assisting in the development of independent skills. The teacher can be informed of the resolution and subsequent plan to review the outcome. Having this type of structure in place is a critical component in the success of peer mediation and conflict resolution approaches. In addition to a designated location in the classroom, it is advisable to have parameters regarding when conferences may be conducted as well as modified problem solving forms that focus on the use of plural pronouns (we, us) in the description of mutually acceptable solutions.

Some teachers advocate the use of classroom meetings within problem-solving approaches. These meetings are viewed as opportunities for group discussion and additional practice of the essential skills for problem-solving, including communication, the acknowledgment of diverse perspectives, and listening skills. To effectively develop the capacity to hold meetings, they should be introduced and presented to the children as a method to express concerns and to provide a forum that will allow them to help in the decision-making process. Nelsen, Lott, and Glenn (1997) suggest eight building blocks for effective classroom meetings. These blocks include recommendations such as the creation and use of an agenda that is based on entries into a notebook of concerns, activities to develop communication skills, and a focus on non-punitive solutions to problems. The meetings should be held on a regular basis and, as with the problem-solving approach in general, should be an integral part of the classroom. As teachers first implement the meetings, they may take a more active, facilitating role in the meeting. However, as understanding of the process as well as proficiency increase, it is recommended that student leaders are given the task of leading the meetings.

Figure 2. *Generic Problem-Solving Worksheet - Individual*

Problem Solving Sheet

Name: _____ **Date:** _____

What was the problem? (Tell how it happened, who was involved, where and when it happened)

_____

_____

_____

What caused the problem?

_____

_____

What could I have done to prevent the problem?

_____

_____

How could I have solved the problem differently? List 2 possible solutions.

1. _____

_____

2. _____

_____

What can I do to keep this from happening in the future?

_____

_____

_____

Student's Signature: _____

Teacher's Signature: _____

School-wide Problem-Solving Strategies

In the current educational context, school-wide approaches that feature problem-solving as component may fall within the broader umbrella of PBIS –Positive Behavior Intervention Support. PBIS is a comprehensive approach to school-wide management that emphasizes direct instruction in and reinforcement of positive behaviors, decision-making based on data, and targeted intervention and support for individuals not responsive to preventive measures (Lewis & Sugai, 1999; Sugai & Horner, 2002). Not all PBIS programs include components of problem-solving nor does the problem-solving approach have to be included within a PBIS system, but when used as a method to reinforce expectations and clearly document and teach responsible behavior, problem-solving represents an important component of PBIS to effectively prevent misbehavior. Examinations of peer mediation, for example, have found schools that have effective programs report a more positive school environment, improvements in the number of disputes that reach a peaceful resolution, and reductions in the number of instances of behavioral disruptions (Jones, 2004; Lane-Garon, Ibarra-Merlo,Zajac, & Vierra, 2005).

Before a school-wide problem solving program can be implemented, several factors need to be present. Notably, there must be a commitment to behavioral interventions that involve the children in decision-making, where the adult functions as a mediator as opposed to the authority figure. This process is not always quick and easy, thus patience and time are often required as is the presence of a committed faculty member who has or is willing to gain expertise in teaching conflict resolution skills to students. Similarly, noting that this is a gradual process, schools must realize that change may take time, especially as all components are taught, practiced, and reinforced. A full description of the programs that feature components and curriculum associated with problem-solving are beyond the scope of the chapter. However, we would recommend examining The Peace Education website (http://www.peace-ed.org/) or Morningside Center for Teaching Social Responsibility website (http://www.morningsidecenter.org/) for curriculum materials and suggestions for implementation.

+ –continuity btw. grades and enrichments

> **Reflect and Act:** –elevates and expands school culture & commun
> **What do you see as the benefits to a school-wide program as opposed to one that is implemented at the classroom-level? Where might the challenges present themselves within a school-wide implementation?**

— – program doesn't serve the student population/
teacher sees need to utilize an alt. progra
in response to his students

APPLICATION WITH DIVERSE LEARNERS

While problem-solving approaches, such as peer mediation and conflict resolution, are not specifically aligned with methods for working with diverse learners, the skills and outcomes associated with the programs represent a viable process to address several goals associated with culturally responsive pedagogy and multicultural education. In regard to the former, Geneva Gay (2010) described culturally responsive pedagogy as being built upon the idea that it is important to facilitate "close interactions among ethnic identity [and] cultural background" (p. 27) and that using students' "personal and cultural strengths, their intellectual capabilities, and their prior accomplishments" (p. 26) will positively impact their success. In using a problem-solving approach, several tenets of culturally responsive pedagogy are inherently included as students learn to acknowledge, appreciate, and interact with one another in a variety of situations. Students are provided opportunities to actively participate in their own learning

(Nieto & Bode, 2012), engage in cooperative tasks (Padron, Waxman, & Rivera, 2002), and develop higher-order thinking skills as they engage both cognitively and metacognitively within the process (Villegas, 1991). Problem-solving approaches also recognize that students bring multiple perspectives, referred to as funds of knowledge (Gonzalez, Moll, & Amanti, 2005), that need to be acknowledged and incorporated into the classroom context. Thus, problem-solving approaches allow the teacher to "maintain a caring, structured, cooperative classroom environment that addresses students' lived experiences and cultural backgrounds" (Adkins-Coleman, 2010, p. 41).

Similarly, problem solving approaches can also serve the goals of multicultural education. As articulated by Howard (1999), multicultural education helps us "learn about and value cultures other than our own [and] to view social reality through the lens of multiple perspectives" (p. 81). As students engage in peer mediation and problem solving, all children will have opportunities to engage in leadership roles and to be full participants in the classroom climate (Banks, 2006; Bennett, 1999). Students also have the opportunity to develop empathy for others, which has been acknowledged as principle and benefit of multicultural education (see Zacher, 2005). In general, both approaches facilitate the capacity to build a community among the learners in the classroom. As educators seek to teach students methods to facilitate the development of cross cultural sensitivity and tolerance among students, problem-solving approaches will help children negotiate the realities of a diverse nation.

CASE STUDY – Problems on the Playground

As Mr. Clark entered his classroom after lunch, several students came up to him to report a problem that had occurred on the playground. Based on the reports that he received, it appeared that two boys, Brady and Andre, had a disagreement while waiting to use the slide on the playground. While his first instinct was to discuss the situation with one of his colleagues, Ms. Martin, who was monitoring recess, he knew that she had a meeting with a parent right after lunch and he did not want to interrupt it. Frustrated by the circumstances as well as by the increasing regularity of incidents between the two boys at recess and elsewhere, Mr. Clark called Andre up to his desk to discuss what happened.

"Andre, can you tell me what happened on the playground today?" asked Mr. Clark.

Andre responded, "There was a long line to go down the slide, so I went to the end of the line to wait my turn, like I am supposed to. Brady came up right after I did and said that he beat me so he should be in front of me. But I didn't let him 'cause I was there first. When it was my turn to go on the steps, Brady bumped me out of the way and cut me. So I grabbed the back of his shirt and pulled him back and got my place in line back. He started yelling at me, but I didn't let him get in front of me. That's when Ms. Martin came over and told us we both had to go to the end of the line. I went to the end of the line, but I think Brady was mad, so he walked away."

"Andre, we've had this conversation several times," Mr. Clark countered. "While I know you were angry, are you supposed to put your hands on someone at any time?"

"No," answered Andre.

"Since this is not the first time this has happened and it seems to be happening more often with Brady lately, tomorrow for recess, you have lost your play privileges and must walk laps instead. If this happens again, the next step will be to hold a phone conference with your mom. Do you understand?"

Andre answered sullenly answered, "Yes." He then walked back to his seat, pointedly looking at Brady as he sat down.

Mr. Clark then called Brady to his desk, asking him, "Brady, can you explain to me what happened at recess today?"

Brady responded, "Andre and I were racing to see who could get to the slide first. I beat him, but he said that he got there first, so he got in front of me. I kept telling him that I was first, but he was ignoring me. Then, when he was supposed to go up the ladder, he got out of line, so I went in front of him. He pulled my shirt and pulled me off the ladder so he could cut in front of me like he did before. So I yelled at him and Ms. Martin heard me. She told both of us go to the back of the line. I didn't want to slide after that, so I went and played tag."

"Brady, when we discussed our recess expectations, what did they say about how we interact with others?" Mr. Clark asked. Without giving Brady time to answer, Mr. Clark answered his own question, "They say that we should respect each other and cooperate. Unfortunately, in this case, yelling at Andre does not demonstrate respectful behavior nor does it show cooperation. While I understand that you had a disagreement with Andre about who should be first, you did not follow the expectations. At recess tomorrow, you are to spend the time walking laps instead of playing."

Obviously, Mr. Carter knew that both boys were presenting their own "unique" version of the story. However, this just also happened to be the fourth time in the last two weeks that something had happened between the two boys while they were at recess and, in each case, the boys' stories did not match. In addition, one of the boys demonstrated some type of physical action, e.g. shoving or pushing/pulling, every time a problem occurred. The first time, Mr. Carter had let the boys off with a warning. In each subsequent case, Mr. Carter had pulled the boys aside, allowed them to explain their side of the story, clarified the classroom expectations in relation to the actions, and administered consequences. It was becoming clear, though, that this was not working and he needed an alternative solution to the problem.

Reflect on the following questions before moving on to the descriptions:

1. What is the problem in this scenario?
2. What actions were taken by Mr. Carter? Do these match previous attempts to solve the problem?
3. How have the boys been involved in resolving the problem?
4. Would you recommend individual problem-solving or some type of conflict resolution or peer mediation approach? Why?
5. How would you handle this situation?

After you have answered the discussion questions and decided how you would handle the situation, read all three of the choices that follow. Select one that most closely matches your ideas. Or if you read one that you like better than your own ideas, choose it as your own. Then follow the directions for the activities that follow the explanations of the options.

Case Study: Response Choices

Choice A

I would handle the situation very similar to how Mr. Carter did. In each case, he listened to both sides of the story and administered consequences, which are important in this situation. As this behavior has been going on for some time, it's important that Mr. Carter clearly and decisively put an end to it. In addition, physical contact should never be tolerated. Consequences are the most effective and efficient manner to take care of the situation. However, I think that Mr. Carter has not followed through enough in administering consequences of increasing severity. It would appear that taking away recess time is not sufficient and I think if the boys had faced consequences that were more severe, they may have stopped already. Unlike Mr. Carter, I would have contacted the students' parents at the second or third instance of the misbehavior since it involved physical contact.

If you chose this option, examine Choice A, which follows at the end of the page, and read the how this relates to the ideas of classroom management theorists.

Choice B

If I were in this situation, rather than telling the students what they did wrong, I would have them complete a problem-solving worksheet individually, conference with each one individually about their answers to the form, and then bring the boys together to discuss the situation. Together we would examine their individual solutions and co-create a new problem-solving form focused on cooperative outcomes. I would also consider the contexts where the conflicts between the two boys most often occurred. Since it appears to be a problem that occurs primarily at recess, I might hold a classroom meeting and lead a discussion about what could be done at recess to eliminate conflicts such as these. As a result of the meeting, with the input of the class, I would implement various procedures to provide appropriate outlets when conflict occurred.

If you chose this option, then turn to page 122 and read the underlying ideas of this response from recognized classroom management theorists.

Choice C

If I were Mr. Carter in this situation, I would set up a hold a conflict resolution or peer mediation conference for the two boys. For the former, I would have the two boys work together to fill out a problem-solving form that was developed for the purpose of conflicts between two or more people. This would be completed during their recess time. They would then present the solution and plan to me. If I chose the peer mediation approach, I would suggest a student who has been successful in mediating disputes in the past. It's important that both Andre and Brady feel that the person is neutral and that they can actively express their views of the situation without being judged. Upon the development of a resolution, I would actively look for demonstrations of the behaviors identified as part of the process and acknowledge these behaviors.

If you chose this option, then turn to page 122 and read the underlying ideas of this response from recognized classroom management theorists.

Case Study: Using TIC-TAC-TOE

Choice A

If your response was aligned with the description in Choice A, your choice is most associated with some of the principles associated with the TIC category. Mr. Carter generally reacted based on elements that would be found in Lee and Marlene Canter's (2002) *Assertive Discipline* and Fred Jones' (1987) *Positive Classroom Discipline* and you feel that these practices are effective. The problem, in your eyes, is that Mr. Carter may not have gone far enough in the administration of consequences of increasing severity, which may have limited his success. Thus, in your eyes, the behaviors would be altered or stopped if parent contact had been made earlier.

While theorists in the TIC category are not traditionally associated with problem-solving techniques as they empower the student, since this is the focus of the chapter, it may be necessary to consider how these may be applied in conjunction with characteristics of TIC. Jones and Jones (2012) note that authoritative approaches to management diminish in their effectiveness as the age of the students increases, thus the ability to incorporate elements that fall outside of the traditional TIC approaches may improve overall management skills through the ability to flexibility respond to each situation. There may be some slight modifications that can be made within the approach to incorporate various elements and still allow you to manage your classroom within the ideas that are most closely aligned with your management style. One of the things that we found notable is that in *Positive Discipline*, Fred Jones (1987) has observed that it is important to teach students to be cooperative and responsible. These skills may be enhanced through the incorporation of questions that ask the student to consider her immediate behavior as well as alternatives, such as would be found in a situation that involves problem-solving, i.e. a problem-solving form. That's not to say that you cannot administer consequences, but by using self-reflection, students may be more likely to consider the implications of their behaviors as well as the potential consequences. In turn, the child may be more likely to solve her own problems.

Choice B

The response emulated by Choice B would fall into the category of the teacher and child (TAC) working together to formulate a solution. Many of the tenets addressed in TAC theories are aligned with the procedures implemented as part of a problem-solving approach, thus this will likely be an important part of your classroom. For example, in an interview with Brandt (1988), William Glasser noted that most children feel they have no power in the classroom environment. Problem-solving approaches, as advocated by Glasser (1988), provide children with a voice and the teacher with an opportunity to listen as well as become attuned to students' needs. When we consider students working with each other and the teacher closely in the development of solutions, we also see elements of Albert's (2003) 3 C's (connected, capable, and contributing) within the classroom.

As you further consider using this approach in your classroom, it's important to think about how the students can be provided the most flexibility to develop their own solutions. In doing so, it will enable them to gain the greatest benefits from the approach. In the choice you selected, each student filled out an individual problem-solving form and then the teacher and students co-created the solution. In potentially considering a more child-centered approach, you may examine additional forms of peer mediation or conflict resolution that will allow students' gain independence, diminishing the role that you have to play in the process. In addition, the notion of classroom meeting is advocated by several theorists in both the TAC and TOE categories. In this case, it is clear that the meeting is led by the teacher, which is aligned with the TAC approach. Consideration may be given to eventually turning over the meeting to students and allowing them to have the primary voice in leading the discussion and solutions that were developed.

Choice C

Choice C would be considered to be effectively aligned with TOE principles. Problem-solving approaches such as peer mediation and conflict resolution are well aligned with the ideas of teacher who identifies with the tenets of TOE. Teachers who espouse this approach look for methods to allow students to empower themselves and generating solutions to problems or engaging with peers in mediation or within conflict resolution fulfills that role. In essence the goal is for the teacher to create students who can think independently and interact effectively with each other within contexts that necessitate complex solutions. In facilitating the capacity to develop these skills, Ginott referred to teachers' ability to communicate in ways that helped validate the students' feelings about situations and themselves, which he called congruent communication (Ginott, 1972). Enabling students to express themselves to the teacher will likely facilitate the process within situations requiring mediation or conflict resolution, allowing students to be more active and confident in the development of the potential solutions. This also helps create what Ginott associated with an effective classroom climate.

While it is not included as part of Choice C, as the classroom teacher and someone who identifies with the TOE philosophy, you may consider holding a classroom meeting in regard to the situation. Alfie Kohn (1996) describes meetings as an effective method to help teach children about community and functioning in a democratic society. In this case, the students could discuss the overall impact of the behaviors on their classroom and during recess and generate a number of solutions that may alleviate the problem within the context of the meeting. They could then decide which of the alternatives may represent the most viable solution and plan to implement it. Again, the ultimate goal is to empower the students to solve problems, enabling them to develop the capacity to think independently and develop decision-making skills that will benefit them later in life.

SUMMARY

In this chapter you have been introduced to various tenets associated with problem-solving in the classroom. It's important to remember that problem-solving is not something that happens on its own – children must be taught how to solve problems and provided with multiple opportunities to practice the steps that lead toward proficiency. You have also read about peer mediation and conflict resolution, which represent problem-solving approaches that involve two or more parties trying to accomplish a resolution to a situation together. These approaches fulfill important roles in teaching students independence as well as communication and listening skills. We also noted that problem-solving approaches will enable you to effectively teach diverse students. Multiple ideas associated with problem-solving approaches are inherently aligned with the principles of culturally responsive pedagogy as well as multicultural education, which will help create an environment that is accepting, open, and values all participants.

MOVING ON: Reflection Assignments

1. Think about the steps in the problem-solving process and, using the form on p. 167, develop a scenario that could be used to introduce these steps. Write the dialogue that might occur as part of the problem-solving conference between a teacher and a student.

2. Further investigate Nelsen, Lott, and Glenn's (1997) building blocks of class meetings. Develop a plan to introduce the idea of holding classroom meeting and describe the process of conducting the first meeting. You may consider developing an agenda for this meeting to assist your planning.

3. Find a local school that uses problem-solving, peer mediation, or conflict resolution procedures. Interview a teacher or administrator in the school to determine how the process is introduced to students and maintained throughout the academic year. Consider asking them their views regarding the components necessary for a successful program.

REFERENCES

Adkins-Coleman, T. A. (2010). "I'm Not Afraid to Come into Your World": Case studies of teachers facilitating engagement in urban high school English classrooms. *The Journal of Negro Education, 79*, 41-53.

Albert, L. (2003). *A teacher's guide to cooperative discipline: How to manage your classroom and promote self-esteem.* Circle Pines, MN: American Guidance Service Publishing.

Banks, J. (2006). *Cultural diversity and education: Foundations, curriculum, and teaching* (5th ed.). Boston: Pearson.

Bennett, C. I. (1999). *Comprehensive multicultural education: Theory and practice* (4th ed.). Boston: Allyn and Bacon.

Brandt, R. (1988). On students' needs and team learning: A conversation with William Glasser. *Educational Leadership, 45*, 38-45.

Canter, L.,, & Canter, M. (2002). *Assertive discipline: Positive behavior management for today's schools* (3rd ed.). Bloomington, IN: Solution Tree.

Crawford, D., & Bodine, R. (1996). *Conflict resolution education: A guide to implementing programs in schools, youth-serving organizations, and community and juvenile justice settings.* Washington, D.C.: U. S. Department of Education.

Gay, G. (2010). Culturally responsive reaching: Theory, research, and practice. New York: Teachers College Press.

Glasser, W. (1988). *Choice theory in the classroom.* New York, NY: Harper Collins.

Ginott, H. (1972). *Teacher and child.* New York: Macmillan.

Gonzalez, N., Moll, L. C., & Amanti, C. (2005). *Funds of knowledge: Theorizing practices in households, communities, and classrooms.* Mahwah, NJ: Lawrence Erlbaum.

Greenwood, R. C., Walker, D., Carta J, J., & Higgins, S. K. (2006).Developing a general outcome measure of growth in the cognitive abilities of children 1 to 4 years old: The early problem-solving indicator. *School Psychology Review, 35*, 535-551.

Howard, G. R. (1999). *We can't teach what we don't know: White teachers, multiracial schools.* New York: Teachers College Press.

Jones, F. H. (1987). *Positive classroom discipline.* New York: McGraw-Hill.

Jones, T. S. Conflict resolution education: The field, the findings, and the future. *Conflict Resolution Quarterly, 22*, 233-267.

Jones, V., & Jones, L. (2012). *Comprehensive classroom management: Creating communities of support and solving problems.* New York, NY: Pearson.

Joseph, G. E., & Strain, P.S. (2010). Teaching young children interpersonal problem-solving skills. *Young Exceptional Children, 13*(3), 28-40.

Kohn, A. (1996). *Beyond discipline: From compliance to community.* Alexandria, VA: Association for Supervision and Curriculum Development.

Lane-Garon, P., Ibarra-Merlo, M., Zajac, J., & Vierra, T. (2005). Mediators and mentors : Partners in conflict resolution. *Journal of Peace Education, 2*, 183-193.

Lewis, T. J., & Sugai, G. Effective behavior support: A systems approach to proactive school-wide management. *Focus on Exceptional Children, 31*, 1-24.

McCluskey, G., Lloyd, G., Kane, J., Riddell, S., Stead, J., & Weeden, E. (2008). Can restorative practices in schools make a difference? *Educational Review, 60*, 405-417.

Meyer, L. H., & Evans, I. M. (2012). *The teacher's guide to restorative classroom discipline*. Thousand Oaks, CA: Corwin.

Nelsen, J., Lott, L., & Glenn, H. S. (1997). *Positive discipline in the classroom*. Rocklin, CA: Prima.

Nieto, S., & Bode, P. (2012). *Affirming diversity: The sociopolitical context of multicultural education* (6th ed.). New York, NY: Pearson.

Padron, Y. N., Waxman, H. C., & Rivera, H. H. (2002). *Educating Hispanic students: Effective instructional practices (Practitioner Brief #5)*. Retrieved from: http://www.cal.org/crede/pdfs/PracBrief5.pdf

Palmer, S. B., & Wehmeyer, M. L. (2003). Promoting self-determination in early elementary school teaching self-regulated problem-solving and goal-setting skills. *Remedial and Special Education, 24*, 115-126.

Shure, M. B., Spivack, G., & Jaeger, M. A. (1971). Problem solving thinking and adjustment among disadvantaged preschool children. *Child Development, 42*, 1791-1803.

Stark, K. D., Hoke, J., Ballatore, M., Valdez, C., Scammaca, N., & Griffin, J. (2005). Treatment of child and adolescent depressive disorders. In E. Hibbs, P. S. Jensen (Eds.), *Psychosocial treatments for child and adolescent disorders: Empirically based strategies for clinical practice* (pp. 239-265). Washington, D.C.: American Psychological Association.

Sugai, G., & Horner, R. H. The evolution of discipline practices : School-wide positive behavioral supports. *Child & Family Therapy, 24*, 23-50.

Villegas, A. M. (1991). *Culturally responsive pedagogy for the 1990's and beyond. Trends and Issues Paper No. 6*. Washington, DC: ERIC Clearinghouse on Teacher Education.

Zacher, J. C. (2005). Effects of a multicultural curriculum in a racially and socioeconomically diverse 5th-grade classroom. In D. McInerney & S. VanEtten (Eds.), *Research on sociocultural influences on motivation and learning: Focus on curriculum* (pp.77–100). Greenwich, CT: Information Age

Zirpoli, T. J. (2005). *Behavior management: Application for teachers* (4th ed.). Boston, MA: Allyn & Bacon.

CHAPTER IX

Bullying
_____

When another person makes you suffer, it is because he suffers deeply within himself, and his suffering

is spilling over. He does not need punishment; he needs help. That's the message he is sending.

Thich Nhat Hanh

In this chapter, we will describe the current educational context in which we find ourselves, where bullying has become a severe problem in many schools. Subsequently, we'll examine characteristics associated with the three primary participants in a bullying situation: the bully, the victim, and the bystander. We will present information on how to work with both bullies and victims to address bullying as well as how schools can develop and sustain programs designed to eliminate it. We conclude the chapter by presenting information on cyberbullying, a relatively new problem that has rapidly developed due to the ubiquitous access to technology and prevalent use of social networking by today's youth.

Guiding Questions

As you read and explore the concepts introduced within this chapter, use the following questions to guide your thinking:

- What are the characteristics associated with the three types of participants within bullying situations?
- What are the signs of children at risk for being bullies?
- How can you recognize when a child might be a victim of bullying?
- What can schools do to prevent or respond to bullying?
- What is cyberbullying?

Reflect and Act: *Socialization and gender norms feed into this.*
Think about the following statements: Bullying is just teasing. Bullying is just part of growing up. Bullies eventually grow out of the behavior. Bullying is more of a problem with males than females.
Which, if any, of the statements are true? What is the rationale you have for your responses?

BACKGROUND

Bullying has become a significant problem in schools in the United States. It has been reported that one in three children is affected by bullying and more than 5 million students have been categorized as a bully, victim, or both (Nansel, Overpeck, Pilla, Ruan, Simons-Morton, & Scheidt, 2001; Smokowski & Kopasz, 2005). In 2009, 28% of 12-18 year olds indicated they have been bullied at school, with the highest percentage occurring in 6th grade at about 39% (Robers, Zhang, Truman, & Snyder, 2012). While there are a variety of behaviors that would be associated with bullying, several of which will be described in a subsequent section, the largest percentage of children reported that they had experienced being "made fun of, called names, or insulted" (Robers, et al, 2012, p. 44). This percentage is more than double the second most pervasive form of bullying behavior, which included physical acts such as pushing or shoving.

Examining bullying at the school level, in 2009-2010, 23% of public schools indicated that bullying occurred daily or weekly (Robers et al, 2012). The problem is so widespread and pervasive that, according to information released in 2011, 21 states had passed legislation to expand school's responsibilities for identifying and eliminating instances of bullying in the school. This is likely due to the connections that have been made between bullying and school violence (Espelage & Swearer, 2003). While bullying itself can often be construed as a violent act, increasingly victims are turning to weapons as a mechanism to equalize power relationships and some feel justified in retaliation through violent means (Henry, 2009). Violent acts at school are now more prevalent that violent acts away from school according to data collected from 1992-2010 (Robers et al., 2012). Incidents such as the Columbine High School tragedy have amplified the necessity of developing mechanisms for educating stakeholders as well as protecting students.

What is bullying and where does it occur?

Before describing how schools and educators can effectively limit or eliminate bullying, it's necessary to establish some basic information regarding it. Bullying is defined as a "conscious, willful, and deliberate hostile activity intended to harm, induce fear through the threat of further aggression, and create terror" (Coloroso, 2002, p. 13). Bullying is multi-dimensional. By this, we mean that it can be exhibited in multiple ways. For example, Tammy can hit Julie, she can tease her verbally to make her feel bad about herself, or she can choose to exclude her from the group. Each of these behaviors would fall into a different category of bullying: verbal (using words), physical (involving a contact), or indirect/relational (completed without direct interaction). While physical and verbal bullying can be intuitively defined and described, relational bullying is more insidious and includes behaviors that are focused on hurting relationships between peers. It has been defined as "harming others through purposeful manipulation and damage of...peer relationships" (Crick & Grotpeter, 1995, p. 711.)

Regardless of its form, though, bullying is remarkably consistent as it is primarily about physical or psychological power over an individual perceived as less powerful (Hazler, Hoover, & Oliver, 1992; Smith & Sharp, 1994). The intent of the more "powerful" bully is to inflict some form of hurt on the victim, sometimes physical, at others, psychological. According to Coloroso (2002), 70% of bullying is verbal, which makes it challenging to detect this form of bullying because it lacks physical evidence. Instead, the damage is emotional (Coloroso, 2002). Bullying that involves physical contact, on the other hand, is the easiest to detect because there is often concrete evidence that can be observed. Interestingly, according to Coloroso (2002), this form of bullying accounts for less than one-third of all bullying.

126

Bullying can occur anywhere, but it is most prevalent in locations where adult supervision is limited, such as outside during recess or at the bus stop. Robers and colleagues (2012) found the highest percentage of students (48%) were bullied in the hallway, with female bullying being more prevalent than male in this location. Males were more likely to report being bullied in locations that were outside, but still on school property, such as the playground. However, it's important to note that bullying can occur anywhere there is a power imbalance, real or perceived, between people.

Who are the participants in situations that involve bullying?

In general, there are three roles that can be identified within the context of bullying: bully, victim, and bystander (Coloroso, 2002). The bully is the perpetrator of the aggressive actions associated with one of the three categories of bullying. The victim is the individual experiencing the intended actions. The bystander is a person who witnesses the actions associated with bullying.

The reasons students become bullies are complex. Explanations range from poor parenting to the influence of media, such as video games. What is clear is that bullies are students who enjoy power and want to feel a sense of control of others. As mentioned previously, the sense of power may be exhibited through physical acts of violence or relational aggression. Behaviors might include, but are not limited to, hitting, threatening, teasing, or rejecting others (Fried & Fried, 1996). Bullies can also be potentially recognized by overly aggressive behavior, an inability to control impulses or anger, and a lack of empathy towards others (Coolidge, DenBoer, & Segal, 2004). Physically, the bully may be older or bigger than other children, but that is not always the case and there are no physically defining characteristics of a bully. In some instances, the bullying behaviors result from being more popular or from having a high level of confidence. In these cases the sense of power is created or enhanced by the audience, which can support or participate in the bullying or fail to stop it, thus perpetuating the sense of power a bully seeks or has established. One thing that may be surprising is that in the early grades, it is very likely that the bully will be popular among students (Smokowski & Kopasz, 2005). However, as children get older, usually beginning in intermediate school or junior high, bullies tend to be less popular and sometimes are even disliked (Smokowski & Kopasz, 2005).

Research has revealed that there are gender differences in bullying. Field (2007) noted, "Boys often use bullying tactics to make a reputation and girls often do so to protect their reputation" (p. 21). Boys are more likely to engage in physical bullying (Olweus, 1993), while girls engage in verbal or indirect bullying (Ross, 2003). The latter involves actions such as alienation from a group, teasing about clothes or appearance, or circulating rumors about an individual (Crick & Grotpeter, 1995). The actions are designed to "significantly damage another child's friendships or feelings of inclusion by the peer group (Crick & Grotpeter, 1995, p. 711) as well as gain social status. For this reason, it is not uncommon for female bullies to be popular and have positive reputations and rapport with adults, which assists them in not being associated with bullying behaviors (Garbarino, 2006). While some researchers have noted that the behaviors associated with each gender are common amongst friendships, it's important to note that when these behaviors are continually and repeatedly manifested towards one individual, they would be described as bullying (Crain, Finch, & Foster, 2005).

As with bullies, victims of bullying do not share physically identifying characteristics – they come in all shapes and sizes. Coloroso (2002) notes that, in general, the only thing all victims share in common is being the target of a bully, However, children who lack assertiveness tend be targeted more often (Dill, Vernberg, Fonagy, Twemlow, & Gamm, 2004). These same students may be more quiet or cautious than their peers, making it increasingly likely that they do not have the support of friends (Smokowski &

Kopasz, 2005). Children who are alone, physically and emotionally, become likely targets of bullies because they lack the mechanisms that protect them from the "power" the bully exhibits over them. They are unable to stand up for themselves. Students who are experiencing bullying may be identified by behaviors such as loss of interests, anxiety, or a sudden drop in grades (Beane, 1999). They may also seem withdrawn and pull away from relationships with peers. Victims are also likely to exhibit behaviors and signs associated with depression, and, as a result, are at a greater risk of committing suicide (Holt, Finkelhor, & Kantor, 2007).

Finally, Coloroso (2002) identifies bystanders as the people who are present when an incidence of bullying occurs. Bystanders are important within the context of bullying because they represent the audience that the bully craves. While many bystanders are uncomfortable or even distressed by events associated with bullying, most simply watch the bullying and do nothing to stop it because they feel it is none of their business (Coloroso, 2002). In essence, when this happens, the bystanders contribute to the problem, not only because they provide the audience, but because their lack of action or intervention allows bullies to continue their hurtful behavior. In some instances, bystanders have actually joined the bully (Coloroso, 2002).

What is the impact of bullying?

Effects of bullying can appear at very young ages and extend through childhood. For example, Crick, Casas, and Ku (1999) found that victims of relational bullying that occurred in preschool experienced problems in developing relationships with peers as well as a lack of development of socialization skills. Furthermore, in middle school, relational bullying resulted in emotional distress and a lack of self-restraint (Crick & Bigbee, 1998). Academically, both bullies and victims are likely to suffer from poor achievement (Smokowsi & Kopasz, 2005). Students from both groups are also more likely to be depressed, experience crime, and be exposed to sexual abuse (Holt, et al., 2007).

The effects of bullying are long-lasting. In his groundbreaking work, Olweus (1978) found that students who are victims remain so for multiple years. Similarly, Smith and colleagues (2004) found that individuals who were victims of bullying as children were more likely to remain victims into their adult years. Being a bully has implications for later in life, too, as individuals who exhibited bullying behaviors in elementary school were still likely to be considered bullies in high school (Sourander, Helstela, Helenius, & Piha, 2000). They are likely to retain the aggressive behaviors that manifested themselves early in life and are likely to exhibit oppositional behaviors, commit crimes, and be physically abusive in relationships (Ashford, LeCroy, & Lortie, 2006; Holt et al., 2007).

Reflect and Act:

Think about a time that you were around a group of children. Did you witness instances of name calling, physical violence, or exclusion from the group? Was there a student who initiated the above actions or "held power" over others? How did the other children react to the dominant child and/or the actions of the child?

THEORY TO PRACTICE

How can we help the victims?

As a teacher, one of the most effective ways to help a victim is be alert to ensure bullying does not begin in the first place. However, while theoretically appealing, we realize that this cannot always be the case and bullying may take place, regardless of how vigilant teachers are. That written, teachers need to be aware of the behaviors of both bullies and victims. This means that it is vital to pay attention to the interactions that occur between students. Do you notice instances of name-calling or physical acts typically taking place with one child often the victim? You must also be aware of the signs that a student may be experiencing behaviors associated with bullying. A brief list was described previously, but this may also include sudden changes in attendance or appearance, a lack of interest in activities that were previously found to be enjoyable, or frequent, unexplained illnesses. When this occurs, it is important to follow up with the student and a parent/guardian as well as other teachers. You will need to identify if the cause of such behavioral changes are induced by bullying.

If you suspect bullying is occurring, it is important to talk to the victim. Often children will not tell adults about bullying (Beane, 1999), thus it's important to think about how you will discuss the situation with the student. Beane (1999) advocates initially approaching "the topic gently and indirectly" (p. 84). The child may not initially want to discuss it. If that is the case, it becomes important for the teacher to convey to the student that she is both willing to listen as well as provide assistance in the matter when/if the student becomes willing or able to talk further. Since you cannot "make" the victim discuss the situation, it's important to periodically follow up and offer opportunities to talk to you or other trusted peers or teachers. Within conversations with the student, it's also important to subtly (and even not so subtly) communicate to the victim that she is not at fault for the bullying, using positive, affirming statements.

If a student is a victim of bullying, teachers can implement a variety of practices to help them. For example, the teacher can help the student:

- develop safety mechanisms (stay calm, walk away);
- develop social skills to help the student make friends (power in numbers);
- develop self-confidence and self-esteem (improving assertiveness);
- develop skills of social value (to increase social standing); and
- become involved in school activities (Beane, 1999).

Beane (1999) also refers to teaching the use of "power skills" as students become more confident and assertive. These include using humor to diminish the gravity of the bullying conflict, using the broken record technique of repeating statements multiple times, or by simply agreeing with whatever the bully says before using one of the safety mechanisms. These should be used with caution, however, as they could potentially escalate a situation too. Teachers may also enlist the help of other educators and school personnel to mentor the victim, which will allow them to monitor the situation as well as the student's interactions with others.

What strategies can be used to address bullying?

Responding effectively to bullying must occur on several levels to be successful in eliminating the behavior. Teachers, students, parents, and administrators can all take actions to address bullying. Since the focus of this book is on developing teaching skills, we will focus on what teachers can do as well as what can be done at the school-level to address this problem and, subsequently, help bullies.

The teacher plays a significant role in not only preventing bullying through effective classroom management policies, but also working with students who may exhibit the potential for or who are bullies. First, the student must be identified. Teachers need to be aware of the characteristics associated with bullies as described above, but especially for students who might demonstrate any of the following traits:

- lack of empathy;
- craving attention (positive or negative);
- refusal to accept responsibility for actions; or
- willingness to utilize power over others to influence them.

This list is by no means exhaustive and these characteristics do not always indicate a student is a bully, but displaying a combination of them likely shows a predilection for bullying. Since identification is the key, it's important to examine additional resources such as Beane's (1999) *The Bully Free Classroom* or StopBullying.gov for more comprehensive lists of traits.

Once identification is made, a likely step in the process of helping the bully is to develop an intervention plan or behavior contract designed to address the specific behaviors exhibited by the student. The plan should clearly state the behaviors to be changed, the replacement behaviors, and any consequences or rewards that may be associated with the plan. The latter should be used with a note of caution, however, as consequences, especially severe ones, may have additional repercussions. It is important to consider this and potentially include the bully in the process of development whenever possible. Contracts and plans will help the bully be fully aware of the expectations, plus it will also allow the teacher to monitor behavior more effectively and provide documentation of the process.

It is recommended that as the student exhibits change, there is a gradual release of responsibility – in other words, the student takes a more active role in monitoring himself and reporting the information to you. The procedures of self-monitoring represent an important component within helping the bully. Not only can students be taught strategies such as anger management or impulse control, but they can also help the bully understand her own actions. Questions such as "Are you picked on by other people around you?" or "How does it make you feel when you say or do something to hurt someone else?" can help the student begin to recognize why she engages in the bullying behavior. Recognition can then lead towards responsibility and, eventually, change (Beane, 1999).

To eliminate bullying, schools must develop and implement a comprehensive plan that focuses on multiple elements at once. These elements include focusing on methods to teach positive behavior and interactions as well as those necessary to limit aggressive behavior. This process can be initiated through a formal assessment, such as an anonymous questionnaire given to students, teachers, and parents (see Beane, 1999, for various examples of surveys) to gain information on the current context and prevalence of bullying. Information can be used to develop a bullying prevention strategy based specifically on the needs associated with the school. This policy could include rules, procedures, and activities to promote awareness.

To be most effective, schools should determine how to involve all stakeholders within the implementation of the selected plan: teachers, administrators, non-teaching personnel, parents, and students. Staff should be trained in bullying prevention and intervention. They need to understand what it looks like, how to respond to it consistently, appropriately, and effectively, and how to work with other stakeholders to prevent future instances of bullying. Adult supervision should be increased in common locations where bullying occurs (Olweus, 1993). Finally, the school should be willing to dedicate portions of classes to educate students about bullying, including how to report it. Olweus (1993) found the frequency of bullying was reduced by half and that fewer new victims of bullying were identified when effective programs that featured many of the aforementioned characteristics were implemented. On the other hand, bullying prevention programs are less effective when peer norms, bystander behaviors, and environmental factors are not addressed (Swearer, Espelage, Vaillancourt, & Hymel, 2010).

Another approach to bully prevention at the school level has been the implementation of a conflict resolution curriculum that teaches communication skills as well as anger management techniques (Daunic, Smith, Robinson, Miller, & Landry, 2000). Research has demonstrated that students are more likely to demonstrate effective coping and problem-solving strategies as well as a greater sense of resilience when a conflict resolution program includes instruction and practice (Johnson & Johnson, 1996). Communication skills seem especially important as they not only help students handle anger and conflict in school, but also extended benefits to interactions with family members (Van Slyck, Newland, & Stern, 1992). We would recommend reviewing Chapter 7 for various problem-solving techniques, including conflict resolution, to determine ways that these strategies can be implemented to help with bullying.

> **Reflect and Act:**
> Conflict resolution programs and peer mediation were addressed in Chapter 7. Conflict resolution has been recommended as an effective method for school-wide approaches to handling bullying, yet peer mediation is not recommended. In your opinion, what is the reason for this?

Cyberbullying

Ubiquitous access to technology has led to a new form of bullying referred to as cyberbullying. It has been defined as "willful and repeated harm inflicted through the use of computers, cell phones, and other electronic devices" (Hinduja & Patchin, 2010, p. 1). Estimates regarding the pervasiveness of cyberbullying vary, yet it appears between 6% and 20% of middle and high school students have been the victim of instances of cyberbullying (Hinduja & Patchin, 2010; Robers, et al., 2012). According to research conducted by the National Crime Prevention Council (NCPC) (n.d.), 16% of females and 18% of males have engaged in some form of cyberbullying. Yet, females are more likely to be cyberbullied than males (Hinduja & Patchin, 2010).

As with what we might refer to as traditional bullying, cyberbullying behaviors vary, and can include actions such as posting hurtful information or videos online, especially on social networking websites, or harassment through a form of electronic communication such as a text or email message. Cyberbulling is largely relational, and the effects on the victim of such bullying generally match our previous description and include withdrawal, diminished self-esteem, depression, and academic problems (Hinduja & Patchin, 2010; NCPC, n.d.). There are several differences between traditional bullying and cyberbullying, however, that might make the latter more problematic. For example, cyberbullying facilitates anonymity for the bully. In traditional bullying, the victim is always able to identify the bully; yet, the cyberbully has the ability through various means to hide his/her identity. In essence, it's easier to bully someone when they can't or won't see you or you don't have to face them (Keith & Martin, 2005). Cyberbullying also vastly expands the audience and location for the bullying as the click of a button allows information to be shared worldwide, while the audience in traditional bullying is represented by the bystanders who are present when the bullying occurs. Students can now effectively be bullied in their own homes, regardless of the location of the bully or time of the message.

When cyberbullying occurs, the NCPC advocates reporting the activity to website administrators and trusted adults as opposed to repeating messages or engaging in cyberbullying in return. Documentation, such as retaining copies of the messages or media, and record keeping are critical to ensure evidence should criminal proceedings become necessary. With the increasing numbers of students possessing smartphones and other web-enabled devices, parents and teachers must continue to be alert for the signals of cyberbullying as well as talk to students about what it is and its impact on others. Parents should also regularly monitor their home computer as well as maintain an open electronics policy where they know students' screen names and passwords. Doing so may diminish the likelihood that a student will engage in or be the victim of cyberbullying.

APPLICATION WITH DIVERSE LEARNERS

Throughout this chapter, it's been established that bullying can vary according to behavior, gender, and age; however, according to information presented on the Teaching Tolerance website (www.tolerance.org), there is a strong relationship between bias and bullying. Prejudice towards specific groups, including those of different races, sexual orientations, gender identities, cognitive abilities, or religious beliefs, are often the cause of the bullying. According to Beane (1999), "most bullying victims are 'different'" from others in some way, making bullies target them. Bullying has been shown to differentially impact students based on their race/ethnicity, language, class, or physical attributes, including disability (Wheeler, 2004). A report published in 2012 indicated that Asian students (10%) were less likely to be bullied in comparison to Caucasian (29%), African-American (29%), or Hispanic peers (26%) (Robers, et al., 2012).

One critical goal of teachers to combat bullying based on differences is to create a culture of acceptance within the classroom. This can be done by activities that are specifically directed towards recognizing, accepting, and teaching about differences. For example, students can examine different disabilities and learn about capabilities of students who may be identified as being affected by them. Similarly, they can encourage students to celebrate their unique attributes, providing them with acceptance and affirmation of the differences amongst the students. Finally, teachers can alleviate bullying towards diverse learners by demonstrating a willingness to talk openly about differences. There are certain parameters and procedures that should be identified and put in place within this process. However, the time will have long-term benefits on students and will likely diminish or eliminate bullying.

CASE STUDY – Bullying

Tommy is a 4th grade boy who is physically much bigger than the other students. He has repeated third grade and is struggling academically only a few weeks into the new school year. He often disengages from instruction and has a tendency to cause disruptions because he repeatedly picks on one boy, Marco, who sits near him. During class he often takes things from the boy, including pencils, toys, and games. If the student or any of his friends argues with Tommy, he is likely to make threatening statements or engage in physical action against them.

Recently, his teacher, Ms. Idol, has noticed Tommy has begun to repeatedly pick on Marco out at recess whenever he can. Ms. Idol has intervened on several occasions, but Tommy is very adept at waiting until no teachers are around. Ms. Idol has heard of several instances of Tommy knocking Marco down and laughing at him (while making it look like an accident), but has not been able to gather proof nor has she witnessed the behavior firsthand.

On this particular day, the two boys appear to be arguing over a set of mechanical pencils. Ms. Idol knows that the pencils do not belong to Tommy because Marco was very proud of them when he brought them in. Most of Tommy's pencils are broken or he "borrows" them from Ms. Idol's pencil jar when he needs one. Hearing Tommy say, 'They're mine,' Ms. Idol begins to walk towards the two boys. At that moment, Tommy pushes Marco very forcefully. Marco falls backwards and hits his head on a chair. Concerned for him, Ms. Idol immediately orders Tommy to go to the office and attends to Marco.

Since this is the second instance Tommy has made physical contact with another student within a three day period, Ms. Idol decides to call Tommy's mom to inform her about the situation. After ringing several times, Tommy's mother picks up the phone.

"Good afternoon, Ms. Marks, this is Ms. Idol, Tommy's teacher," says Ms. Idol when she hears the connection is made.

Tommy's mother responds by saying, "What's Tommy done now? The only time I hear from anybody there is when he has done something wrong."

Ms. Idol informs her, "Tommy recently pushed another student down after taking one of his pencils. The other child hit his head and, as a result, spent the afternoon with an icepack on the bump. I am concerned for several reasons, but primarily because Tommy has been behaving very aggressively towards other children recently, especially this child, in particular. This is the second time he has pushed him down and I have observed him making fun of him at recess and in the classroom. In this particular case, when I asked him why he took the pencils and pushed the other student down, his reply was that he wanted the pencils. When I asked him if they were his, he said no, but that he liked them and decided that he should take them because the other boy didn't need them anyway."

"Yeah, that sounds about like what happens at home with his older brothers," Ms. Marks replied. "Since he's the youngest, he is usually the one who gets pushed around and his brothers pick on him quite a bit, especially since he was held back. They even nicknamed him "Tool" and that's what he's used to being called around the house by his brothers. There's not much I can do about it since they never listen to me when I tell them to stop."

"I see," Ms. Idol responded. "I must admit that the behaviors I am seeing from him would be classified as bullying based on the school's established policy. If they continue, I will need to ..."

At this point, Ms. Marks seemed to get angry and cut off Ms. Idol before she could finish. She responded, "Tommy is NOT a bully. He's just a boy who may be a little rough with other kids. That other kid needs to toughen up. Look at Tommy, his brothers pick on him, but he takes it and moves on. It's just boys being boys, that's all."

Reflect on the following questions before moving on:

1. What do you think about the behaviors being exhibited by Tommy? Do they constitute bullying?
2. What should happen when physical contact between students occurs? Should it warrant an immediate trip to the principal as was the case in this scenario?
3. If you were Ms. Idol, how would you have approached and prepared for the conversation with Ms. Marks.?
4. How should Ms. Idol respond to Ms. Marks final comments?
5. Do you feel that Tommy might be a bully? If you were Ms. Idol, how would you handle this situation?

After you have answered the discussion questions and decided how you would handle the situation, we encourage you to participate in a discussion with your peers in class to facilitate an understanding of the various factors that impact how Ms. Idol might address the situation. First, there is the situation involving the students, but, due to the potential conflict with Mrs. Marks, it will be important to consider a variety of perspectives. Due to the severity of any situation that might involve bullying, within the description that references TIC-TAC-TOE that follows, we will not address the scenario. Instead we will establish how various elements of the theories highlighted across the continuum can be considered simultaneously to provide a multifaceted approach to bullying.

Case Study: Using TIC-TAC-TOE

Throughout the book, we've focused your attention on various ways to consider your philosophy within the context of a Case Study that exemplified a particular situation relevant to the topic of the chapter. However, we feel that bullying represents a behavior that necessitates a reaction from the educator that intersects each of the philosophies. We acknowledge that sometimes it is challenging to step outside your chosen philosophy, but to effectively deal with bullying, you must make additional considerations relevant to the parties involved as well as have multiple strategies at your disposal.

Perhaps most consistent with the TIC approach is the necessity of clearly communicating consequences as part of your management plan, but especially when bullying is suspected. We feel, and other experts agree, that students must be well aware of the consequences that will occur if they engage in behaviors associated with bullying. To ensure this, you should verbally present the consequences for bullying with students. This should be followed by discussions of what constitutes bullying behaviors as well as role plays that involve demonstrations of behaviors consistent with bullying. Finally, the consequences should be visibly posted somewhere on the room. Beane (1999) describes consequences that are:

- practical
- logical, e.g. related to the behavior
- inevitable and consistently enforced
- predictable
- immediate (p. 126)

While Beane's work is not aligned with any particular theory within our continuum, there are definite parallels with Fred Jones' (1987) *Positive Discipline* within this approach, beyond simply administering consequences. For example, Jones advocates setting clear expectations, engaging in an immediate response when misbehavior occurs, and consistently enforcing expectations. Similarly, both Jones (1987) and Canter and Canter (2002) advocate consequences of increasing severity based on the misbehavior. Therefore, the greater the intensity of the bullying, the more severe the consequence. While acknowledging that some teachers who don't subscribe to TIC philosophies may not readily identify with the use of consequences, bullying situations call for certain principles that will effectively address bullying behaviors.

When considering TAC in previous chapters, we've examined information relevant to Curwin and Mendler on multiple occasions. We will do so once again in regard to bullying, yet the specific component from the theory is not being applied within the context in which it was designed. Curwin and Mendler (1999) judge "zero tolerance" policies as ineffective practices when it comes to classroom management. In their opinion, they affect large numbers of children and put teachers and administrators in situations where they have to react in the same manner to problems or situations that don't warrant the same consequence. For example, bringing a pocketknife to school because it was accidently left in the pocket of a Cub Scout uniform would warrant the same penalty as bringing a gun to school. Similarly, on the StopBullying.gov website, it has been proposed that these "zero tolerance" policies may actually inhibit the reporting of bullying and do not represent the type of intervention that students who are further at-risk for such behaviors as fighting and theft need. Instead, as advocated by several TAC theorists (e.g. Albert, Curwin and Mendler) and Beane (1999), the consequence must be logically related to the bullying behavior. For example, for students who bully or are at-risk to bully because they are unable to enact the social skills necessary to for typical adolescent relationships, we may assign them a positive, encouraging adults to partner with as a mentor. In essence, the adult would provide a model who effectively demonstrated pro-social behaviors. Similarly, the teacher or adult could work closely with children who may be bullies or victims to differentially promote positive behaviors, such as making and keeping friends, seeing others' perspectives, and, in the case of the victim, providing affirmation (see Faye & Funk, 1995). As personal relationships are established, bullies and victims may feel more capable and accepted, diminishing negative behaviors for bullies and improving mechanisms that will allow victims to more effectively handle situations with bullies.

Finally, teachers whose views most align with the TOE philosophy, which is focused on the empowerment of students, can utilize elements consistent with Ginott (1972) and Coloroso (2002). One strategy, primarily associated with Ginott (1972) is the use of I-messages. Teaching the use of I-messages to victims allows them to state their feelings in a neutral manner. For example, the student should not say to the bully, "You are being a jerk." Instead, the student can state, "I feel (expression of feeling, e.g. angry) when you (action that causes feeling, e.g. when you pick on me) because (explain the effect of the action)." The focus is not on the person, but the feeling, leading towards a potential sense of empowerment within the victim. Helping the victim become comfortable using such statements may take some time and a great deal of practice, but doing so may improve the assertiveness of the child. The resulting decision to stand up to the bully may effectively stop the bullying behavior.

In *The Bully, the Bullied, and the Bystander*, Coloroso (2002) has written extensively about how to help both the bully and the victim through empowerment. The bully can be taught and provided with opportunities to demonstrate non-bullying behaviors as well as how to develop friendships. For the victim, on the other hand, Coloroso describes strengthening the child's sense of self through affirmation and to help him or her develop and keep at least one good friend. Interestingly, somewhat analogous to what we see from the TIC theorists, Coloroso recommends intervening immediately with disciplinary action, i.e. consequences. However, she also believes in the 3 R's – restitution, resolution, and reconciliation – to potentially diffuse these situations in the future. This means that whatever the bully does, she must correct the situation, potentially by issuing an apology to the victim as part of the process and developing a plan to help alleviate the problem in future situations.

SUMMARY

In this chapter you were introduced to a problem that has garnered increased attention in recent years. In review, bullying situations involve three participants: the bully, the victim, and the bystander. Bullies seek power over victims, while the victims lack assertiveness or social attributes necessary to break the bully's power. Bystanders, on the other hand, generally constitute the audience within a bullying situation. The effects of bullying are long-term as bullies are more likely to commit criminal acts, while victims were more likely to experience lingering social problems later in life. We also presented how schools and teachers can take steps to stop and eliminate bullying, but the effort must begin with the identification of the problem as well as a significant investment in time and effort to maximize the results of any program or effort. Finally, cyberbullying represents a new form of bullying that has arisen from school-age children ubiquitous access to and use of various forms of technology. It represents an important development that has tremendous implications due to the access to large audiences on the Internet as well as the anonymity it affords the bully.

MOVING ON: Reflection Assignments

1. Since legislation has been passed in 21 states that specifically deal with bullying, it's important to become familiar with the current policies of your state to ensure you are aware of your role and the expectations of the school in regard to bullying. Access the department associated with education in your state, e.g. Department of Public Instruction, to determine the bullying policy of your state or to examine whether one is currently in place. When present, become familiar with the policy. If your state has not enacted a specific policy, find a state nearby that might have and examine that policy.

2. You are speaking with a parent whose child appears to be bullying other children. However, the parent refuses to acknowledge the behaviors, stating, "Boys will be boys. It's just part of growing up." How would you respond to this parent?

3. Think about the characteristics associated with bullies. Teachers typically yield nearly unlimited power in their classrooms. Can teachers be bullies? Read the article found at: http://www.tolerance.org/bully-at-blackboard. Describe how you would handle a situation where a colleague was using her power to intimidate students, exhibiting similar characteristics as those described in the section on bullies.

REFERENCES

Ashford, J.B., LeCroy, C.W., & Lortie, K.L. (2006). *Human behavior in the social environment.* Belmont: Thomson Brooks/Cole.

Beane, A. L. (1999). The bully free classroom: Over 100 tips and strategies for teachers K-8. Minneapolis, MN: Free Spirit Publishing, Inc.

Canter, L.,, & Canter, M. (2002). *Assertive discipline: Positive behavior management for today's schools* (3rd ed.). Bloomington, IN: Solution Tree.

Coloroso, B. (2002). *The bully, the bullied, and the bystander.* Toronto: HarperCollins Publishers Ltd.

Coolidge, F. L., DenBoer, J. W., & Segal, D. L. (2004). Personality and neuropsychological correlates of bullying behavior. *Personality and Individual Differences, 36,* 1559-1569.

Crain, M. M., Finch, C. L., & Foster, S. L. (2005). The relevance of the social information processing model for understanding relational aggression in girls. *Merrill - Palmer Quarterly, 51*(2), 213-250.

Crick, N. R., & Bigbee, M. A. (1998). Relational and overt forms of peer victimization: A multiinformant approach. *Journal of Consulting and Clinical Psychology, 66,* 337-347.

Crick, N. R., Casus, J. F., & Ku, H. C. (1999). Relational and physical forms of peer victimization in preschool. *Developmental Psychology, 35,* 376-385.

Crick, N. R., & Grotpeter, J. K. (1995). Relational aggression, gender, and social-psychological adjustment. *Child Development, 66,* 710-722.

Curwin, R. L., & Mendler, A. N. (1999). Zero tolerance for zero tolerance. *Phi Delta Kappan, 81,* 119-120.

Daunic, A. P., Smith, S. W., Robinson, T. R., Miller, M. D., & Landry, K. L. (2000). School- wide conflict resolution and peer mediation programs: Experiences in three middle schools. *Intervention in School and Clinic, 26,* 94-100.

Dill, E. J., Vernberg, E. M., Fonagy, P., Twemlow, S. W., & Gamm, B. K. (2004). Negative affect in victimized children: The roles of social withdrawal, peer rejection, and attitudes toward bullying. *Journal of Abnormal Child Psychology, 32,* 159-171.

Espelage, D. L., & Swearer, S. (2003). Research on school bullying and victimization: What have we learned and where do we go from here? *School Psychology Review, 23,* 365-383.

Fay, J., & Funk, D. (1995). *Teaching With Love and Logic: Taking Control of the Classroom.* Golden, CO: The Love and Logic Press, Inc.

Field, E. M. (2007). Bully blocking: Six secrets to help children deal with teasing and bullying (Revised Edition). London: Jessica Kingsley Publishers.

Fried, S., & Fried, P. (1996). *Bullies & victims: Helping your child through the schoolyard battlefield.* New York, N.Y.: M. Evans and Company, Inc.

Ginott, H. (1972). *Teacher and child.* New York: Macmillan.

Garbarino, J. (2006). See Jane hit: Why girls are growing more violent and what we can do about it. New York, N.Y.: The Penguin Press.

Hazler, R. J., Hoover, J. H., & Oliver, R. (1992, November). What kids say about bullying. *Executive Educator, 14,* 20-22.

Henry, S. (2009). School violence beyond Columbine: A complex problem in need of an interdisciplinary analysis. *American Behavior Scientist, 52,* 1246-1265.

Hinduja, S., & Patchin, J. (2010). Cyberbullying fact sheet: Identification, prevention, and response. Cyberbullying Research Center. Retrieved from http://www.cyberbullying.us/Cyberbullying_Identification_Prevention_Response_Fact_Sheet.pdf

Holt, M.K., Finkelhor, D., & Kantor, G.K. (2007). Hidden forms of victimization in elementary students involved in bullying. *School Psychology Review, 36*, 345-360.

Johnson, D. W., & Johnson, R. T. (1996). Conflict resolution and peer mediation programs in elementary and secondary schools: A review of the research. *Review of Educational Research, 66,* 459-506.

Jones, F. H. (1987). *Positive classroom discipline.* New York: McGraw-Hill.

Keith, S. & Martin, M. E. (2005). Cyber-bullying: Creating a culture of respect in a cyber world. *Reclaiming Children and Youth, 13*(4), 224-229.

Nansel, T. R., Overpeck, M., Pilla, R. S., Ruan, W. J., Simons-Morton, B. & Scheidt, P.(2001). Bullying behaviors among U.S. youth: Prevalence and associations with psychosocial adjustment. *Journal of the American Medical Association, 285*, 2094–2100.

National Crime Prevention Council. (n.d.). Cyberbullying: What is it? Arlington, VA: Author. Retrieved from:
http://www.ncpc.org/topics/cyberbullying/cyberbullying-tip-sheets/NCPC%20Tip%20Sheet%20-%20What%20Is%20It.pdf

Olweus, D. (1978). *Aggression in the schools: Bullies and whipping boys.* Washington, DC: Hemisphere.

Olweus, D. (1993). *Bullying at school.* Oxford: Blackwell Publishers.

Robers, S., Zhang, J., Truman, J., & Snyder, T. D. (2012). *Indicators of School Crime and Safety: 2011.* Washington, DC: United States Department of Education.

Ross, D. M. (2003).*Childhood bullying, teasing, and violence: What school personnel, other professionals, and parents can do*? Alexandria, VA: American Counseling Association.

Smith, P. K., & Sharp, S. (1994). The problem of school bullying. In P. K. Smith, & S. Sharp (Eds.), *School bullying*, (pp. 1-19). London: Routledge.

Smith, P. K., Talamelli, L., & Cowie, H. (2004). Profiles of non-victims, escaped victims, continuing victims and new victims of school bullying. *British Journal of Educational Psychology, 74,* 565–581.

Smokowski, P.R., & Kopasz, K.H. (2005). Bullying in school: An overview of types, effects, family characteristics, and intervention strategies. *Children & Schools, 27*, 101-110.

Sourander, A., Helstela, L., Helenius, H., & Piha, J. (2000). Persistence of bullying from childhood to adolescence – A longitudinal 8-year follow-up study. *Child Abuse & Neglect: The International Journal, 24,* 873-881.

Swearer, S. M., Espelage, D. L., Vaillancourt, T., & Hymel, S. (2010). What can be done about school bullying? Linking research to educational practice. *Educational Research, 39,* 38–47.

Van Slyck, M. R., Newland, L. M. & Stern, M. (1992), Parent-child mediation: Integrating theory, research, and practice. *Conflict Resolution Quarterly, 10,* 193–208.

Wheeler, E. (2004). Confronting social exclusion and bullying. *Childhood Education, 81*(1), 32L-32W.

CHAPTER X

Summary and Conclusions

As a general rule, teachers teach more by who they are than by what they say.

Unknown

This chapter will review the main points of the styles of management (TIC, TAC, TOE), summarize the importance of creating your own classroom management plan, and provide the outline to create your plan. First, we will review the rationale for having a classroom management plan. We will describe the components and present information on how to implement your personal discipline plan. Finally, we will share a sample plan for your learning environment.

This book has served as a foundation and guide for creating your own classroom management plan. Each chapter has provided an introduction to the idea that classroom management represents more than the traditional notion of discipline – after reading previous chapters, you know it encompasses multiple facets within the classroom. We also described how classroom management models and philosophies can be represented on a continuum of philosophical views. This is TIC, TAC, TOE. As you read this book, you were introduced to relevant vocabulary, presented with philosophical underpinnings for classroom management, and introduced to pertinent concepts. In sum, if you read, reflected, and completed the assignments, the information should have helped you consider the answer to the question "How will I manage my classroom?" Now it is your turn to synthesize what you have learned and create your own plan for managing the learning environment.

Guiding Questions

In chapter one, we asked you what was meant by the term classroom management. We asked about different philosophies of classroom management, and we asked you describe the style of management that best matches what you envision for your own classroom. The guiding questions for this chapter are a review:

- What is your own philosophy of management?
- What are the main points of the styles of management (TIC, TAC, TOE)?
- What is the importance and rationale of creating your own classroom management plan?
- What does a sample classroom management plan look like?

Reflect and Act:

Think about what you have learned about classroom management. Write a definition for classroom management, then develop a short list of 5-10 items that describes your knowledge of and perceptions about classroom management, including why it may be difficult or challenging for teachers. Compare this answer to what you might have written when you began studying classroom management.

BACKGROUND

Statement of Philosophy

In order to begin developing a classroom management plan or personal discipline plan, it is advisable to begin with an examination of your own philosophy (or position statement) of teaching. The following guidelines can be used as a guide to help you to draft your own position statement. First, consider a quote that represents you and your teaching philosophy. Each of the chapters in this book begins with a quote related education and management. Think of a quote that may provide a relevant start to set the tone for your philosophy statement. Perhaps a former teacher, coach, or mentor could be quoted or maybe a hero, author, political figure, or other significant person from history has a quote that resonates with your position on education.

Next, consider your opinion of the broad goals of education, your hopes for your students, and what you want them to remember about your class. Think of what you want the students to do you and what you want them to achieve, feel, accomplish, etc. Write about these reflections, share examples, and support your ideas. The position statement can include a reflection on your role in your student's learning, how you think children learn best, and share a rationale for the values you will promote in your classroom. Finally, as you conclude your position statement, describe the environment you will create in your classroom. Include mention of the feedback and praise you will offer students as they work. Consider your views on praise, rewards, punishment.

As was discussed in the first chapter, traditionally, classroom management is primarily associated with the organization of the classroom, the creation of rules, routines, and procedures, the engagement of students during instruction, and interventions for displays of improper behavior (Doyle, 2006; Evertson & Weinstein, 2006). Teachers need to be effective managers. Bloom, (2009) and Jones & Jones (2012) have proposed effective managers:

1. Demonstrate caring
2. Communicate regularly and clearly with students
3. Have established rules or behavioral guidelines
4. Hold high expectations
5. Model positive behavior
6. Are proactive, rather than reactive
7. Utilize procedures and routines that provide structure to activities
8. Teach students methods to develop self-control and responsibility
9. Create an engaging curriculum

Teachers who are successful in this area also understand students' needs and react accordingly, treating each as individuals (Horne, 2003). Now that you have finished the text and are ready to create your own classroom management plan, use the above list as a checklist for your own philosophy statement and use as a guide when you create your plan.

Reflect and Act:

Think about your own elementary school experience. Could you tell if your own elementary school teachers had a classroom management plan? What was their style of management? Would they fit with *Teacher in charge, Teacher and child*, or were they wanting you to move *toward ownership and empowerment*? How could you tell? Often, teachers teach the way in which they were taught. Is that ok?

THEORY TO PRACTICE

Before any teacher can implement a system of classroom management, questions regarding his or her views of the role of the teacher, the child, and the interaction between the two need to be examined. The previous section helped you to consider your philosophy or position on how you feel children should be taught. The next section will provide some advice and guidelines for your classroom management plan. If you can answer the following in your CMP- you will be ready for your classroom- think about your philosophy statement, rules, protocols, intervention strategies, consequences, prevention and implementation. You should also reflect on relevant literature related to your plan.

Rules, Procedures, and Routines

First, your rules should be observable, measurable, understandable, attainable, and reasonable. The authors encourage establishing rules early in the school year with the students. Harry & Rosemary Wong in their book *The First Days of School* stated, "The function of a rule is to prevent or encourage behavior by clearly stating student expectations." Teachers should take whatever time is necessary to make clear the classroom rules (Jones, 1987). Please see earlier chapters regarding establishing rules for your classroom. When considering the protocols- or activity procedures for your classroom you can think of the phrase, "This is how we do things in our class". Take time to consider what you will do and expect from the children during the following situations:

1. Entering and leaving the room
2. Beginning and ending the day or class period
3. Getting students attention (verbal, non-verbal, visual, etc)
4. Student interaction (when can students speak to one another)
5. Using areas of the room- pencil sharpener, supplies, centers, etc.
6. Using areas of the school- drinking fountain, restroom, cafeteria, recess
7. Working individually and together
8. How will the students go about obtaining your help?
9. What do the students do when they are done with their work?
10. What will be the responsibilities of taking care of the room? Who will share these responsibilities?
11. How will you and the students handle disruptions?
12. What about materials checkout? Library, in the class, labs, etc.

When you are considering whether your room is set up for all learners and room arrangement, think of the acronym, VACUUM (Kyle & Rogien, 2004):

Visibility: Can everybody see everything? Can you see them and what they are doing?

Accountability: Does your room arrangement allow for anyone to get away with things? Is everyone included?

Communicability: Can you communicate with all? can you move swiftly and easily between seats and tables, working the crowd?

Understandability: Your room arrangement reflects your philosophy your style and your climate for teaching. Is your arrangement giving the message you want to give, is it open? Is it closed? Collaborative? Individualized? Does it match the instruction?

Usability: Where are the supplies? Can you get to everything you need? Are things accessible to all?

Movability: If there is an emergency- can everyone move safely around the room and out? Quick and safe exits and entrances?

Daily Procedures

As you continue working on your own classroom management plan, there are many protocol items to consider. In addition to reviewing the relevant chapters, please review the following questions regarding your daily procedures and routines:

How will students line up?

How will you handle the transition times, what will be your verbal and nonverbal cues? How will attendance be taken?

What are the procedures for packing up and checking work/homework? Will you assign homework? What is your position on this?

How will you determine seating arrangements? How should the students expect to be treated each day?

How will the students know about the daily schedule?

Will there be announcements? Newsletter?

How will you help the students to take responsibility for their actions in the classroom? Will you have contracts?

What is your specific routine for the start of class?

Where will you post assignments?

Is consistency part of your protocols…

Will you call roll? Or will there be magnets, pins, nametags, etc.?

Will your procedures be revisited throughout the year? Please mention how you will discuss, model, and define your protocols and procedures until they become better routine- and you will reflect and change anything that is not working.

Will you utilize online management tools such as classdojo.com? If so, how?

Daily Procedures, continued

It can be overwhelming thinking of everything required of a teacher during the school day. How will textbooks be distributed? What about materials? Where will they be stored? How will they be shared- will each student have their own? How will materials in the classroom be kept? Is there a book checkout- or book bags?

In addition to materials manager, you are a coach, and guide. It is your job to motivate and inspire. It is your responsibility to invite families and to create a welcoming environment for communication and collaboration with families and stakeholders. How will you convey to the students that you are excited about their learning, you expect success, and ensure your confidence in their success? Decide on a home note connection procedure, email, newsletter, website, and phone call protocol. How will you invite parents and families into the learning experience?

A teacher is to teach every child in the classroom and embrace differences. How will you establish a fair setting for learning? How will you ensure culturally responsive teaching? How will these procedures embrace respect for all classroom members? Will your procedures be reasonable? How will you make it clear that the children are expected to contribute in many ways? How will you get to know the individuals in your classroom? How will you decide when to accommodate a students' differences and when to push the child toward assimilation to the larger community? Please take the utmost care in reflecting on this. How will your classroom accommodate for differences. Think about the use of interest inventories, individual conferences, and time with your students. Think about one on one time with your children- and how will you prioritize this.

Preventative Measures Discipline Procedures

The next section to consider will be your preventative strategies. This is where you reflect on planning active and meaningful learning experiences. Remember, powerful lessons are engaging- where there will not be time for misbehavior. Your instruction and management will be linked, if you can assume a role or ask the students to participate in experiential exercises where they assume roles and take an active part in the learning. For example, the students will be "pirates" to use a map to hunt for treasure, and learn geography skills. The students will participate in a classroom economy where they will earn "paychecks" or "good bucks" for the experience of understanding scarcity, sacrifice, saving, investing, and choice.

When you want to prevent, you will need to model appropriate behavior at all times. You will keep the goal of discipline in mind- self-discipline- and you will trust and support your students. Here are ways to create a preventive environment:

1. Make the learning relevant.
2. Foster positive relationships with peers and adults in the classroom
3. You will TEACH behavior management skills.
4. Conflict resolution, empathy, tolerance, and respect will be a part of your preventative strategies. They can be the foundation of your class.
5. Preventive atmospheres are inclusive and can strengthen self-confidence and self-efficacy
6. You will help students have a low stress environment.
7. Prevention includes hope. Instill hope and a positive attitude with your students.

Prevention, continued

In addition, to the items mentioned above, you can pace your lessons properly. This comes with experience and practice. The authors recommend video recording your teaching experiences. When you watch the video back, you will be able to note your pacing, body language, voice, attention to certain students, and other teacher behaviors. By displaying "withitness" you will prevent behavior problems. (Kounin, 1970).

We advise your planning and management go together. Plan your lessons well, have variety and interest in your lessons, keep the momentum going, call on students regularly. You can use name cards, multitask, utilize the ripple effect (good behavior can spread- so can poor) have smooth transitions, clarify expectations, and decide how you will manage student work, papers, uploads, etc. Your room arrangement can be preventive and so can the way you "work the room"…"working the crowd" (Jones, 1987).

Implementation Plan

When you consider how all of this will be implemented, what will you do first? Communication with families, administrators, and colleagues is important. It is advisable to visit with a mentor teacher in advance of the school year, if possible, to see how a plan is implemented. Of course, this implementation is a process, not a one-time event.

It may help to again, consider the individuals you will be working with, your students, when you consider how what you have planned will be implemented. Please reflect on what it was like to be a student, empathize, and treat them with respect as you begin your year. It is true, if you give respect, you are more likely to get respect in return. On the first day of school, the student should know:

1. Am I in the right place- do I feel safe here?
2. Where do I sit?
3. Where do I put my things?
4. How can I expect to be treated here?
5. What will I learn in this class?
6. How will I be evaluated? Graded?
7. What sort of person is the teacher?
8. Will students be involved in the procedures?
9. Will they be invited to learn? Respected? Valued?

What are your expectations for learning in your classroom?

What are some icebreakers or ways you can teach your plan and get to know your students? Begin a collection of "first days" experiences that will set the stage for a successful year. Bookmark those websites with teacher ideas.

Reviewing the Continuum

The authors feel it is important to review the definition of the continuum in this final chapter. Teachers typically exhibit beliefs relating to classroom management (and children's behaviors) that fall into a consistent pattern. This general pattern is easily shown in a continuum which reflects varying levels of power in the teacher/student relationship. Figure 1 provides a visual reference to the management continuum. In general, teacher-in-charge (TIC) would be described as teacher behaviors which utilize assertive or controlling techniques to cause students to change their behavior to better match what is desired by the educator or educational setting. In the center of the continuum is the Teacher-and-Child (TAC) philosophy. Here the relationship could be described as mutually inclusive as the teacher and students communicate to develop and agree upon behaviors and interventions. The final section of the continuum is Toward Empowerment/Ownership (TOE). Teachers who exhibit this orientation, ultimately cede the majority of control of power to the students in the classroom, providing them an authentic environment to experience problem-solving and relationship-building.Figure 1. Continuum of Classroom Management Philosophy

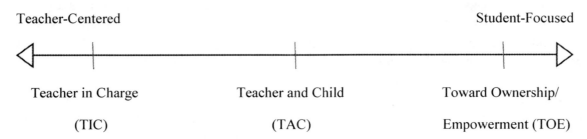

144

Teacher in Charge (TIC)

The Teacher in Charge would be most aligned with a behavioristic orientation towards effective classroom management. Teachers with this philosophy envision the classroom as an orderly, structured environment and are like to emphasize a system of reinforcement or consequences to increase the likelihood that children demonstrate acceptable behavior. In short, students who demonstrate appropriate behavior are reinforced, either tangibly or verbally, while inappropriate behavior is extinguished or diminished with the use of punishments that increase in the level of severity as the magnitude or significance of misbehavior rises.

Teacher and Child (TAC)

Teacher and Child is exemplified by a partnership between the teacher and students. The ultimate goal of the teacher in such a system is to help children take responsibility for their own behavior while simultaneously altering behavior that results from children's lack of understanding of methods to fulfill their own needs. The teacher may also use logical consequences to inappropriate conduct. For example, if a student wrote on a desk, he may have to clean the desk. —natural consequences

— restorative in nature

Toward Ownership/Empowerment (TOE)

Towards Ownership/Empowerment is characterized by students have an active part in determining the overall classroom climate with respect to management. For example, teachers who subscribe to this philosophy may utilize classroom meetings where the classroom collaboratively develops rules or discusses a solution to a classroom situation.

Previous research has established other names for the continuum of classroom management and linked the various theories to the levels of control. For example, Glickman and Tamashiro (1980) described the levels as Interventionist (TIC), Interactionalist (TAC), and Non-Interventionists. Table 1 lists several theorists which could be associated with of each categories of the continuum. It is important to note that the various theorists may espouse actions/strategies that may align at various points along the continuum. The location in the table is meant to demonstrate the level of the continuum that the theory is most aligned with.

145

comfort level starts here ↓ → *moving here*
- *collaborative*
- *balanced*

Table 1. Theories and Theorists Aligned with TAC-TAC-TOE Continuum
- *grow from mistakes*

Teacher in Charge (TIC)	Teacher and Child (TAC)	Toward Ownership/Empowerment (TOE)
Assertive Discipline Lee and Marlene Canter

Positive Discipline Fredric Jones

Behavior Modification B.F. Skinner | **Positive Discipline in the Classroom** Jane Nelsen, Lynn Lott, and H. Stephen Glenn

Cooperative Discipline Linda Albert

Discipline with Dignity Richard Curwin and Allen Mendler

Noncoercive Discipline William Glasser

Win-Win Discipline Spencer Kagan, Patricia Kyle, and Sally Scott | **Beyond Discipline** Alfie Kohn

Teaching with Love and Logic Jim Fay and David Funk

Discipline as Self-Control Thomas Gordon

Inner Discipline Barbara Coloroso |

need for control

✳ **Reflect and Act:**
Re-examine your definition of classroom management. Has it changed? Where do you fall on the continuum? With this in mind, write three statements that will form a foundation for your classroom management plan, e.g. Students in my classroom will take an active part in establishing the behavioral standards that will be enforced in my classroom.

CASE STUDY

In the beginning of Miss. Estrada's 6th year of teaching her principal asked if she would teach by looping, a self-contained 6th grade class. The class consisted of 31 students, varying in ability levels and behavior disorders. The classroom is small, in the basement, and in need of repair. There is no two-way intercom in the classroom, and the office is on the third floor. The desks are crammed together and no room is available for a teacher space or desk. Three windows are broken and covered with duct tape and cardboard. Twelve of Miss Estrada's students have IEP's, all students have failed at least one portion of the state proficiency exam, and several have emotional and behavioral problems.

One child, in particular, Robert, has been diagnosed with paranoid schizophrenia, tactile dysfunction, and obsessive compulsive disorder. Robert is a likeable child who struggles at school. He is smaller than other boys his age, but older. He has greasy hair and is not very coordinated. Children in other classes make fun of him. His whole world is in flux, much like most adolescent boys, however in addition to the normal physical, emotional, and social turmoil of early adolescence, he has a very difficult psychological disorder. He takes several strong medications, including Depakote for the hallucinations and the voices he hears. Every day is different with Robert-he is responsible for getting himself ready for school in the morning and sometimes, does not take his medication. Robert and Miss Estrada have an ok relationship, on some days. They have tried several strategies to help him to improve his behavior and self-discipline.

There are several challenges with Robert. Miss Estrada chooses to focus on his behavior during transition times within class. Robert does not like change, the OCD and Paranoia require that he have incredibly consistent schedule and few distractions. She teaches with integrated themes so the students are not going text to text, bell to bell...but when instructions are given and the class begins to move into action-Robert will exhibit any or all of the following behaviors: Yelling out, profane language, hitting himself, breaking pencils, or staring into space while talking in nonsense.

In the past, Ms. Estrada has tried to handle these behaviors individually. If he yelled out, she would say, "Robert, please, no yelling." If he broke pencils she would take them away. She would say, "Abuse it-Lose it". She would also often be heard saying, "Robert, stay in your own space" or "Give Respect-Get Respect". This would only work sometimes and he would mock me and move on to someone or something else. The teacher realized she was not helping him to learn proper behavior. What should Miss Estrada do?

The baseline data Miss Estrada has tells her his behaviors are worse in the afternoon and more frequent during transition times within the classroom, when there is a lot of movement in the classroom. The parents are divorced and remarried. Robert has older step brothers who tease him and are not good step brothers and sisters. They encourage him to get into trouble and Robert loves the attention because he thinks they are "cool". They once gave Robert a gun to shoot small animals randomly in the back yard of their suburban neighborhood. The parents are frustrated at home, with Robert, and the mother often calls crying and not knowing what to do. The family moves frequently, works long hours, and do not check on meds. The family has refused the doctor's analysis that Robert should NOT be in a public school setting.

Some potential stereotypes Miss Estrada needs to be aware of, include: a) Robert's mother is a young mother and more concerned with her personal life and social events than with her son's well-being, b) Robert is not clean or well-dressed, c) He would often wear several items of his clothes layered, even on a 90 degree day, because of the paranoia. Robert's thinking is that someone would steal his clothing while he was at school. The clothes would begin to smell, because he refused to take them off for weeks at a time. Miss Estrada had to have the nurse speak to him about personal hygiene. Miss Estrada was originally afraid to have Robert in her class, because other teachers would tell "nightmare" stories about this disturbed child. Apparently he tried to burn his neighbor's barn, and threatened to burn and kill children and pets in the neighborhood.

Miss Estrada will have to admit that her previous experiences with Robert have not been implemented with his best interest in mind. Her management with him consisted of acknowledging negative behaviors and taking things away. Miss Estrada was not helping Robert to learn about his own complicated behaviors. Her previous management also developed from ignorance, and a somewhat stereotypical reaction to paranoid schizophrenia. She had to research paranoid schizophrenia, obsessive compulsiveness, and feel better equipped for Robert. She has taken time to schedule one-on-one time with Robert at lunch and throughout the week.

Her future plans with Robert include implementing a personalized behavior management plan involving a head set, music, non-verbal signs, and books on tape.

Plan of action:

1. Robert and the teacher decided on their own private "sign".

2. Robert will be allowed to use a personal radio or IPod, Walkman, portable device, during transition times.

3. Before Miss Estrada gives the new instruction to the rest of the class signaling to move, she gives Robert the sign. The sign is Spiderman's web fingers.

4. He knows he is allowed to put on his headset, listen to books on tape, music, or the radio. The books on tape aown voice and she has personalized the stories for Robert. He reads on about a 1st grade level.

5. The plan will be implemented for two weeks, she will collect some frequency data, reflect, and reevaluate.

Daily Interventions: Robert's Rockin' Plan

Date:_____

	8:00	8:20	8:40	9:00	9:20	9:40
Spidey Sign Intervention						
On-Task Behavior (yelling, breaking, profanity) Tallies						

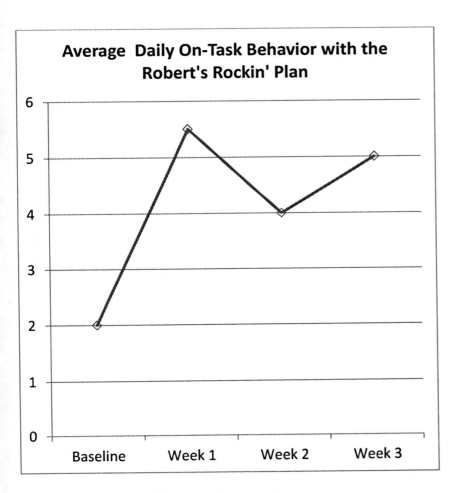

Robert's Rockin' Reward Chart

I will make smart choices this week by completing my assignments and remaining on-task. I understand that if I make smart choices then I will earn additional time with my IPod.

_____ (Student signature)   _____ (Date)

6 signatures a day = 5 extra minutes of recess each day

	Monday	Tuesday	Wednesday	Thursday	Friday
Morning Work					
Specials: Art, music, PE					
Math Small Group					

Reading Group					
Science					
Social Studies					
Recess					

Reflect on the following questions before moving on to the descriptions:

1. What are some of the behaviors being exhibited by Robert?
2. What actions has Miss Estrada taken to help Robert?
3. What are some potential reasons Robert may be exhibiting the behaviors?
4. If you were Robert's teacher, how would you have handled this situation?
5. Do you feel that Robert was treated fairly?
6. Where is Miss Estrada on the TIC, TAC, TOE continuum?

CONCLUSION

In this chapter you were provided a summary of TIC, TAC, TOE. In review, you have defined classroom management, reviewed the TIC, TAC, TOE continuum of classroom management, and have reflected on your own management style with theories in mind. As stated throughout the book, the continuum and connection to other theories of managing the learning environment can provide a context as you develop and design your own management plan. Please continue to reflect on your own answer to the question, "How will I manage my classroom?" you are now closer to creating and implementing a plan that is successful with all children in your classroom. Remember, every year is different you should continually reflect on how you can improve your management as a leader in the classroom.

MOVING ON: Reflection Assignments

1. Form a discussion group whose members represent all three options. Discuss together everyone's answers to the Discussion Questions you answered before selecting an option.
2. Create a Venn Diagram with a circle representing each of the three management perspectives. Fill in the diagram noting similarities and differences between the potential and actual responses by a teacher representing each of the perspectives.
3. Individually, describe in writing how you could use observation as an important component within classroom management to help limit misbehaviors.

4. Complete the CMP.

Appendix A: Reflect and Act

Teachers need to be effective managers. In this chapter, 9 characteristics of effective managers were described. Choose three characteristics and sketch something showing the characteristic and list how you will demonstrate you have the trait or characteristic.

Appendix B: Complete and Share: The Management Intervention Study (Putting It All Together)

The CMP is a required piece of evidence for the Master's degree program. The CMP is a research study on behavioral interventions that requires you to:

- examine and synthesize literature (theoretical and practitioner-focused) relevant to classroom management
- design a behavioral intervention for a specific student or group of students based upon your examination of literature and the completion of a needs assessment;
- implement the intervention and collect data to document the results;
- create an artifact documenting the research process, including an abstract, a literature review, methodology, and a self-reflection;

This project will be completed in stages as the semester progresses. Candidates will be required to submit assignments on a regular basis that will comprise the final project. The final point total indicated above represents the sum of the various components. For example, in the previous chapters, you have been asked to identify a child's behaviors, and compile literature relevant to helping the child. Completion of the CMP will be accompanied by a presentation, i.e. workshop, using a digital artifact for candidates to discuss their finding and implications of the CMP for school-wide and personal use.

REFERENCES

Albert, L. (2003). A teacher's guide to cooperative discipline: How to manage your
classroom and promote self-esteem (rev. ed.).   Circle Pines, MN: American Guidance Service Publishing.

Brophy, J. (2006). History of research on classroom management. In C. M. Evertson and C. S. Weinstein (Eds.), *Handbook of Classroom Management: Research, Practice, and Contemporary Issues* (pp. 17-43). Mahwah, NJ: Lawrence Erlbaum Associates.

Canter & Associates. (1998). First-class teacher: Success strategies for new teachers.
Bloomington, IN: Solution Tree.

Canter, L.,, & Canter, M. (2002). Assertive discipline: Positive behavior management
for today's schools (3rd ed.). Bloomington, IN: Solution Tree.

Chambers, S. M. (2003, February). *The impact of length of student teaching on the self-efficacy and classroom orientation of preservice teachers.* Paper presented at the Annual Meeting of the Southwest Educational Research Association, San Antonio, TX. Retrieved from http://www.eric.ed.gov/PDFS/ED477509.pdf

Curwin, R. L., & Mendler, A. N. (1999). Discipline with dignity. Alexandria, VA: Association for Supervision and Curriculum Development.

Doyle, W. (2006). Ecological approaches to classroom management. In C. M. Evertson and C. S. Weinstein (Eds.), *Handbook of Classroom Management: Research, Practice, and Contemporary Issues* (pp. 97-126). Mahwah, NJ: Lawrence Erlbaum Associates.

Evertson, C. M., & Weinstein, C. S. (2006). Classroom management as a field of inquiry. In C. M. Evertson and C. S. Weinstein (Eds.), *Handbook of Classroom Management: Research, Practice, and Contemporary Issues* (pp. 1-16). Mahwah, NJ: Lawrence Erlbaum Associates.

Ginott, H. (1972). Teacher and child. New York: Macmillan.

Glickman, C. D., & Tamashiro, R. T. (1980). Clarifying teachers' beliefs about discipline. *Educational Leadership, 37*, 459-464.

Jones, F. H. (1987). Positive classroom discipline. New York: McGraw-Hill.

Kohn, A. (1996). Beyond discipline: From compliance to community. Alexandria, VA: Association for Supervision and Curriculum Development.

Kounin, J. S. (1970). Discipline and group management in classrooms. Austin, TX: Holt, Rinehart, & Winston.

Kyle, P. B., & Rogien, L. R. (2004). *Opportunities and Options in Classroom Management: Effective Teaching, Preventive Strategies, Corrective Strategies, Supportive Techniques*. Upper Saddle River, NJ: Pearson..

McCormack, A. C. (2001). Investigating the impact of an internship on the classroom management beliefs of preservice teachers. *The Professional Educator, 23*(2), 11-22.

Moore, R. (2003). Reexamining the field experiences of preservice teachers. *Journal of Teacher Education, 54*, 31-42.

National Education Association. (2010). *Status of the American public school teacher 2005-2006*. Washington, D.C.: National Education Association.

Pianta, R. C. (2006). Classroom management and relationships between children and teachers: Implications for research and practice. In C. M. Evertson and C. S. Weinstein (Eds.), *Handbook of Classroom Management: Research, Practice, and Contemporary Issues* (pp. 685-710). Mahwah, NJ: Lawrence Erlbaum Associates.

Rinke, C. (2007). Understanding teachers' careers: Linking professional life to professional path. *Educational Research Review, 3*, 1–13. doi:10.1016/j.edurev.2007.10.001

Veenman, S. (1984). Perceived problems of beginning teachers. *Review of Educational Research, 54*(2), 143-178.

Wentzel, K. R. (2006). A social motivation perspective for classroom management. In C. M. Evertson and C. S. Weinstein (Eds.), *Handbook of Classroom Management: Research, Practice, and Contemporary Issues* (pp. 619-643). Mahwah, NJ: Lawrence Erlbaum Associates.

Chapter 1

Reflect and Act:

Think about what you already know about classroom management. Write a definition for classroom management, then develop a short list of 5-10 items that describes your knowledge of and perceptions about classroom management, including why it may be difficult or challenging for teachers.

Definition:

Routines, expectations, and cause-effect consequences established and explicitly detailed in a classroom community.

Classroom management ideas:

1. Transparent
2. No surprises
3. clear expectations & routines
4. Practice to get into "rhythm"
5. Class promise/covenant created together
6.
7.
8.
9.
10.

Reflect and Act:

Create a list of the behaviors that will be strictly forbidden in your classroom. Discuss the list with a colleague. How do the two lists differ? Together, form a list to represent the most common forms of misbehavior that you think you will see in the classroom.

List of forbidden behaviors:

1. unkindness towards peers
2. stealing
3. lying
4.
5.

Reflect and Act:

Re-examine your definition of classroom management. Has it changed? Where do you fall on the continuum? With this in mind, write three statements that will form a foundation for your classroom management plan, e.g. Students in my classroom will take an active part in establishing the behavioral standards that will be enforced in my classroom.

New definition of classroom management:

Foundational statements:

1. Students will be empowered in the classroom and take
2. ownership for their learning.
3. Consequences are logical and within "scale" to students' choices
   Expectations are created in partnership

Reflect and Act:
Think about what you already know about building positive relationships with your own family, friends, and community. What are characteristics of a successful relationship? Design a T-chart describing positive and negative behaviors that influence caring relationships.

Positive behaviors	Negative behaviors

Reflect and Act: Reflect and Act:

Creating positive relationships with your students can start with an examination of your own personality and your own behaviors. List how others would describe you. Create a graphic where you brainstorm your attributes. What would others say about you?

Chapter 3

Reflect and Act:

What rules do you think every classroom needs? Why? List the classroom rules you will present, teach, and gain commitment in your classroom. Are they observable, measurable, and few?

Reflect and Act:

Map out your classroom. How would you like your room arranged?

Chapter 4

Reflect and Act:

Draft an introductory letter to families regarding you and your classroom.

Chapter 5

Reflect and Act:

Create an IF/THEN chart for how you will respond to students' positive and negative behaviors:

If a student in my class does this:	Then this will happen:

Chapter 6

Use the Functional Behavior Assessment form (below) to complete several observations of a student in a classroom. Develop a list of potential causes for the behavior, choosing one to address within an individual behavior plan.

Functional Behavior Assessment
Student_____

Step 1 – Describe the behavior.

What does the behavior look like?

How often does the behavior occur? How long does it last?

What is the setting where the behavior is most likely to occur?

Step 2 – Describe the antecedents.

Date	Location	Activity	Behavior	Intensity
				Low High 1 2 3 4 5
				Low High 1 2 3 4 5
				Low High 1 2 3 4 5
				Low High 1 2 3 4 5
				Low High 1 2 3 4 5
				Low High 1 2 3 4 5
				Low High 1 2 3 4 5

Step 3 – Describe the consequence.

What happens as a result of the problem behavior? (Include the subject's, teacher's, and other students' reactions as well as the specific events, e.g. removal to the school office)

Step 4 – Summarize the information.

Antecedent (Predictor)	Behavior (of concern)	Consequence (of adult, peers, etc)

Step 5 – Propose a function for the behavior in each of the ABC sequences listed above.

1.
2.
3.

Using the information obtained through the behavioral analysis completed on the preceding pages, use Individual Behavior Plan Template to create and document and Individual Behavior Plan for the student.

Individual Behavior Plan

Student_____   Date _____

Step 1 – Summarize the behaviors to be targeted.

Step 2 – Establish behavioral goals (observable and measurable).

Step 3 - Determine progress-monitoring procedures.

Goal	Data Collection Procedures	Person Responsible	Dates

Step 4 – Establish a review date.

This plan will be reviewed on _____.

Step 5 – Collect signatures of responsible parties.

_____
Student

_____
Parent (when applicable)

_____
Teacher

_____
(Responsible party #1 – when applicable)

_____
(Responsible party #2 – when applicable)

Venn Diagram for comparing functional behavior assessments in **MOVING ON: Reflection Assignments.**

Think about the steps in the problem-solving process and develop a scenario that could be used to introduce these steps. Write the dialogue that might occur as part of the problem-solving conference between a teacher and a student.

Chapter 8

Reflect and Act:
Reflect on the behaviors that you think might be most associated with students who would be characterized as "chronic rule breakers". Write a list of 3-5 of these behaviors and share them with a colleague.

1.

2.

3.

4.

5.

Use the space below to write a scenario in which a student (or students) engage in one of the behaviors listed at the beginning of the chapter (e.g. profanity, aggressions towards another student or teacher). Be sure to include strategies the teacher would demonstrate to effectively handle the situation.

Chapter 9

Chapter 10

Reflect and Act:

Teachers need to be effective managers. Bloom, (2009) and Jones & Jones (2012) proposed 9 characteristics of effective managers.
Choose three characteristics. Sketch something showing the characteristic and list how you will demonstrate you have the trait or characteristic.

Effective Manager

Appendix B: Constructing the Management Intervention Study

Chapter 2

Annotated Bibliography

Think of one child in your classroom who's behavior is challenging you as a teacher. Define his or her behaviors. Create a professional resource list with 5-7 resources related to these behaviors and strategies for discipline and opportunities to teach the child to behave or learn replacement behaviors. This is an annotated bibliography of articles that could be used to create your literature review for the Management Intervention Study.

Chapter 3 – Review of Literature

The Review of Literature serves two purposes: to describe your classroom management philosophies and plan and to explain research-based classroom management interventions for relevant behavioral issues. Part 1 should describe: your philosophy of management, the rationale for the development of your rules and procedures, and your overall procedures for discipline (consequences/preventive measures). Part 2 should provide the educational and personal rationale for your project and background information describing research on the behavioral intervention(s) you've chosen to implement to enable the student in your classroom to be more successful. The literature should conclude with personal reflections on what your research of the literature has revealed in light of your experiences.

Please include a minimum of 5-7 research articles within your sources, many of which will likely come from the Annotated Bibliography.

Chapter 4 – Collaboration

When helping a child to behave, it requires collaboration with families and stakeholders. Write a reflection of your collaborative efforts to help the student in your classroom.

Chapter 6 – Research Plan & Data Collection

Functional Behavior Assessment Student_____				
Step 1 – Describe the behavior.				
What does the behavior look like? How often does the behavior occur? How long does it last? What is the setting where the behavior is most likely to occur? 				

Step 2 – Describe the antecedents.

Date	Location	Activity	Behavior	Intensity
				Low High 1 2 3 4 5
				Low High 1 2 3 4 5
				Low High 1 2 3 4 5
				Low High 1 2 3 4 5
				Low High 1 2 3 4 5
				Low High 1 2 3 4 5
				Low High 1 2 3 4 5

Step 3 – Describe the consequence.

What happens as a result of the problem behavior? (Include the subject's, teacher's, and other students' reactions as well as the specific events, e.g. removal to the school office)

Step 4 – Summarize the information.

Antecedent (Predictor)	Behavior (of concern)	Consequence (of adult, peers, etc)

Step 5 – Propose a function for the behavior in each of the ABC sequences listed above.

1.
2.
3.

Using the information obtained through the behavioral analysis completed on the preceding pages, use Individual Behavior Plan Template to create and document and Individual Behavior Plan for the student.

Individual Behavior Plan

Student_____   Date _____

Step 1 – Summarize the behaviors to be targeted.

Step 2 – Establish behavioral goals (observable and measurable).

Step 3 - Determine progress-monitoring procedures.

Goal	Data Collection Procedures	Person Responsible	Dates

Step 4 – Establish a review date.

This plan will be reviewed on _____.

Step 5 – Collect signatures of responsible parties.

_____
Student

_____
Parent (when applicable)

_____
Teacher

_____
(Responsible party #1 – when applicable)

_____
(Responsible party #2 – when applicable)

Research Plan

To complete the activities associated with Chapter 6, you will develop a research plan documenting the process that will be used for the intervention. It should encompass the following:

1. Evidence of Behavior Analysis
   a. Address what it was about the student's behavior that made him/her a likely candidate for intervention.
   b. Describe the data collected to reinforce your selection and document the rationale. You may include functional behavior analysis form included in this appendix as documentation.

2. Description of Intervention
   a. Explain exactly (or as accurately as possible) what you are going to do for your intervention. Visit this website:
   http://oldweb.madison.k12.wi.us/sod/car/car5wandh.html
   The 5 W's are appropriate to include here (the "H" should be on your mind, but is not necessary until the end of the intervention).
   b. This should also explain how data collection and analysis will be conducted. You may submit the Individual Behavior Plan Template as documentation for this portion of the research plan.

3. Collaboration - This has been included and developed within Chapter 4. You may need to document further efforts as necessary.

4. Timeline
   a. Addresses all activities that need to be completed as part of the intervention. This includes collection of baseline data (as necessary), data collection as part of the intervention, and data analysis.

Chapter 9 – Data Analysis & Action Plan

When you have collected your data from observing your student, please share data analysis and implications for the student here. As part of the analysis, describe:

- What was successful in your intervention? What is the underlying reason of the success? What evidence do you have that could document this success?
- What did not work? What limited the success of this portion of the intervention?
- Was your chosen form of data effective for determining overall behavior change? How do you know?
- Describe any changes you made to the intervention. What was been the impact on the intervention (overall)?
- What changes do you still foresee as being necessary in the future to enable a more successful intervention?
- What insights have you gained so far as part of the intervention (self-reflection)? How will this intervention study impact your long-term practices?
- How will you continue to work with this student (or others) in the future?

Chapter 10 – The Management Intervention Study (Putting It All Together)

Part 1 – Evidence Summary

A. Summary of the overall intervention and research
   a. Review of Literature
   b. Research plan - modified to reflect any changes that occurred within implementation and documentation of the results
B. Peer Feedback
   a. Describe evidence that the information from the intervention was presented to peers and feedback was collected. The rubric that follows can be used in the process. A reflection on the peer feedback is included
C. Collaboration with Stakeholders
   a. Further documents ongoing communication with parents to facilitate understanding of the ongoing process and results of the intervention. It also conveys the implications of the impact of the intervention to the parents, both behavioral and academic.
D. Discussion of Changes
   a. Describe how the intervention could have been improved. What would you have done differently? How could you have made the intervention more successful? What do you wish you knew at the beginning that would have influenced the process?
E. Plan of Action
   a. Describes how you will proceed with professional development or additional interventions based on completed intervention, self-reflection, and feedback. (Answers questions such as: What should be done next? What additional interventions might still be necessary? How will you proceed with future interventions for the student who was the focus of this intervention or additional, different students? How will you conduct these interventions? What data will be collected?)

Part 2 - Reflections

A. Personal Practice
   a. Discuss your personal reflections about the intervention, including the process, results, and implications for your professional practice. Include information on your growth as a classroom manager as a result of completing the intervention.
B. Implications for P-12 Learner
   a. Discuss the effectiveness and impact of the intervention on the student's behavioral and academic goals

Part 3 - References and Appendices

Peer Feedback Rubric

Presenter _____

1. Presentation of literature/theoretical basis   1   2   3   4   5

Comment:

2. Description of Intervention   1   2   3   4   5

Comment:

3. Description of data collection and analysis   1   2   3   4   5

Comment:

4. Presentation of results   1   2   3   4   5

Comment:

5. Implications for future research/action plan   1   2   3   4   5

Suggestions for future research/interventions:

6. Other Comments: